Simply
Vegetarian
Thai
cooking

Simply Vegetarian Thai cooking

125 real Thai recipes

Nancie McDermott

Robert
ROSE

For complete cataloguing information, see page 240.

Disclaimer
The recipes in this book have been carefully tested by our kitchen and our tasters. To the best of our knowledge, they are safe and nutritious for ordinary use and users. For those people with food or other allergies, or who have special food requirements or health issues, please read the suggested contents of each recipe carefully and determine whether or not they may create a problem for you. All recipes are used at the risk of the consumer.

We cannot be responsible for any hazards, loss or damage that may occur as a result of any recipe use.

For those with special needs, allergies, requirements or health problems, in the event of any doubt, please contact your medical adviser prior to the use of any recipe.

Design and Production: Martina Hwang/PageWave Graphics Inc.
Editor: Carol Sherman
Proofreader: Karen Campbell-Sheviak
Photographer: Colin Erricson
Associate Photographer: Matt Johannsson
Prop Stylist: Charlene Erricson
Food Stylist: Michael Elliot

Cover image: Red Hot Vegetable Stir-Fry (page 120)
Other photographs: Crispy Spring Rolls with Sweet and Hot Garlic Sauce © iStockphoto.com/h3ct02; Wild Lime Leaves © Shutterstock.com/successo images; Shallots © iStockphoto.com/sandoclr; Galanga © iStockphoto.com/-lvinst-; Chiles © iStockphoto.com/enviromantic; Straw Mushrooms © iStockphoto.com/umbertoleporini; Cilantro © iStockphoto.com/MmeEmil; Tome Yum Soup © iStockphoto.com/darrenwise; Lime © iStockphoto.com/AlexStar; Lemongrass © iStockphoto.com/shawn_hempel; Star Anise © Shutterstock.com/Sebastian Duda; Curry Pastes © Shutterstock.com/zkruger; Dried Shiitake Mushrooms © iStockphoto.com/kcline; Sataw Beans © Shutterstock.com/kongkieat suraka; Sticky Rice © iStockphoto.com/Paul_Brighton; Coconut Ice Cream © iStockphoto.com/Mustang_79; Thai Iced Tea © Shutterstock.com/pick

The publisher gratefully acknowledges the financial support of our publishing program by the Government of Canada through the Canada Book Fund.

Published by Robert Rose Inc.
120 Eglinton Avenue East, Suite 800,
Toronto, Ontario, Canada M4P 1E2
Tel: (416) 322-6552 Fax: (416) 322-6936
www.robertrose.ca

Printed and bound in USA

1 2 3 4 5 6 7 8 9 CKV 23 22 21 20 19 18 17 16 15

DEDICATION

This book is dedicated to my friends and fellow Peace Corps volunteers Kathy Judd, Mary Claire Peceny, Kay Strong and Sandi and Dudley Younkin, with gratitude for the humor, adventure, insight, generosity and good company with which they provided me during the years we spent in Thailand.

ACKNOWLEDGMENTS

My thanks to Phillis Carey, Jill O'Connor and Fiona Urquhart for their excellent work in bringing this book to life, both in the kitchen and on the page. Their efforts have made the book indescribably better and the process a lot more fun. I am grateful to my family as well for cheering me on and for making life sweet while I worked on this book and every day since.

I would be delighted to hear what you think of this book and its recipes. You can visit my website, www.nanciemcdermott.com, and click on "Contact Nancie." There you'll find a form to fill out and your comments will swiftly fly to my e-mail.

I'd love to be in touch via social media as well, so look for me on Facebook, on Twitter @nanciemac, and on my blog at www.nanciemcdermott.com

Contents

Acknowledgments 5

Introduction. 8

Appetizers and Snacks 17

Salads 49

Soups 69

Curries 87

Stir-Fries and Other Main Dishes 103

Rice and Noodles 133

Sweets and Drinks 157

Basic Recipes 177

Suggested Menus 212

Glossary 214

Resources 230

Index. 232

Introduction

This is a book about the remarkable food of the remarkable kingdom where I had the good fortune to spend three years of my life. I went to Thailand not to explore an extraordinary cuisine in its vibrant context, but to teach English as a second language to Thai adolescents in an upcountry junior high. In fact, I did both during my stay, as well as receiving an education in eating, laughing, shopping, linguistics, friendship, art, agriculture, cooking, economics, conversation and enjoying life.

Had I foreseen that I would turn to writing cookbooks and teaching Thai cooking classes, I would have asked questions, sought out experts and made notes about the innumerable feasts, everyday suppers and snacks I savored during my stay in Thailand. When I set out to write my first cookbook, *Real Thai: The Best of Thailand's Regional Cooking,* I longed to turn back the clock and relive my time in Thailand as an official student of its cuisine. I regretted that my culinary concerns had run no further than finding a dynamite version of *paht Thai, som tum* or *tome yum* soup, and making brownies on a bucket-shaped charcoal stove. But now I consider this a blessing, because I absorbed the foundation of my knowledge of Thai food and culture like a child, soaking up a whole world along with the plain jasmine rice I ate morning, noon and night.

Although I am not a vegetarian, I wanted to write a cookbook for people who love Thai food but who do not eat meat. It was a great pleasure to create these recipes, coming up with delicious versions of traditional Thai dishes while respecting the commitments of the vegetarian kitchen. To do so I quickly found I had to veer away from the framework of authenticity within which I love to explore Thai cooking, for unlike India, China and Japan, Thailand lacks a strong indigenous vegetarian tradition.

Despite the fact that the majority of Thais are devoted to the teachings of Theravada Buddhism, vegetarian practice is rare. Even the Theravada Buddhist monks may be unable to follow a vegetarian diet, since they vow to live simply, subsisting on whatever the people provide for them. The people establish merit toward future incarnations by making daily offerings of food and other necessities of life to the monks.

Although vegetarianism is not widespread in Thailand, there are those who refrain from eating flesh. Followers of *ahahn mahng-saha-wiraht*, a religious practice with origins in the traditions of ayurvedic medicine and the teachings of Hinduism, forsake the eating of meat, although they may find eggs and dairy foods acceptable. They generally do not consider it necessary to maintain separate utensils to prepare and serve food.

A more common tradition of vegetarianism in Thailand is *ahahn jay*. The first word means "food," and the second refers to Chinese vegetarian practice. The Thai phrase *Kin jay* conveys that you do not eat meat. Chinese vegetarianism is rooted in Mahayana Buddhist practice and around it has sprung up a highly developed cuisine of tofu, wheat gluten and other protein-rich foods that are created to resemble meat in shape and texture. Within *ahahn mahng-saha-wiraht*, the emphasis is on eating vegetables for their own sake, while within the tradition of *ahahn jay*, cooks use meatlike foods to "vegetarianize" beloved dishes that are traditionally made with meat.

While they may not embrace vegetarianism as a way of life, each year many Thai-Chinese people abstain from eating meat for a period of time. These Mahayana Buddhists see vegetarianism as a means of purification, a route to mindfulness through temporary abstinence and sacrifice, much like the Christian observance of Lent. Believers forego meat and animal products in any form and food must be prepared and served using special pans, plates and utensils. This ten-day celebration is most prominent in southern Thai cities, particularly Phuket, where a large Thai-Chinese population has kept numerous Chinese cultural practices thriving for generations. In Bangkok and other large cities where the Chinese influence is strong, you will find a few Chinese vegetarian cafés and even street vendors who specialize in snacks made of tofu and gluten, sold in charming little cups fashioned from banana and bamboo leaves.

Within the last decade or so, a small number of Thais have adopted vegetarianism and have begun reinventing Thai cuisine without the use of meat or fish. Enthusiasm for this approach is growing, for health as well as religious reasons. Visitors to Thailand can sample this vegetarian work in progress at a few restaurants in Bangkok and in the fabled northern Thai city of Chiang Mai.

I created these recipes using no meat, fish, seafood or any condiments containing them. This meant omitting the fish sauce that seasons virtually every savory dish prepared in a Thai kitchen. Simply substituting an equal amount of soy sauce did not do the job: Soy sauce is heavy and rich by comparison and it takes over a dish. To replace the fish sauce, I arrived at a simple formula of increasing the salt while adding vegetable broth and a little soy sauce. In some cases, where an especially pungent, over-the-top saltiness is required, a touch of Asian bean sauce can be included. I also played with the scrumptious French mushroom creation called *duxelles,* to invent an alternative to the minced pork mixture flavored with cilantro, garlic and pepper that is used extensively in Thai food. The result is Mushroom Mince (page 192) and it is used in savory dishes throughout this book. These adaptations worked beautifully, enabling me to create a vegetarian way of cooking within the traditions of Thai cuisine.

For vegans, Thai food is easy to enjoy, since dairy products are virtually unknown in the traditional cuisine of almost every Asian country except India, where yogurt and ghee are widely used. Eggs are quite popular and not limited to breakfast, but in most cases they are left whole; consequently, substitutions and omissions are easy to make. In most of the recipes that use eggs, I have given adaptations for vegan readers in the notes that follow the recipes.

During my time in Thailand, I lived in Thatoom, a town of ten thousand people on the Mun River in the northeastern Thai province of Surin. Like the Thai provinces of Buriram and Sri Saket, its neighbors to the east and west, Surin was part of Cambodia through the centuries during which the Khmer empire dominated the region. By the fifteenth century, Thailand had taken control of these three provinces. Today, they make up a small portion of Pahk Issahn, Thailand's large northeastern region, which retains cultural and linguistic ties to neighboring Laos. Strong traces of Cambodian influence endure in Surin and its neighbors, particularly in the form of traditional silk weaving and in the Khmer dialect spoken in upcountry homes.

I shared a house with several students from our school, whose villages were too far from Thatoom to permit them a daily commute. In a traditional Thai arrangement, I provided room and board while my students took care of household chores and kept a huge, barrel-shaped jar in my kitchen supplied with jasmine rice from their family larders. The house I rented was a spacious wooden structure in the typical Thai style, with the living quarters raised one story off the ground on sturdy posts and the kitchen and bathroom down below. This keeps everyone high and dry during the monsoon season, when flooding of up to a foot or so is common. Upstairs, a long sitting room ran the length of the house, with three bedrooms taking up the remaining space. The room opened onto a porch lined with benches, with wide steps leading down to the cement patio beneath the house.

This sheltered space under the house is where country people can park their plows and shelter their water buffalo, oxen, ducks and chickens through the night. Here we parked bicycles and shoes, lawn chairs, low tables and straw mats lined with pillows. In this shady oasis, we often waited out the melting heat of a weekend afternoon, sustained by oscillating fans, conversation, the BBC World Service and Thai iced tea. One-third of this downstairs patio was enclosed to form a small bathroom and a simple but spacious kitchen, with huge wooden shutters over windows and doors. These were sealed up tight each night and flung open again each morning, creating an almost alfresco room in which to cook and eat. A picket fence enclosed our small yard, which contained two beautiful mango trees, big plump jars to catch rainwater for drinking and cooking and a well that provided water for household use.

Rising at dawn is standard operating procedure all over Thailand. I quickly grew fond of the cool, soft ambience of those morning hours, and an early start helped me take it slow in the harsh light and heat of afternoon. It also pays to show up at the market as early as possible. In a modest market like ours, cabbage, cucumbers, cauliflower and chiles were always available, but laggards were sure to miss out on sweet, crunchy snow peas, ears of baby corn in diminutive husks, small piles of fresh straw mushrooms and any unusually good batches of curry.

I pedaled my bicycle to the market each morning, never in the first wave of shoppers but always early enough to merit only modest teasing from passing neighbors on their way home. I picked up some curry and a little soup or chile sauce to supplement our breakfast rice, along with whatever we needed to cook supper. I topped off my tote bag with *kanome,* delicious Thai snacks made by enterprising townsfolk who had risen to cook them a good bit earlier than dawn. My personal favorite was *dao suan,* a warm, sweet mung bean pudding made with palm sugar and coconut milk, but banana leaf packets of coconut sticky rice with custard could also turn my head, and it was almost impossible to walk by the fried banana lady without trading a few *baht* for a cluster of warm, crunchy *gluay kaek.* This would keep us patient till the morning's rice was ready.

In my absence, my students had risen, bathed and dressed and then turned to morning chores. The boys drew water, the girls lit the charcoal stoves, put on the rice pot and got breakfast started and everyone pitched in on the sweeping and on washing down the wooden floors upstairs. While I got ready for school, the two girls, Onjan and Titimah, finished cooking and set out our morning meal, spreading out thick straw mats to transform the kitchen floor into the scene of a homey feast. When five plates heaped with steaming jasmine rice ringed the circle of half-a-dozen savory dishes, we gathered for a quick meal before heading off, striving to be in our appointed places at school in time for the playing of the national anthem and the raising of the flag.

Left behind in our quiet kitchen were the simple appointments of Thai home cooking. A pair of bucket-shaped charcoal stoves stood on a low platform that raised them to the perfect height for cooking. A handy straw fan helped us crank up the heat as needed and a covered bucket stood by with tongs, accepting deposits of live coals when we wanted to turn it down. A worktable held two mortars, one a tall, deep clay cone with a wooden pestle for green papaya salad and the other a squat, sturdy bowl of blue-green granite for curry pastes. Beside it were the cutting board, a thick pale round of hardwood cut from a sturdy tamarind tree and a no-nonsense cleaver and assorted paring knives. A stack of enameled-tin dinner plates stood by, along with a basket of silverware. This consisted of the forks and large spoons Thais use for eating. Diners scoop up rice and its accompaniments onto the spoon, using the fork to direct the tidbits of food. The basket also contained chopsticks, both long ones for cooking and regular ones for eating, on those occasions when we brought home noodle dishes from the corner noodle shop.

Pots, pans and a shallow, lightweight Thai-style wok hung on the wall, along with two steamers—a large, metal Chinese-style steamer and a cone-shaped, woven bamboo steamer for Laotian-style sticky rice. Nearby hung various utensils along with market bags and copious supplies of the ubiquitous twin elements of Thai cooking, listed in recipes simply as *hohm-gratiem,* "garlic and shallots." Both are tiny compared to their Western cousins, flavor-packed and tinged with a deep, lovely shade of pink.

On the far wall stood our *thoo,* a dead ringer for my Granny Suitt's pie safe, but with screen wire lining the doors rather than embossed tin. Here we kept condiments and food screened away from pesky flies and cordoned off from tenacious ants by a quartet of ceramic cups in which the four legs of the cabinet stood. Each cup provided a little moat filled with water. This fended off creatures with a mind to crawl up the *thoo* leg for a picnic without immersing the cabinet's wooden legs in water, which would rot them over time. In the two far corners stood waist-high glazed jars, one filled with rainwater for cooking and drinking and the other holding about 50 pounds (23 kg) of jasmine rice.

My kitchen was simple and sensible, and most of its equipment, or a good substitute, is easily found in the West. Many Thai ingredients can be found in supermarkets and specialty grocery stores, as well as in Asian markets. Fresh herbs present the biggest challenge, especially wild lime leaves *(bai makrut)*, galanga and holy basil. See Resources (page 230) for companies that may be able to send you ingredients you need, and look for Asian markets when you have time to explore. I have offered suggestions on substitutions whenever possible and I salute your efforts to work out your version of a dish with whatever you have available if you cannot find choices A and B. Check the Resources for some excellent purveyors of Asian ingredients and equipment. Thailand's cuisine owes much to that of India and China and any acquaintance you make with Chinese and Indian cooking will serve you well as you cook Thai food.

To organize this book in a truly Thai culinary spirit, I would need only four chapters, defined by the respectful relationship Thais automatically create between rice and everything else they eat. Rice and Noodles would be Chapter One, Good Stuff to Set Our Rice Aglow would be Chapter Two, Snacks and Sweets to Enjoy between Rice-Centered Meals would be Chapter Three and Basic Recipes would be Chapter Four.

Of these four chapters, Chapter Two would be the largest, encompassing the range of what Thais call *gahp kao, gahp* meaning "with" and *kao* meaning "rice." I have broken this category Western-style into Soups, Salads, Curries, and Stir-Fries and Other Main Dishes to make it easier to find favorite dishes and to put a vegetarian Thai menu together. Chapter One, the Rice and Noodles chapter, might not even exist, since every Thai person old enough to light an upcountry charcoal stove learns how to cook a pot of rice and since noodles are savored in noodle shops rather than cooked at home.

Instead, this book is organized into eight chapters, beginning with Appetizers and Snacks, followed by Salads and then Soups. In these three chapters you will find dishes that are light in spirit, often appropriate for a first course, a nibble with which to welcome guests or a simple lunch or supper for one or two people. Next comes Curries, with a roundup of saucy, spectacular dishes, each with a Thai-style curry paste as its flavorful base. Stir-fries and Other Main Dishes offers grilled vegetables and an array of stir-fries. As with curries, you will want to serve these dishes along with lots of unseasoned rice, either jasmine rice or Laotian-style sticky rice. Both serve as a pleasing foil for the array of intense flavors that compose a Thai meal.

Next comes a savory chapter on Rice and Noodles. Here you will find basic rice recipes, seasoned rice dishes such as fried rice and coconut rice and a delicious array of noodle dishes. You can enjoy *paht Thai* and Thai-style fried rice as one-dish meals or serve them along with other dishes as is often done in Thai restaurants in the West. Sweets and Drinks follows, where you will find classics such as Cool, Crisp Rubies in Coconut Milk and Thai Iced Tea, as well as irresistible East-West creations, including Thai Coffee Ice Cream, Coconut Rice Pudding and Fresh Lemongrass Lemonade. The final chapter, Basic Recipes, is a compendium of condiments and other dishes called for in recipes throughout the book. Here you will find instructions for dipping sauces, curry pastes, Roasted Rice Powder and Tamarind Liquid, as well as advice for those of you who want to make coconut milk from scratch.

Following this final chapter of recipes are three appendices: suggested vegetarian menus; a glossary containing information about the ingredients you will encounter in this book; and a resource section, where you will find information on vendors who can supply you with herbs, spices and utensils.

For a traditional Thai approach to a vegetarian menu, try to think in terms of a few principles rather than a list of specific dishes. Think of a typical home-style Thai meal as an edible solar system, with lots of delicious little planets revolving around the sun. The latter, for our purposes, is an abundance of naturally fragrant unseasoned jasmine rice. The planets must not only nourish us and taste good, they must also delight us in their variety, orbiting in a harmonious vegetarian dance, which we are free to choreograph in a number of ways.

Foremost is variety of flavors. You have probably heard that Thai people love chiles, but even a Thai with the proverbial asbestos palate wants only one or two incendiary dishes to set the meal aflame, not a tableful, because then the balance is gone. Pick a chile-hot curry as your centerpiece dish and add contrasting planets to your universe, with something sour such as Lemongrass Soup with Rice and Basil Chez Sovan, something sweet such as Son-in-Law Eggs and something salty such as Dao Jiow Lone Dipping Sauce with a rainbow of vegetables.

Another way to ensure variety is to avoid repetition of ingredients. Do not make tofu or mushrooms, for example, a major player in more than one dish. Also, you will want to vary textures and cooking methods. Rather than preparing several stir-fries, pick one and round out the menu with something deep-fried for a rich, crispy note, something liquid such as clear soup for a simple resonance and perhaps a salad for a cool hit and a raw vegetable crunch.

Finally, I add my personal mission to achieve variety in the amount of effort I must expend to put forth the meal. If I am making labor-intensive Sweet Potato Wonton Soup with Crispy Garlic and frying delicious Mung Bean Fritters to welcome my guests, I will take every possible shortcut for the rest of the meal, from assigning someone else to bring a salad and drinks, to serving a fruit tart or brownies from my favorite bakery for dessert.

Keep in mind that these are guidelines and not commandments. If you take anxiety into the kitchen, it will get in the food. Thai people make a national pastime out of surrendering to the universe and following their hearts. Just pick a recipe, start cooking and you will be doing it right.

My goal is to put words about Thai food on paper in such a way that you will long to taste it and thus be driven to cook it to life. I hope these recipes will create delicious vegetarian Thai food for you and for those who share your table. May this book bring you pleasure and pass along to you some of the magic I have found in the world of food, cooking and all things Thai.

Appetizers and Snacks

Pineapple Bites 20

Mung Bean Fritters 21

Curried Corncakes with Sweet and Hot
Garlic Sauce 22

Garlicky Mushroom Turnovers 23

Vegetable Curry Puffs 24

Chewy "Pearl" Dumplings with
Mushroom Mince and Crispy Garlic 26

Delectable Lettuce Bites 28

Dao Jiow Lone Dipping Sauce with Vegetables 30

Crispy Spring Rolls with Sweet and Hot
Garlic Sauce 32

Roasted Eggplant Dip with Thai Flavors 35

Two-Potato Curry Pot Stickers 36

Sweet Potato Shiao Mai 38

Satay Peanut Sauce with Grilled Vegetables,
Fried Tofu and Toast 40

Spicy Cashews with Chiles, Cilantro and Lime 43

Crispy Rice Cakes 44

Fried Peanuts with Green Onions and Chiles 46

Sweet and Spicy Nuts 47

Appetizers and Snacks

Early in my three-year sojourn in Thailand, I made the common observation that Thai people seem to eat all the time. This custom pleased me enormously, since food has always been of great interest to me. I also wanted to make up for time lost in growing to adulthood in a world without the blessing of Thai food.

From the bluish hour before sunrise until the bullfrogs and cicadas serenade the last night owls off to sleep, the people of Thailand are cooking, buying provisions at the market, eating square meals, snacking on an endless array of tidbits, toting food to someone else for sharing or talking about food. Many of the dishes that comprise these rituals fit into the category of *ahahn wahng,* with *ahahn* meaning "food" and *wahng* meaning "free," alluding to leisure, free time and the appeal of passing a little time nibbling and chatting with friends and family.

On returning to my desk in the teacher's room after a seventh-grade English class, I was certain to find edible reinforcements on the conference table: cool, juicy chunks of ripe pineapple for dipping in a tiny mountain of salt laced with dried red chiles, silver dollar–sized pancakes of freshly grated coconut known as *kanome ping,* crispy fried bananas called *gluay kaek.* The teachers enjoying the treats would quickly beckon, calling out an invitation to each returning colleague to take a moment to visit and enjoy a bite. If I were the one heading out on my break to bicycle to the post office or the bank, I kept an eye out for something sweet or savory to bring back, lest I return empty-handed. I loved this custom and still do, for the company as well as the food. During our training, we greenhorn Peace Corps volunteers learned that eating while strolling down the street was considered poor manners. I imagine the rationale is not the incongruous prissy attitude I surmised at the time, but a respect for food and an appreciation of its intrinsic pleasure and the benefits of eating with people one enjoys.

Most of the recipes in this chapter are for street food—the appealing, portable snacks that fuel Thai people between their three daily meals centered on rice. The custom of ordering a first course in a restaurant or serving one as part of a special meal at home is more Western than Thai. Certainly you will be offered food within minutes of arriving at someone's home, but this hospitality would be shown whether or not a meal was soon to follow.

These dishes work well as informal appetizers before a meal or as snacks any time the urge strikes you for the taste of Thai food. Have *miang kum*—Delectable Lettuce Bites—ready when guests arrive, for nibbling while you command the grill and pour tempting tumblers of Thai Iced Tea. Fry up a sizzling saucer of Two-Potato Curry Pot Stickers to go with the popcorn while you watch the playoff games or present lovely Pineapple Bites for a sparkling note at the next potluck.

All but two of the recipes in this chapter are my vegetarian versions of traditional Thai dishes. I created the Garlicky Mushroom Turnovers to showcase Mushroom Mince, the scrumptious filling found in the Basic Recipes chapter that you will use many times in the course of cooking recipes from this book. The other, Sweet and Spicy Nuts, was inspired by peanut brittle and honey-roasted nuts and carried to Thai heights with the addition of red curry paste, roasted cumin and toasted shredded coconut. You will need to make these in advance and you may need to do as I do and have an un-bribable family member hide them so that some remain to serve to your guests. The pot stickers, Sweet Potato Shiao Mai, Fried Peanuts with Green Onions and Chiles and Crispy Spring Rolls with Sweet and Hot Garlic Sauce are Thai-Chinese dishes that entered Thailand's culinary landscape centuries ago as part of the great Chinese legacy to Thai cuisine.

The amount of time and the degree of skill required to prepare the recipes vary widely. The two dipping sauces, Roasted Eggplant Dip with Thai Flavors and Dao Jiow Lone Dipping Sauce, are simple to make, as are Pineapple Bites and Sweet and Spicy Nuts. Curried Corncakes, Mung Bean Fritters and Fried Peanuts with Green Onions and Chiles are straightforward but require the care and effort demanded by deep-frying. The *shiao mai,* pot stickers and spring rolls involve the challenge of filling, rolling and shaping each piece and then steaming or frying the result, but the rewards will be great. Keep in mind as you try your hand at making these "greatest hits" of the world of Thai street food that you are venturing where Thai home cooks seldom go, since these good things are commonly purchased from vendors, experts for whom making spring rolls or dumplings is a daily task.

Pineapple Bites

This classic Thai snack goes by the mysterious name mah haw. *The first word means "horse" and the second refers to the Haw people, who migrated to northern Thailand from the southwestern Chinese province of Yunnan centuries ago. While I am still working out the connection to horses, Haw people and a royal-style Thai snack, I can say with certainty that almost everyone loves these. Fresh pineapple is lovely, canned pineapple is easy and using either one produces a great taste. If you choose fresh pineapple, reserve the leafy top, place it on the serving platter as a garnish and surround it with a flotilla of tiny Pineapple Bites.*

MAKES ABOUT 36 BITES

Tips

You will need only ½ recipe Mushroom Mince for this dish, but I usually make a full recipe and enjoy the rest tossed with pasta or rice, in an omelet or spread on a grilled vegetable sandwich.

The classic presentation for this dish is to arrange 2 small slivers of pepper in an X over the filling. But as long as you have the splash of red and green you will have an appealing appetizer.

1	small ripe pineapple, or 1 can (14 oz/400 mL) pineapple rings or chunks, drained	1
1 cup	Mushroom Mince (page 192) (see Tips, left)	250 mL
1 tbsp	finely chopped salted dry-roasted peanuts	15 mL
½	red bell pepper	½
½	bunch fresh cilantro	½

1. Carefully peel pineapple and cut it crosswise into slices about ¼ inch (0.5 cm) thick. Cut each slice in half and then remove and discard its tough core. Cut each slice into little tiles or wedge-shaped bite-size pieces. Cut canned pineapple rings in the same way.

2. In a small bowl, combine Mushroom Mince and peanuts and stir well. Cut red pepper into slivers ½ inch (1 cm) long. Tear off a handful of small whole cilantro leaves.

3. Carefully top a pineapple piece with about ½ tsp (2 mL) of the Mushroom Mince mixture, then garnish with a cilantro leaf and a piece or two of red pepper. Place on a serving platter and repeat until all the ingredients are used. Serve at room temperature.

Mung Bean Fritters

These crunchy golden tidbits are delicious, appealing and simple to make. Yellow mung beans are the hulled and split yellow centers of round green mung beans. Serve these fritters with one of the Thai sauces I have suggested or with any favorite tangy dipping sauce.

MAKES ABOUT 48 FRITTERS

Tips

If you are pressed for time, you can bring unsoaked yellow mung beans to a boil, reduce the heat to low and simmer until tender enough to mash, 5 to 10 minutes.

You can prepare the batter up to 1 day in advance, cover and refrigerate until cooking time.

If you need to cook the fritters in advance, you can keep them warm for 30 minutes or so in a 250°F (120°C) oven. Or set them aside to cool to room temperature, transfer to an airtight container until serving time and then loosely wrap them in foil and reheat in a 250°F (120°C) oven until heated through, 10 to 15 minutes.

- Steamer basket
- Baking sheet, lined with paper towels
- Candy/deep-fry thermometer
- Asian-style wire strainer or slotted spoon

1 cup	dried yellow mung beans	250 mL
½ cup	all-purpose flour	125 mL
1 tbsp	curry powder	15 mL
1 tsp	salt	5 mL
4	green onions, thinly sliced crosswise	4
	Vegetable oil for deep-frying	
	A handful of fresh cilantro sprigs	
	Tangy Tamarind Sauce (page 207) or Sweet and Hot Garlic Sauce (page 206)	

1. Place beans in a bowl and add warm water to cover by about 2 inches (5 cm). Let soak for 3 hours and then drain well. Meanwhile, combine flour, curry and salt in a bowl, mix well with a fork and set aside.

2. Place soaked beans on a steamer basket and steam until soft enough to mash with a spoon, about 15 minutes. Transfer to flour mixture and mix well, stirring, scraping and mashing to combine everything into a fairly smooth paste. Stir in onions and mix well.

3. To cook fritters, form thick batter into walnut-size lumps and then pinch each lump into a football shape. You should have about 48 balls. Pour oil into a large, deep heavy skillet or wok to a depth of 3 inches (7.5 cm). Place over medium heat for 5 to 10 minutes. The oil is ready when a bit of batter dropped into the pan sizzles and floats at once. (The oil should register 360° to 375°F/182° to 190°C on the thermometer.) Gently lower about 6 fritters into oil and cook until beautifully browned and crisp, 1 to 2 minutes. Using wire strainer, remove fritters, holding briefly over pan to drain and then set aside on prepared baking sheet. Cook remaining fritters in the same way.

4. When all the fritters are done, transfer to a serving platter. Garnish with cilantro and serve at once with a small bowl of sauce.

Curried Corncakes with Sweet and Hot Garlic Sauce

Like most Asian people, Thais seldom eat corn and when they do it tends to be sturdy roasting ears grilled over charcoal or plump kernels floating in coconut milk–based sweets. But this vegetarian version of the popular Thai fritter of ground fish called tod mun *is wildly popular throughout the kingdom. In this* tod mun kao pode, *fresh corn is ideal, but frozen kernels work fine, if given time to thaw before cooking.*

MAKES ABOUT 24 CORNCAKES

Tip

Rice flour is sold in health food stores and Asian markets and makes the fritters crispier, but you can omit it and use 5 tbsp (75 mL) all-purpose flour instead.

- ♦ Baking sheet, lined with paper towels
- ♦ Candy/deep-fry thermometer
- ♦ Asian-style wire strainer or slotted spoon

2 cups	fresh or thawed frozen corn kernels	500 mL
3 tbsp	rice flour (see Tip, left)	45 mL
2 tbsp	all-purpose flour	30 mL
2 tsp	Red Curry Paste (page 180)	10 mL
½ tsp	soy sauce	2 mL
½ tsp	salt	2 mL
1	egg, lightly beaten	1
	Vegetable oil for deep-frying	
	Sweet-and-Sour Cucumber Salad (page 61)	
	Sweet and Hot Garlic Sauce (page 206) or Tangy Tamarind Sauce (page 207)	

1. In a bowl, combine corn, rice flour, flour, curry paste, soy sauce, salt and egg and stir to mix well. The batter will be thick, wet and nubby. Set aside.

2. Pour oil into a large, deep heavy skillet or wok to a depth of 3 inches (7.5 cm). Place over medium heat for 5 to 10 minutes. The oil is ready when a bit of batter dropped into it sizzles and floats at once. (The oil should register 360° to 375°F/182° to 190°C on the thermometer.) Using a large spoon, scoop up about 1 tbsp (15 mL) of the batter and carefully slip it into the hot oil. Add 2 or 3 more spoonfuls and cook until the cakes are nicely browned on the bottom, about 2 minutes. Carefully turn them to brown the top, about 1 minute. Using the wire strainer, remove fritters, holding briefly over the pan to drain and then set aside on prepared baking sheet. Cook the remaining fritters in the same way.

3. When all the fritters are done, transfer to a serving platter. Serve at once with small bowls of salad and sauce on the side.

Garlicky Mushroom Turnovers

Here are plump little pockets filled with a savory mixture of tofu and mushrooms, seasoned with the traditional Thai flavor combination of garlic and cilantro. Make the dough first and then make the filling while it rests.

MAKES ABOUT 36 TURNOVERS

Tip

If you have time to fill these tiny pastries a day ahead of serving, you can refrigerate the unbaked turnovers and then bake them just before the festivities begin.

* Baking sheet, lined with parchment paper or lightly greased
* 2½-inch (6 cm) round cutter

Pastry

2½ cups	all-purpose flour	625 mL
1 tsp	salt	5 mL
⅔ cup	vegetable oil	150 mL
⅓ cup	water	75 mL

Filling

2 cups	Mushroom Mince (page 192)	500 mL
2 tbsp	minced green onions	30 mL
2 tbsp	minced fresh cilantro	30 mL

A handful of fresh cilantro sprigs
Sweet and Hot Garlic Sauce (page 206)

1. *Pastry:* In a large bowl, combine flour and salt and stir to mix well. In a measuring cup, combine oil and water and pour over flour and salt. Using a fork, stir until mixture comes together. Continue working dough with fork or your fingers until it can be gathered into a ball. Divide dough in half and form each half into a flat disk. Wrap each disk in plastic wrap and let stand at room temperature for 20 minutes.

2. *Filling:* In a small bowl, combine Mushroom Mince, green onions and cilantro and stir to mix well. Cover and refrigerate until ready to form turnovers.

3. Preheat oven to 400°F (200°C). Place 1 pastry disk between 2 large sheets of plastic wrap. Roll out pastry about ⅛ inch (3 mm) thick. Using round cutter, cut dough into rounds. Repeat with remaining disk. You should have about 36 rounds.

4. Place about 1 tsp (5 mL) filling on a pastry round. Fold it in half to form a half-moon and pinch the edges together firmly to seal. Crimp the sealed edge with the tines of a fork and place on the prepared baking sheet. Repeat with the remaining pastry rounds and filling. Bake until lightly browned, about 20 minutes. Transfer to a serving platter. Garnish with cilantro and serve warm with sauce.

Vegetable Curry Puffs

Thais depend on complex curry pastes for most of their curry dishes, but they also often make use of curry powder, known as pong kah-ree. *It probably entered the Thai pantry via the Chinese- and British-influenced kitchens of neighboring Malaysia and Singapore, and its familiar golden hue appears in savory snacks such as these delicious turnovers. They are traditionally made with a double-layered lard-based pastry, but here I use the shortcut of frozen puff pastry dough, widely available in Western supermarkets. You could also use a homemade samosa-type dough.*

MAKES ABOUT 40 PUFFS

Tip

Frozen puff pastry makes an excellent, speedy substitute for the double-layered, flaky dough used for this popular snack throughout Southeast Asia. Made with shortening or lard, it is time-consuming to prepare, which is why this dish is primarily a street food treat or celebration snack, prepared by professional cooks. Look for puff pastry dough in the freezer section of well-stocked supermarkets. Shortening-based puff pastry is the most common but butter-based is also available. Remove what you need and let it stand on a baking sheet until thawed enough to handle, about 15 minutes. Wrap and freeze any remaining pastry for up to 2 months.

- Preheat oven to 400°F (200°C)
- Skillet with tight-fitting lid
- Baking sheet, lined with parchment paper

2 tbsp	vegetable oil	30 mL
1	large baking potato, peeled and cut into ¼-inch (0.5 cm) cubes	1
1	carrot, peeled and cut into ¼-inch (0.5 cm) cubes	1
1	onion, finely chopped	1
10	green beans, trimmed and cut crosswise into thin slices	10
2	large cloves garlic, minced	2
2 tbsp	curry powder	30 mL
1 tbsp	granulated sugar	15 mL
1 tsp	soy sauce	5 mL
1 tsp	salt	5 mL
½ cup	Vegetable Stock (pages 189 and 190) or store-bought	125 mL
1	package (about 1 lb/500 g; 2 sheets) frozen puff pastry, thawed (see Tip, left)	1
¼ cup	finely chopped fresh cilantro	60 mL
1	egg mixed with 1 tbsp (15 mL) water	1
	Sweet and Hot Garlic Sauce (page 206)	

Tips

You can prepare these curry puffs and then set them aside for baking later. Arrange them on a plate or baking sheet, close together but not touching. Cover them airtight and refrigerate for up to 1 day before baking as directed.

While these curry puffs are at their delicious best when freshly baked, they are still tasty at room temperature, which is how they are usually enjoyed in Thailand.

Variation

You could use sweet potatoes or winter squash in place of white potatoes, and parsnips instead of carrots.

1. In a skillet, heat oil over medium heat until a bit of garlic added to the pan sizzles at once. Add potato, carrot, onion, green beans and garlic and sprinkle with curry powder. Cook, tossing often, for 2 minutes. Add sugar, soy sauce, salt and stock and bring to a gentle boil. Reduce heat to low, cover and cook until vegetables are tender, about 5 minutes.

2. Uncover pan, increase heat to medium and continue to cook, tossing often, until all the liquid has evaporated, 3 to 4 minutes. Transfer vegetable mixture to a plate and spread out and let cool to room temperature.

3. Meanwhile, roll out 1 sheet of the puff pastry on a lightly floured board, shaping into a 15- by 12-inch (38 by 30 cm) rectangle ¼ inch (0.5 cm) thick. Cut pastry into twenty 3-inch (7.5 cm) squares.

4. Add cilantro to the cooled vegetable mixture and toss well. Spoon about 2 tsp (10 mL) of the curry filling onto each pastry square. Brush 2 adjacent sides of the square with egg mixture and fold the square to form a triangle, enclosing the filling. Pinch and stretch the dough as needed to seal tightly. Crimp the edges of the triangle with a fork and place on the prepared baking sheet. Repeat with the remaining pastry squares, curry filling and puff pastry sheet until all the ingredients are used.

5. Brush the tops of the curry puffs with the remaining egg mixture and bake in preheated oven until a rich, golden brown, 15 to 20 minutes. Serve hot or warm with Sweet and Hot Garlic Sauce.

Chewy "Pearl" Dumplings with Mushroom Mince and Crispy Garlic

Inside these chewy little dumplings is a garlicky mushroom filling studded with chopped peanuts for crunch. Known in Thai as saku sai heht, *they are placed on a leaf of lettuce, topped with crispy garlic, a few leaves of fresh cilantro and a burst of fresh green chile heat and then enjoyed in one or two glorious bites. Tiny tapioca pearls, a traditional Thai ingredient found in even the smallest market town, are used in sweets as well as savory dishes such as this one. During its bath of steam, the chalky white tapioca dough is transformed into a silvery noodle-like covering. These irresistible treats are best when freshly made, so if you need to prepare them in advance, shape the balls, chill for a few hours and then steam briefly an hour or so before serving, so they will be at room temperature.*

MAKES 32 BALLS

Tip

When the dumplings are hot, stickiness can be a problem. If they stick when you try to remove them from the steamer, dip your utensils in water or lightly grease any surface they touch.

- Steamer basket

Filling

2 tbsp	finely chopped salted dry-roasted peanuts	30 mL
¾ cup	Mushroom Mince (page 192) (approx.)	175 mL

Dough

2 cups	small tapioca pearls	500 mL
1½ cups	warm water	375 mL
32	leaf lettuce cups or small lettuce leaves	32
½ cup	loosely packed fresh cilantro leaves	125 mL
1	fresh green serrano chile, thinly sliced crosswise or 10 tiny Thai bird's-eye chiles, optional	1
¼ cup	Crispy Garlic in Oil (page 203)	60 mL

1. *Filling:* In a bowl, stir together peanuts and Mushroom Mince, combining well. Set aside.

2. *Dough:* Place tapioca pearls in a medium bowl. Slowly add warm water while kneading the tapioca pearls with your hands for several minutes to soften and coax them to absorb the water. You should end up with a thick, sticky, chalk-white paste. Let stand for 5 minutes and then knead until the dough is a soft, malleable clay that comes together and "wipes" the bowl clean, about 1 minute longer. Shape dough into a log and cut into 32 equal pieces, about 1 tbsp (15 mL) each. Roll each piece into a ball, moistening your hands as needed to work and shape the dough.

You can mask the steaming rack with a banana leaf or leaves of cabbage or sturdy lettuce if you like; the leaves may lessen the stickiness. If you have a small basket steamer, simply cook the dumplings in batches.

If you have trouble filling the balls as directed, try flattening each ball into a little pancake on your palm. Place the filling in the center and then pinch the edges together to enclose it, taking care to keep the center of the pancake thick enough to cover the filling without splitting once it is sealed.

3. Hold a ball in the palm of one hand and poke the thumb of your other hand into its center to hollow out a tiny chamber. Add about ½ tsp (2 mL) of the mushroom mixture and then carefully pinch and press the dough back over the filling to seal up and smooth. Moisten your fingers lightly if needed to ease this task and use bits of moistened dough to seal any broken patches. Try to keep the dough an even thickness all around, although it will be somewhat thicker at the seam. Set aside on a platter while you continue forming the remaining dough and filling into balls.

4. Fill the bottom of a steamer or a heavy saucepan with 3 inches (7.5 cm) of water and bring it to a rolling boil over medium heat. Meanwhile, place balls on a lightly oiled steamer basket, taking care that they do not touch one another or the sides of the basket. When the steam is steady and strong, place balls over the steam, cover and adjust the heat to maintain a steady head of steam. Cook until balls turn from small, dry golf balls into plump, translucent dumplings, 12 to 15 minutes. Check the water level and add very hot water as needed, increasing the cooking time to cover any time lost while the water returns to a steamy boil. Test for doneness by cutting open a dumpling. The wrapping should be chewy and the filling heated through. Remove the steaming basket from the heat and set aside for about 5 minutes.

5. Lightly grease a platter (or moisten it with cold water) and transfer dumplings to it, placing them an inch (2.5 cm) or so apart. Let cool to room temperature.

6. To serve, mound dumplings on a platter along with the lettuce cups, cilantro leaves, and chiles, if using, and pour Crispy Garlic in Oil over dumplings. To eat, place a lettuce cup in your palm, top with a dumpling and sprinkle on a little cilantro and some chiles, if you like. Fold the leaf into a packet and enjoy it in a bite or two. Alternatively, arrange small lettuce leaves on 1 or 2 platters and place a dumpling on each leaf. Spoon a little Crispy Garlic in Oil over each dumpling and top with a few cilantro leaves. Set out the chiles for diners to add to taste.

Delectable Lettuce Bites

Known as miang kum—miang *means "leaf" and* kum *means "a small mouthful"—this unique dish provides a beautiful centerpiece and a mouthwatering nibble that can be prepared hours in advance. In Thailand, each guest prepares his or her own portions, but you may want to assemble several lettuce bites to start. That way your guests will have an idea of how they go together before they begin making their own. Make 1 cup (250 mL) of the Toasted Coconut, since it is used for both the sauce and the treats. The sauce needs time to cool to room temperature and it keeps well for several days, so you may want to make it in advance and then assemble the treats just before serving.*

SERVES 10

Tips

Ideal lettuce varieties include Boston, butter, limestone or iceberg lettuce. Large fresh spinach leaves can also be used. You want diminutive cup-shaped leaves or palm-sized leaves that can be folded into large bite-size packets. Belgian endive spears make a chic, practical substitute for the lettuce.

You can also serve these with the ingredients already portioned out into the leaves. You can leave the sauce on the side or dollop the sauce in first before adding the other ingredients.

◆ Mini food processor or blender

Sauce

½ cup	Toasted Coconut (page 199)	125 mL
3 tbsp	coarsely chopped peeled fresh gingerroot	45 mL
2 tbsp	coarsely chopped shallots	30 mL
1 tbsp	Asian bean sauce	15 mL
¾ cup	Vegetable Stock (pages 189 and 190) or store-bought	175 mL
1 cup	palm sugar or brown sugar	250 mL
¼ cup	Tamarind Liquid (page 191)	60 mL
1 tsp	soy sauce	5 mL
1 tsp	salt	5 mL

Treats

½ cup	Toasted Coconut (page 199)	125 mL
½ cup	cut-up peeled fresh gingerroot (¼-inch/0.5 cm chunks)	125 mL
½ cup	cut-up limes, including peel (¼-inch/0.5 cm chunks)	125 mL
½ cup	cut-up shallots or red onions (¼-inch/0.5 cm chunks)	125 mL
2 tbsp	thinly sliced fresh green chiles such as Thai bird's eye, serrano or jalapeño	30 mL
½ cup	salted dry-roasted peanuts	125 mL
½ cup	salted sunflower seeds	125 mL
1	head lettuce with cup-shaped leaves (see Tips, left)	1

Some traditional versions of this sauce call for fresh galanga rather than fresh ginger and roast both the galanga and the shallots before grinding them with the coconut and bean sauce. A spoonful of finely ground peanuts is also sometimes added. Try these variations if you have the ingredients and the time.

1. *Sauce:* In mini processor or blender, combine coconut, ginger, shallots and Asian bean sauce and pulse to grind to a fairly smooth paste. Scrape down the sides as you work, adding a little of the vegetable stock as needed to move the blades.

2. In a saucepan over medium heat, combine coconut-ginger paste, vegetable stock, sugar, tamarind, soy sauce and salt. Stir well and bring to a rolling boil, stirring often. Boil for 2 minutes, stirring and adjusting heat as needed to be sure sauce does not boil over. Reduce heat to maintain a gentle boil and simmer, stirring and scraping the sides down occasionally, until sauce is dark brown, thickened to a medium syrup and well combined, about 10 minutes.

3. When sauce reaches room temperature it should be a little thicker than real maple syrup and a good bit thinner than honey. Transfer to a bowl and set aside, uncovered, and let cool to room temperature. You should have about $1\frac{1}{4}$ cups (300 mL). (At this point the sauce can be tightly covered and refrigerated for 3 or 4 days.)

4. *Treats:* Arrange coconut, ginger, limes, shallots, chiles, peanuts and sunflower seeds in separate heaps on a platter or in small separate bowls. Separate lettuce leaves and arrange a platter of pretty, cup-shaped leaves nearby. Place sauce in a small deep serving bowl and provide a small serving spoon.

5. To eat, take a lettuce leaf, add small amounts of each treat to it and then top with a dollop of sauce. Fold into a small packet, pop it into your mouth and chew, chew, chew! It's a mouthful, but biting it daintily tends to spill the whole business all over you and the idea is to get the extraordinary flavor combination in one grand explosion.

Dao Jiow Lone Dipping Sauce with Vegetables

The word lone *identifies this sauce as one of the rich, pungent dipping sauces made with coconut milk that are typical of the cuisine of central Thailand.* Lone *dishes are elegant members of the larger family of* nahm prik *dishes, intensely flavored dipping sauces generally fiery with chiles. All these spunky sauces exist to flavor fresh vegetables and plain jasmine or sticky rice. This lone stars the super-salty bean sauce Thais inherited from the kitchens of China.*

SERVES 10 TO 12

Tip
Although *lone* and *nahm prik* dishes are always presented with raw vegetables for dipping, there is usually rice as well.

◆ Mini food processor or blender

Sauce

¾ cup	coarsely chopped tofu	175 mL
1 tbsp	Asian bean sauce	15 mL
⅓ cup	Vegetable Stock (pages 189 and 190) or store-bought	75 mL
½ cup	minced shallots, divided	125 mL
1 tbsp	vegetable oil	15 mL
2 tbsp	coarsely chopped garlic	30 mL
½ cup	finely chopped red onion	125 mL
⅔ cup	unsweetened coconut milk	150 mL
2 tbsp	palm sugar or brown sugar	30 mL
1 tsp	soy sauce	5 mL
¼ tsp	salt	1 mL
2 tbsp	Tamarind Liquid (page 191) (approx.) (see Variation, right)	30 mL

Vegetables

3	small cucumbers or 1 large hothouse cucumber, peeled, halved lengthwise and cut into thick slices	3
3	wedges green cabbage, about 2 inches (5 cm) wide at their widest point	3
15	green beans, cut into 3-inch (7.5 cm) lengths or whole snow peas	15
½	red bell pepper, cut into long thin strips	½
10	carrot sticks	10
5	large radishes, trimmed and halved lengthwise	5

Variation

Lime juice sweetened with a little brown sugar can replace the tamarind liquid in a pinch.

1. *Sauce:* In mini processor or blender, combine tofu, Asian bean sauce, vegetable stock and half of the shallots and pulse to grind to a fairly smooth paste, stopping to scrape down the sides as needed to grind evenly. Transfer to a small bowl and set aside.

2. In a small skillet over medium heat, warm oil until a bit of garlic added to the pan sizzles at once. Add garlic and onion and cook, tossing often, until fragrant, shiny and tender, about 2 minutes. Stir in coconut milk and bring to a gentle boil. Adjust the heat to maintain an active simmer and cook until coconut milk thickens slightly and releases its sweet fragrance, 5 to 7 minutes.

3. When coconut milk is ready, add tofu paste and cook, stirring occasionally, for 3 minutes. Add remaining shallots, sugar, soy sauce and salt. Cook, stirring occasionally, for 2 minutes, then remove from heat. Stir in tamarind. Taste the sauce. Seeking a pleasing balance of salty, sour and sweet, adjust to your liking with a little more salt, tamarind or sugar, if needed. You should have about $1\frac{1}{4}$ cups (300 mL).

4. Let sauce cool until slightly warm or to room temperature. Transfer to a small bowl and place on a serving platter. Arrange the vegetables around the bowl of sauce and serve. Store any extra sauce in an airtight jar in the refrigerator for up to 2 days.

Crispy Spring Rolls with Sweet and Hot Garlic Sauce

You are in for some work when you make these spring rolls, as you will need to stir-fry the noodle filling, shape the rolls and then deep-fry them shortly before serving. Believe me when I tell you that they are worth every bit of the effort and are worlds better than the ho-hum spring rolls many Asian restaurants serve. To lighten the load of preparing them, follow the Thai tradition of recruiting a friend or two to help you. The effort becomes entertainment when you have good company and once you become famous for your Thai spring rolls, you will have volunteers. If you roll them up in advance and then deep-fry them just before your guests arrive, you will have time to enjoy the party.

MAKES ABOUT 24 SPRING ROLLS

Tip

To prepare the spring rolls in advance, cook the filling, cover it and store in the refrigerator for up to 2 days. Or you can store the uncooked spring rolls, covered airtight, in the refrigerator for up to 2 days, providing that you have just made the filling. You can also freeze the uncooked spring rolls for up to 1 month. To cook frozen spring rolls, do not thaw them, but allow an extra minute or two in the oil.

- ◆ Candy/deep-fry thermometer
- ◆ Baking sheet, lined with paper towels
- ◆ Asian-style wire strainer or slotted spoon

4 oz	bean thread noodles	125 g
6	dried shiitake mushrooms or Chinese mushrooms (about ½ oz/15 g) (see Tip, right)	6
	Vegetable oil for sautéing and deep-frying	
2	eggs, lightly beaten, divided	2
8 oz	fresh button mushrooms, thinly sliced	250 g
1 tbsp	soy sauce	15 mL
1 tsp	granulated sugar	5 mL
½ tsp	salt	2 mL
½ tsp	freshly ground black pepper	2 mL
1	package (1 lb/500 g) frozen spring roll wrappers (25 to 30 wrappers)	1
1 tbsp	coarsely chopped garlic (4 to 6 cloves)	15 mL
¼ cup	finely chopped shallots or onion	60 mL
1 cup	shredded carrots	250 mL
½ cup	minced green onions	125 mL
¼ cup	minced fresh cilantro	60 mL
	A handful of fresh cilantro as garnish	
	Sweet and Hot Garlic Sauce (page 206)	

1. Place noodles in a large bowl, add warm water to cover and soak until tender, about 30 minutes. Place dried mushrooms in another bowl, add warm water to cover and soak until softened, about 30 minutes.

2. Meanwhile, heat 1 tsp (5 mL) oil in a nonstick skillet and place a plate next to the stove. Add half of the beaten egg to the pan and swirl so the egg covers the bottom in a thin sheet. Cook until set and opaque, about 30 seconds. Transfer egg sheet to the plate and repeat with another 1 tsp (5 mL) oil and remaining egg. When egg sheets have cooled, roll them up, slice them into thin shreds and set aside.

3. Drain noodles and mound on a cutting board in a plump log, horizontal to you. Cut crosswise into 2-inch (5 cm) lengths. Do not fret about precision, as the point is to make these extremely long noodles more manageable for stir-frying. Transfer noodles to a bowl, toss to separate and set aside with egg strips.

4. Drain softened dried mushrooms and cut away and discard the tough stem ends. Slice into long, thin shreds and set aside along with sliced button mushrooms.

5. In a small bowl, combine soy sauce, sugar, salt and pepper and stir well. Set next to the stove, along with garlic, shallots, dried and fresh mushrooms and carrots. Have ready a large platter to hold the cooked filling.

6. To wrap spring rolls, remove spring roll wrappers from the freezer and let thaw for about 30 minutes. Set out a baking sheet on which to place the finished spring rolls and a small bowl of water to use for sealing the filled rolls. Gently separate the stack of wrappers into 3 or 4 piles and cover them with a damp kitchen towel or plastic wrap while you work. Carefully peel off 1 wrapper and place it on a clean, dry work surface, smooth side down. Position the wrapper like a diamond, with one point toward you.

7. Heat a wok or large, deep skillet over medium-high heat. Add 1 tbsp (15 mL) oil and swirl to coat the surface. When a bit of garlic added to the pan sizzles at once, add garlic and shallots and stir and toss for 1 minute. Add dried and fresh mushrooms and stir-fry until shiny and softened, about 3 minutes. Add carrots and cook, tossing once, for 1 minute. Stir soy sauce mixture and add to pan, tossing to coat everything well.

continued on page 34

8. Add noodles and egg strips to pan and cook, tumbling and turning everything to combine well, until noodles are transformed from stiff, white, wiry threads into transparent, soft, curly strands, about 2 minutes. Once noodles are tender and evenly coated with sauce, turn off the heat. Add green onions and minced cilantro and toss well. Transfer the filling to the platter, spread out in an even layer and let cool.

9. Place about 3 tbsp (45 mL) of the filling on the wrapper, centering it on the half of the diamond closest to you. Use your fingers to shape it into a log about 3 inches (7.5 cm) long. Fold the point closest to you up, over and around the filling and then tightly roll the wrapper over once to the center of the diamond. Fold the right and left points in toward the middle, completely enclosing the filling and then continue rolling. When you reach the topmost point, moisten its edges with water and seal the roll like an envelope. Set the roll aside on the baking sheet, seam side down. Continue filling and rolling until you have used all the filling mixture. Space the rolls so that they do not touch and separate the layers with plastic wrap if you stack them. Seal any unused wrappers airtight and return them to the freezer at once (see Tip, page 32).

10. To fry the spring rolls, pour oil into a wok or large, deep heavy skillet to a depth of 3 inches (7.5 mL). Place over medium-high heat for 5 to 10 minutes. The oil is ready when a bit of spring roll wrapper dropped into it sizzles and floats at once. (The oil should register 350° to 365°F/180° to 185°C on the thermometer.) Carefully add a spring roll by sliding it gently down the curved side of the wok or lowering it carefully into the skillet. Add 2 or 3 more rolls, but do not crowd the pan. Cook, turning the rolls occasionally to brown them evenly, until golden brown, about 3 minutes.

11. Using slotted spoon or wire strainer, remove each spring roll, holding it briefly over the pan to drain and set it on prepared baking sheet. Cook remaining rolls in the same way. When all the spring rolls are done, arrange them on a serving platter. Garnish with cilantro and serve with individual bowls of Sweet and Hot Garlic Sauce.

Roasted Eggplant Dip with Thai Flavors

Lime, cilantro and chile paste impart a Thai sizzle to the natural richness of roasted eggplant. Enjoy this as a dip for thick strips of cucumber, green sweet pepper, carrots or blanched broccoli, asparagus or green beans. Or serve it as a spread for Crispy Rice Cakes (page 44).

MAKES ABOUT 1½ CUPS (375 ML)

Tip

If you do not have a food processor, place the flesh of the roasted eggplant on your cutting board and chop it to a fine, moist, fairly smooth mush. Transfer to a bowl and add sugar, soy sauce, salt, Roasted Chile Paste and lime juice. Stir to dissolve sugar and combine everything well, then mix in chopped cilantro and green onions.

- Preheat oven to 400°F (200°C)
- Baking sheet, lightly greased
- Food processor (see Tip, left)

1	large eggplant (about 1¼ lbs/625 g)	1
1 tbsp	palm sugar or brown sugar	15 mL
1 tsp	soy sauce	5 mL
½ tsp	salt	2 mL
2 tbsp	Roasted Chile Paste (page 204) or store-bought	30 mL
2 tbsp	freshly squeezed lime or lemon juice	30 mL
¼ cup	finely chopped fresh cilantro leaves	60 mL
2	green onions, thinly sliced crosswise	2
	A small handful of fresh cilantro leaves	

1. Cut eggplant in half lengthwise, stem and all and place on prepared baking sheet, cut side down. Bake in preheated oven until the flesh is soft and the purple skin is a dark, burnished brown, about 30 minutes. Remove from oven and set aside and let cool to room temperature.

2. Scoop out the flesh and transfer to a food processor fitted with metal blade. Add sugar, soy sauce, salt, Roasted Chile Paste and lime juice and pulse to a thick, coarse purée, stopping to scrape down the sides as needed to grind evenly.

3. Transfer to a bowl and stir in chopped cilantro and green onions. Serve at room temperature, garnished with cilantro leaves.

Two-Potato Curry Pot Stickers

Pot stickers appear in Thailand among the array of dim sum goodies offered in upcountry Chinese cafés and as part of the Chinese menus offered in hotels. Make up these tasty bites in advance and then fry them up after your guests arrive for a hot starter that will get you back to the party quickly.

**MAKES ABOUT
40 POT STICKERS**

Tip

Gyoza are the Japanese version of pot stickers. Gyoza wrappers are thicker than wonton wrappers and are round rather than square. If gyoza wrappers are unavailable, trim the corners from a package of wonton wrappers and use them in the same way, handling carefully as they are more likely to tear.

◆ Medium skillet with tight-fitting lid

1 cup	Mushroom Mince (page 192)	250 mL
¾ cup	mashed cooked white potatoes	175 mL
¾ cup	mashed cooked sweet potatoes	175 mL
½ cup	bread crumbs	125 mL
1	egg, lightly beaten	1
1 tsp	soy sauce	5 mL
½ tsp	curry powder	2 mL
¼ tsp	granulated sugar	1 mL
¼ tsp	salt	1 mL
2	green onions, finely chopped	2
¼ cup	finely chopped sturdy greens such as bok choy, napa cabbage or green head cabbage	60 mL
⅓ cup	coarsely chopped fresh cilantro	75 mL
1	package (10 oz/300 g) gyoza wrappers (about 42 wrappers) (see Tip, left)	1
	Sweet and Hot Garlic Sauce (page 206)	
4 tbsp	vegetable oil, divided (approx.)	60 mL
½ cup	Vegetable Stock (pages 189 and 190) or store-bought, divided	125 mL
	Chopped fresh cilantro for garnish	

1. In a bowl, combine Mushroom Mince, white and sweet potatoes, bread crumbs, egg, soy sauce, curry powder, sugar, salt, green onions, greens and cilantro. Stir until all ingredients are evenly distributed. Set up a workspace with a clean, dry cutting board, a baking sheet, a small bowl of water, gyoza wrappers and two-potato filling.

Vegan Variation

Vegan readers can omit the egg and add an additional 2 tbsp (30 mL) bread crumbs to the sweet potato mixture. The filling will be quite soft, so handle the dumplings carefully.

2. Place a gyoza wrapper before you on cutting board and place about 2 tsp (10 mL) filling in center. Dip your finger in water and moisten edges of wrapper. Fold in half to form a half circle, enclosing the filling and pinch together the top center point to seal. Now form 2 pleats in the left side of the wrapper close to you and press to seal closed. Form 2 pleats in the right side of the wrapper and press to seal closed. Now tap the pot sticker on cutting board to flatten its base and help it stand upright with its sealed, pleated edge pointing skyward. You can also shape the gyoza by simply folding them into half circles, sealing without the pleats and then standing them up and tapping them on the cutting board to form a sturdy base with the fold standing straight up like a crest. Place on baking sheet. Fill and shape remaining pot stickers in the same way. Place them without touching on baking sheet.

3. Place a small bowl of Sweet and Hot Garlic Sauce on a serving platter and position it by the stove to hold the pot stickers when they are done. In a skillet with a tight-fitting lid, heat 2 tbsp (30 mL) of the oil over medium-high heat for about 1 minute. Add pot stickers, placing them with flattened base down, tucking them close together and fitting about 12 into pan. Cook until bottoms are golden brown, 1 to 2 minutes. Add ¼ cup (60 mL) of the vegetable stock, cover and cook until most of the liquid evaporates and the wrapper is translucent, tender and ready to eat, 2 to 3 minutes. Flip pot stickers out onto the platter, sprinkle with some of the cilantro and serve at once with the dipping sauce. Cook remaining pot stickers in batches in the same way, using remaining oil and vegetable stock as needed.

Sweet Potato Shiao Mai

These delicious Chinese tidbits are a familiar feature in Thailand, both as street food and at dim sum feasts. Thais call them kanome jeep, *enjoying them when they find them, but never bothering to make them at home. They look fabulous standing at attention on a plate and garnished with a bouquet of cilantro leaves. Accompany them with a small saucer of soy sauce kissed with a little vinegar and sugar and sprinkled with minced green onions.*

MAKES ABOUT 48 DUMPLINGS

Tip

You can mask the steaming rack with a banana leaf or leaves of cabbage or sturdy lettuce if you like; the leaves may lessen the stickiness. If you have a small basket steamer, simply cook the dumplings in batches.

- Steamer basket
- Asian-style wire strainer or slotted spoon

1 cup	Mushroom Mince (page 192)	250 mL
1 cup	mashed cooked sweet potato	250 mL
½ cup	bread crumbs	125 mL
1	egg, lightly beaten	1
1 tsp	soy sauce	5 mL
¼ tsp	granulated sugar	1 mL
¼ tsp	salt	1 mL
2	green onions, finely chopped	2
2 tbsp	minced fresh mint	30 mL
1	package (12 oz/375 g) wonton wrappers	1
	Soy sauce, seasoned to taste with white vinegar, sugar and green onions, for dipping	

1. In a bowl, combine Mushroom Mince, sweet potato, bread crumbs, egg, soy sauce, sugar, salt, green onions and mint. Mix very well. Set up a work space with a clean, dry cutting board, a baking sheet, a small bowl of water, wonton wrappers and sweet potato filling.

2. Divide stack of wonton wrappers into thirds and trim away the four corners of each stack, reserving the little pasta triangles to toss into your next pot of boiling soup. Place 3 of the now-octagonal wrappers before you on the cutting board. Place about 2 tsp (10 mL) filling in center of each wrapper. Now, your job is to coax each wrapper into a tiny, slender version of a paper baking cup filled with cupcake batter. Begin by using a table knife to spread filling on each wrapper as if it were peanut butter on bread. Stop just short of the edge, leaving a thin border of pasta all the way around. Then place one wrapper in your palm and, using the fingers of your other hand, pinch its sides up into a cup. Tap its base on the cutting board to firm it up. Next, work your way around the exterior, pressing the dull side of the table knife

into the sides to even up the little folds and give the dumpling an upright shape, like a column holding up a roof. Tap base again and set the tall but diminutive "cupcake" aside on baking sheet. Fill and shape the remaining dumplings in the same way. Place them without touching on baking sheet. At this point, you can seal the dumplings airtight and refrigerate them for 1 to 2 days or freeze for up to 1 month. They can be steamed directly from the refrigerator or freezer.

3. To steam dumplings: Fill bottom of a steamer or a heavy saucepan with 3 inches (7.5 cm) of water and bring to a rolling boil over medium heat. Meanwhile, place a batch of dumplings on a steamer basket. When steam is steady and strong, place dumplings over steam, cover and adjust heat to maintain a steady head of steam. Cook until filling firms up and wrappers are tender and cooked, about 15 minutes. Transfer carefully to a serving platter. Serve warm with seasoned soy sauce.

Satay Peanut Sauce with Grilled Vegetables, Fried Tofu and Toast

Serving grilled vegetables and fried tofu with peanut sauce is my vegetarian adaptation for the classic skewers of satay; but the toast is 100 percent Thai. You will find this West-meets-East touch in upcountry Thailand, where it is offered alongside standard meat kebabs as a traditional means of soaking up every last bit of scrumptious sauce. Put the zucchini and other vegetables in their marinade while you prepare the peanut sauce and cucumber salad. The sauce can cool to room temperature and the salad can develop its tangy flavors while you grill foods to enjoy along with them.

SERVES 6 TO 8

Tip

Bamboo skewers come in several lengths, with 6-inch (15 cm) ones and foot-long (30 cm) ones the most common. Long ones are more traditional, but use whatever is easiest and appeals to you. Cover them completely with food, embedding the tip in something and leaving the handle end exposed.

* Barbecue or grill
* Bamboo skewers (see Tip, left and right)
* Candy/deep-fry thermometer
* Plate, lined with paper towels
* Asian-style wire strainer or slotted spoon

Satay Peanut Sauce

½ cup	unsweetened coconut milk	125 mL
2 tbsp	Red Curry Paste (page 180)	30 mL
¾ cup	Vegetable Stock (pages 189 and 190) or store-bought	175 mL
2 tbsp	palm sugar or brown sugar	30 mL
¼ cup	freshly ground salted dry-roasted peanuts or peanut butter	60 mL
2 tbsp	Tamarind Liquid (page 191) or freshly squeezed lime or lemon juice	30 mL
½ tsp	salt	2 mL

Sweet-and-Sour Cucumber Salad (page 61)

Vegetables and Tofu

6	zucchini	6
6	Japanese eggplants	6
3	red bell peppers	3
20	small fresh button mushrooms	20
⅓ cup	vegetable oil, plus additional oil for deep-frying	75 mL
2 tsp	curry powder	10 mL
1 tsp	soy sauce	5 mL
½ tsp	salt	2 mL
6	white bread slices	6
8 oz	firm tofu	250 g

Soak the bamboo skewers for an hour or so to discourage them from catching fire. You can also use the professional satay vendor's method of shielding the skewers from the charcoal fire by placing them at the edge of the grill surface, so that the food rests on the grill while the skewers extend out toward you into thin air and can be easily grasped and turned as needed. Finally, if the skewers need to be close to the center of the grill to cook well, you can mask the area where the skewers rest with foil before you heat the grill.

1. *Satay Peanut Sauce:* In a saucepan over medium heat, warm coconut milk until a gentle boil. Simmer, stirring occasionally, until fragrant and thickened slightly, about 5 minutes. Add curry paste and cook for 3 to 4 minutes, mashing and scraping to dissolve paste and mix everything well. Add vegetable stock and sugar and simmer, stirring once or twice, for 5 minutes. Add peanuts or peanut butter and cook for 3 minutes, stirring as needed to dissolve peanut butter into sauce. Remove from heat and season with tamarind and salt, stirring to mix well. Set aside and let cool to room temperature. At this point, sauce can be covered and refrigerated for up to 2 days. Reheat gently and thin with a little vegetable stock before serving.

2. Make the cucumber salad and set it aside to allow the flavors to blend.

3. To prepare the vegetables, trim ends from zucchini and eggplants and cut in half lengthwise. Stem and seed bell peppers and cut into 2-inch (5 cm) squares. Trim base of each mushroom stem but leave whole.

4. In a medium bowl, combine $1/3$ cup (75 mL) of the oil, curry powder, soy sauce and salt and mix well. Add zucchini, eggplants, peppers and mushrooms and toss to coat well. Set aside for 30 minutes. (They can also be covered and refrigerated as long as overnight, tossing occasionally.)

5. When you are ready to cook vegetables, prepare a very hot fire in a grill. Thread sweet peppers and mushrooms on bamboo skewers and place on grill rack, along with zucchini and eggplant halves, cut side down. Cook until tender and nicely charred, turning often to cook evenly, about 5 minutes. Transfer to a platter and let cool until warm or at room temperature, 5 minutes or longer.

6. Meanwhile, place bread slices on grill rack and toast on both sides to a handsome, golden crunchy state. Remove from grill and cut each twice on the diagonal into 4 triangles. Remove crusts first if you want the most traditional look and leave on if you like the crust as I do. Set aside near the cooling vegetables.

continued on page 42

Variation

Serve with Roasted Tomato-Chile Sauce (page 211) instead of the Satay Peanut Sauce.

7. In a skillet, pour in oil to a depth of 3 inches (7.5 cm) and place over medium-high heat for about 10 minutes. While it heats, cut tofu in half horizontally to form 2 blocks. Cut each block lengthwise into thirds and then crosswise in half. This will give you 12 thick rods of tofu. Blot them dry on a clean kitchen towel and set aside.

8. When the oil is hot, 350° to 365°F (180° to 185°C) on the thermometer, gently slide 3 rods of tofu into oil and cook, turning once or twice, until crispy and golden brown, about 3 minutes. Using slotted spoon or wire strainer, remove from oil, draining briefly over pan and transfer to prepared plate to drain well. Continue cooking remaining tofu in the same way.

9. To serve, make up two or more platters, putting a small bowl of peanut sauce, a small bowl of cucumber salad and a beautiful assortment of grilled vegetables, fried tofu and toast triangles on each. The vegetables, tofu and toast are all delicious dipped in the sauce.

❀ *Thai Tales*

Thais learned this sauce from Malaysian cooks and while the dish has southern Thai roots, it has spread to every corner of the kingdom. Street vendors make up their signature sauces in the morning and then travel to every gathering place. There they set up shop, fan charcoal into hellish flames to grill skewered foods and dish out little saucers of peanut sauce and piquant cucumber salad to garnish each platter.

Spicy Cashews with Chiles, Cilantro and Lime

This is the kind of dish you might order in a café, as you get settled in with a big happy group, order a round of something cool to sip, and begin to ponder a menu to accompany a rice meal. It comes quickly to the table, and disappears almost as fast. You can often find raw cashews in health food stores and other specialty food shops, as well as many Asian markets.

SERVES 4

Tip

Serve these nuts with spoons for scooping onto individual plates, for eating with small spoons, Thai-style, or as finger food.

* Plate, lined with paper towels
* Asian-style wire strainer or slotted spoon

	Vegetable oil for frying	
2 cups	fresh raw cashews (about 8 oz/250 g)	500 mL
1 tsp	salt	5 mL
3 tbsp	coarsely chopped shallots	45 mL
3 tbsp	thinly sliced green onions	45 mL
2 tsp	hot pepper flakes or finely chopped fresh hot green chiles	10 mL
2 tbsp	freshly squeezed lime juice	30 mL

1. Set prepared plate and strainer by the stove. In a wok or a large, deep heavy skillet, heat 2 to 3 inches (5 to 7.5 cm) of vegetable oil over medium heat until a bit of raw cashew sizzles as it drops into hot oil, 4 to 5 minutes. Set aside 2 or 3 raw cashews on a plate by the stove (this will help you judge the color of the nuts as they fry).

2. Carefully add raw cashews to oil, stirring gently. Cook, stirring often, until golden brown, 2 to 3 minutes. Scoop out onto prepared plate and let cool slightly.

3. Transfer warm cashews to a medium bowl. Add salt and toss well. Add shallots, green onions and pepper flakes and toss well. Add lime juice, toss once more, and mound on a serving platter. Serve warm or at room temperature.

Crispy Rice Cakes

This old-time treat traveled across the Mekong River and into Thailand from her cultural first-cousin and neighboring kingdom, Laos. The puffy white rafts of crunchy rice are crowned with a palm sugar spiral for a homey, satisfying snack. Thais call them kao taen *in the northern region, where they are particularly popular and* nahng leht *elsewhere in the kingdom. For a savory treat, leave off the palm sugar adornment and use the cakes as edible platforms for scrumptious Thai sauces. Spread them with Roasted Chile Paste (page 204) or serve them with Roasted Eggplant Dip with Thai Flavors (page 35), Satay Peanut Sauce (page 40) or Tangy Tamarind Sauce (page 207).*

MAKES 24 TO 36 RICE CAKES

Tips

If an all-day sunbath is too slow or otherwise not practical for you, simply dry your rice disks in a 150°F (70°C) oven for about 3 hours. Check every hour and remove as soon as dry. They should not brown at all. You can also leave them out on your kitchen counter for 1 or 2 days, turning occasionally.

Plan ahead for this recipe, keeping in mind that the cooked sticky rice, which is used to make the rice cakes, takes more time to prepare than regular rice; 3 hours of soaking time and 30 to 40 minutes of cooking time. It also requires that you be ready to shape the rice cakes as soon as the soaked rice has finished steaming and is tender. Once shaped, the cakes must dry for several hours more. It's simple, but requires a set timeline, a little attention several times throughout the day.

- ◆ Candy/deep-fry thermometer
- ◆ Baking sheet, lined with paper towels
- ◆ Asian-style wire strainer or slotted spoon

1½ cups	long-grain white sticky rice (see Tips, left)	375 mL
	Vegetable oil for deep-frying	
1 cup	palm sugar or brown sugar	250 mL

1. Cook rice as directed on page 137. Turn hot rice out onto a large tray or baking sheet. Quickly and gently spread it into a shallow layer to release some of the steam and moisture. As soon as rice is cool enough to touch, shape into several dozen small thin disks, each 2 to 3 inches (5 to 7.5 cm) in diameter and only 3 or 4 grains thick. Wet your hands with water as needed to ward off stickiness and make the disks as thin as you can. Resist the urge to press them too firmly into submission or they will be very hard. Work fast, knowing that your cakes need not be perfectly round; a raggedy edge is fine.

2. Place your shaped disks on cooling racks or trays to air-dry as you work. When all the disks are formed, set out in the full sun until brittle and very dry, turning over several times to dry evenly, 6 to 8 hours. (See Tips, left, for two easy, practical substitutes if this extended sunbath is not workable for you.)

Tip

You may want to try a method many Thai cooks use for decorating the cakes: Form a piece of banana leaf into a cone, with a small hole at the pointed tip. Fill this Thai-style pastry bag with a nice dose of the warm, caramelized sugar syrup and let it ooze out over each rice cake in a spiral design.

3. *To fry cakes:* In a large, deep skillet pour in oil to a depth of about 3 inches (7.5 cm). Place over medium heat for 5 to 10 minutes. The oil is ready when a small piece of rice cake dropped in sinks and then immediately floats to the top. (The oil should register 350° to 365°F/180° to 185°C on the thermometer.) Gently slide 3 cakes into oil and let float and swell into thick, white rice crackers. When they stop swelling on the first side, turn and cook until fully puffed, 1 to 3 minutes total. Do not let them brown. Using slotted spoon or strainer, remove each cake, holding briefly over pan to drain and set on the prepared baking sheet. Cook remaining disks in the same way.

4. Place sugar in a small, heavy saucepan and bring to a gentle boil over medium heat. Simmer, stirring occasionally, until sugar melts into a syrup and turns a rich caramel color (somewhere in color and texture between real maple syrup and honey), 5 to 10 minutes. When ready, syrup should fall in a shiny ribbon when spoon is lifted.

5. Quickly drizzle some of the syrup in a spiral design onto each rice cake, starting at the center and twirling out to the edge. Let rice cakes dry at room temperature until syrup sets. Store in an airtight container for up to 1 week.

❋ Thai Tales

This recipe comes from Laos, and is a signature street food snack throughout Northern and Northeastern Thailand. Market vendors fry up these popular rice cakes in quantity to sell in upcountry markets. Home cooks make them as a way to use up the brown, crispy crust of rice that often forms when rice is cooked the old-fashioned way, on a stove rather than in an electric rice cooker (see Rice crusts, page 223). This can happen over charcoal, gas or electric heat. In Thailand, these rice crusts are always in demand by one family member or another, to enjoy along with supper.

Fried Peanuts with Green Onions and Chiles

Yes, these are rich, but they are spectacularly good and worth the culinary splurge. Look for raw peanuts in Asian markets and health food stores. Remove the red husks by rubbing the peanuts between your hands. You can substitute raw cashews here with terrific results. Make yourself a pitcher of lemonade or limeade while this delicious snack cools down, stirring a little salt into the pitcher if you want to enjoy it Thai style.

SERVES 4

Tip

If you deep-fry food now and then, treat yourself to a long-handled Asian-style wire-mesh strainer. The bamboo handle and beautiful golden mesh bowl are perfect for handling hot food in quantity deftly and quickly. You can find these in Asian markets and through many of the Resources, page 230.

◆ Large bowl or baking sheet, lined with paper towels
◆ Asian-style wire strainer or slotted spoon
◆ Candy/deep-fry thermometer

	Peanut oil or other vegetable oil for deep-frying	
8 oz	raw whole peanuts	250 g
20	small dried red chiles	20
1 tsp	salt	5 mL
3	green onions, thinly sliced crosswise	3

1. Place prepared baking sheet, a small plate and strainer near the stove. In a wok or deep, heavy skillet, pour in peanut oil to a depth of about 3 inches (7.5 cm). Place over medium-low heat for 5 to 10 minutes. The oil is ready when a bit of green onion dropped in sizzles at once. (The oil should register 300° to 325°F/150° to 160°C on the thermometer.) Carefully add peanuts to the oil and stir gently. Cook, stirring and lifting them up out of the oil occasionally with the scoop or spoon, for about 5 minutes. When peanuts are a rich, deep reddish gold, scoop out, holding over oil briefly to drain. Then transfer to prepared bowl or baking sheet to drain well.

2. Meanwhile, place chiles in strainer or slotted spoon, lower them into oil for about 30 seconds and then lift out. Repeat this process, giving chiles short baths, until darkened slightly and have a rich, roasted aroma. If they burn, discard and try again with a new batch. When they are ready, turn off heat, lift out and set aside on a small plate to cool.

3. Transfer hot, drained peanuts to a clean bowl and sprinkle with salt, tossing at the same time to mix well. Toss in chiles and set aside and let cool for about 5 minutes, then transfer to a serving plate. Sprinkle with green onions and serve at once.

Sweet and Spicy Nuts

This nontraditional dish is a delectable combination of Thai spices and nuts—scrumptious and simple to make. It is a dandy gift for friends and neighbors, if you can resist eating too many as you pack them up. You can use all almonds, all cashews or all pecans if you are nuts about a particular nut.

**MAKES ABOUT
3 CUPS (750 ML)**

Tips

To toast ground cumin: Toast cumin in a small dry skillet over medium heat until fragrant and a little darkened, about 1 minute.

These delectable tidbits will leave behind a dusting of their crunchy coating on the baking sheet. I like to scrape it into a small bowl and set it aside to enjoy over ice cream.

You can use raw or roasted nuts in this recipe.

- Preheat oven to 400°F (200°C)
- Baking sheet, lightly greased

1 cup	granulated sugar	250 mL
1 cup	water	250 mL
2 tsp	ground ginger	10 mL
1 tsp	ground cardamom	5 mL
1 tsp	ground cinnamon	5 mL
1 tsp	ground cumin, toasted (see Tips, left)	5 mL
½ tsp	ground nutmeg	2 mL
½ tsp	ground cloves	2 mL
2 tsp	Red Curry Paste (page 180) (approx.)	10 mL
½ tsp	chile-garlic sauce or Red Chile Purée (page 209)	2 mL
1 cup	unsalted whole cashews	250 mL
1 cup	unsalted whole pecans	250 mL
1 cup	unsalted whole almonds	250 mL
3 tbsp	butter or margarine	45 mL
1 cup	Toasted Coconut (page 199)	250 mL

1. In a large heavy saucepan, combine sugar, water, ginger, cardamom, cinnamon, toasted cumin, nutmeg, cloves, curry paste and chile-garlic sauce. Bring to a gentle boil over medium heat and cook, stirring occasionally, until a thin syrup forms, about 3 minutes.

2. Add cashews, pecans and almonds and cook over medium heat, stirring constantly, until nuts have absorbed most of the syrup and are beginning to clump together, about 5 minutes. Add butter and stir until melted, about 1 minute. Remove from heat and place nuts onto prepared baking sheet. Spread out in a single layer but still touching. Bake in preheated oven until fragrant and coating is bubbly, about 15 minutes. Remove from oven and sprinkle with Toasted Coconut. Set aside on baking sheet and let cool to room temperature, about 30 minutes. Store airtight at room temperature for 2 to 3 weeks.

Salads

Oyster Mushroom Salad with Chiles and Lime 52

Shredded Bamboo Salad, Issahn-Style 53

Green Papaya Salad 54

Muslim-Style Salad with Peanut Dressing 56

Kao Yum Rice Salad, Southern-Style 58

Sweet-and-Sour Cucumber Salad 61

Pickled Cabbage 62

Green Salad with Spicy Thai Citrus Dressing 63

Kale Salad with Thai Flavors 64

Thai Fruit Salad 65

Orange Salad in Ginger Syrup with Fresh Mint 66

Pink Grapefruit Salad with Toasted Coconut,
Fresh Mint and Lime 67

Salads

THAIS RELISH RAW VEGETABLES AND FRUITS, INCLUDING THEM often as an accompaniment to rice-centered meals. The dishes that would be considered salads in Western terms are *yums*. These are hearty and substantial combinations of meat or seafood served with a tangy lime juice dressing liberally anointed with hot pepper flakes. Lots of greens—for nibbling as well as for presentation—cradle a typical *yum* and it is generally garnished with cucumber rounds, cherry tomatoes and cabbage wedges.

Yum is actually a verb and it describes the action of taking an array of seasonings, including the chiles mentioned above, plus sugar and lime juice and mashing and mixing them all up by hand into an explosion of hot, sweet and tangy flavors. The classic Thai soup *tome yum* is the same culinary concept in liquid form, with tome meaning "boiled."

In Thailand, *yums* are often served as stand-alone dishes, as snacks enjoyed by a group. They are often accompanied with Thai whiskey, beer or home brew, while diners contemplate whether or not to progress to a proper meal. I like to serve them just as I would a salad in a Western meal.

For vegetarians it is a simple task to place tofu, sautéed tempeh or wheat gluten in a salad's starring role and treat it to the typical *yum* flavors. You can also serve countless vegetables in this same way with delicious results.

This chapter begins with my favorite vegetarian *yum,* Oyster Mushroom Salad with Chiles and Lime. The mushrooms are cooked briefly to make them tender before their immersion in a sparkling dressing laced with herbs. This is followed by *soop naw mai*, a unique toss of bamboo shoots with garlic, shallots and a shower of fresh mint. Both these dishes share a *yum* trademark—Roasted Rice Powder. Thai cooks dry-fry whole raw grains of rice in a hot skillet to a rich, wheaty brown. The grains are pounded to a coarse powder and tossed into *yum* dishes to provide a sandy crunch and a rustic flavor on the pleasurable side of burnt.

Both the bamboo shoot salad and Green Papaya Salad are trademark dishes of the northeastern region of Thailand known as *Pahk Issahn*. Green refers to the hard, raw, unripe state of the papayas used for this dish. Home cooks and street vendors keep a steady drumbeat going throughout the kingdom from dawn until nightfall, pounding up pale, sturdy shreds of green papaya and seasonings with mighty pestles in tall heavy mortars designed specifically for this job. The details vary around a basic formula of garlic, chiles, sugar, tomato, green beans and a burst of lime. You will want to serve these traditional Thai salads with their typical companion: sticky rice. It is finger food and the classic foil for both bamboo and green papaya salads on their home turf, the Lao- and Cambodian-influenced region of northeastern Thailand.

Salaht kaek, a dish of Indian origin beloved in southern Thailand, packs well for a picnic, as it is essentially raw vegetables and a peanut dressing for dipping. Sweet-and-Sour Cucumber Salad is the classic accompaniment to satay and peanut sauce and it is a satisfying partner for grilled or fried dishes. Winding up this chapter are two Thai-inspired fruit salads that can be made in advance and enjoyed along with volcanic dishes or as desserts when you want sweetness without a heavy note.

You may want to add a Thai touch to your Western green salads by using one of the sauces in my Basic Recipes chapter to boost the flavor of your favorite dressings. Try a dollop of Tangy Tamarind Sauce in your favorite vinaigrette or fire up a bowlful of baby lettuce and halved cherry tomatoes with a little Sweet and Hot Garlic Sauce and a squeeze of lime.

You can also create a salad course in the style of the Thai dishes called *nahm prik,* an array of hot and pungent chile dipping sauces served with raw or blanched vegetables and usually eaten with rice. Check the Appetizers and Snacks chapter for Roasted Eggplant Dip with Thai Flavors or Dao Jiow Lone Dipping Sauce and present a bowl of either dip along with the traditional Thai accompaniments of cucumber rounds, green beans and wedges of cabbage or with a rainbow of radishes, carrot sticks, sweet peppers and blanched broccoli, asparagus or snow peas.

Oyster Mushroom Salad with Chiles and Lime

This is my mushroom version of the salads that fall under the single Thai umbrella of yum. *Here, sautéed mushrooms, onions, fresh herbs, chiles, sugar and lime juice are coaxed into an explosion of delicious contrasts of sweet and sour, salty and spicy hot. Enjoy it as a dynamite starter or serve it alongside other dishes on a menu anchored with rice.*

SERVES 4

Tips

I like to serve these sprightly salads Thai style, that is, right after they are tossed together with their seasonings. If you would like to prepare the salad in advance, you can toss everything together except roasted rice powder, cover and refrigerate for up to 1 day. You can then serve it chilled or at room temperature, adding rice powder shortly before serving. Or you can cook the mushrooms, let them cool completely and then cover and refrigerate them for up to 1 day. To serve, heat the vegetable stock and proceed as directed. In this case, the completed salad can be covered and refrigerated for an additional day.

This salad is terrific even if you substitute additional button mushrooms for the oyster mushrooms.

2 tbsp	vegetable oil	30 mL
1 tbsp	coarsely chopped garlic (4 to 6 cloves)	15 mL
½ cup	coarsely chopped onions	125 mL
½ tsp	salt, divided	2 mL
8 oz	fresh button mushrooms, thickly sliced	250 g
9 oz	fresh oyster mushrooms	270 g
⅓ cup	Vegetable Stock (pages 189 and 190) or store-bought	75 mL
3 tbsp	freshly squeezed lime juice	45 mL
2	green onions, thinly sliced crosswise	2
2 tbsp	finely chopped fresh mint	30 mL
1 tbsp	finely chopped shallots	15 mL
1 tbsp	Roasted Rice Powder (page 198)	15 mL
2 tsp	granulated sugar	10 mL
½ tsp	soy sauce	2 mL
½ tsp	hot pepper flakes or more to taste	2 mL
	Lettuce leaves	

1. In a medium skillet over medium-high heat, warm oil until a bit of garlic dropped in sizzles at once. Add onion and cook, tossing often, until fragrant, shiny and beginning to brown, about 2 minutes. Add garlic and ¼ tsp (1 mL) of the salt, toss well and add button mushrooms. Cook, tossing often, for 2 minutes. Add oyster mushrooms and continue cooking, tossing often, until mushrooms are tender, nicely browned and reduced in volume, about 3 minutes. Transfer to a plate. Set aside and let cool to room temperature.

2. In a saucepan over medium heat, bring stock to a gentle boil. Add mushrooms, toss for about 1 minute to warm. Remove from heat. Add lime juice, green onions, mint, shallots, rice powder, sugar, soy sauce, hot pepper flakes and remaining ¼ tsp (1 mL) salt. Mix well, using your fingers or a large spoon. Transfer to a bed of lettuce and serve at once.

Shredded Bamboo Salad, Issahn-Style

This traditional dish marries the cool, country crunch of rice powder and bamboo shoots with the hot, sharp sizzle of chiles, lime and mint. Its Thai name is soop naw mai. *The result is a bracing little platter of summery flavors and it is especially suited to toting along on picnics and serving on buffets, as it comes together quickly and keeps well for several hours at room temperature. Thais enjoy it with grilled foods and Sticky Rice (page 137), the classic fare of the country's northeastern Pahk Issahn region. Roasted Rice Powder imparts a traditional rustic texture, but the salad will still be tasty if it is omitted.*

SERVES 4 TO 6

Tips

You can use the ubiquitous canned sliced bamboo shoots sold in the Asian section of major supermarkets. If you have the time, check out Asian markets for a wider selection of varieties and forms of this beloved Asian vegetable, which is generally sold loose in the refrigerated section or in cans on the shelf.

This dish is traditionally hot stuff. Crank up the amount of hot pepper flakes if you love fiery food or cut it to ¼ tsp (1 mL) if you want pleasing sparks with only a mild flame.

1	can (14 oz/400 mL) whole or sliced bamboo shoots (see Tips, left)	1
2 tbsp	finely chopped shallots	30 mL
1 tbsp	finely chopped garlic (4 to 6 cloves)	15 mL
2	green onions, thinly sliced crosswise	2
2 tbsp	Vegetable Stock (pages 189 and 190) or store-bought	30 mL
2 tbsp	freshly squeezed lime juice	30 mL
1 tbsp	Roasted Rice Powder (page 198)	15 mL
2 tsp	granulated sugar	10 mL
½ tsp	salt	2 mL
½ tsp	hot pepper flakes or more to taste	2 mL
	A handful of fresh mint sprigs	
2	wedges green cabbage, each about 2 inches (5 cm) wide at the widest point	2
9	green beans, trimmed and halved crosswise	9

1. Drain bamboo shoots, rinse and drain again. Shred or cut lengthwise into very thin strips, about 2 inches (5 cm) long. Place in a bowl and add shallots, garlic, green onions, stock, lime juice, rice powder, sugar, salt and hot pepper flakes and toss well. Reserve a few beautiful mint sprigs for garnish. Remove leaves from remainder and shred crosswise into thin strips. Add to bowl and toss well. Taste and adjust with more lime juice, sugar or salt, if you wish.

2. Transfer salad to a small, deep serving plate and arrange cabbage wedges and green beans on one side. Garnish with reserved mint sprigs. Serve at room temperature or cover and chill for up to 1 day.

Green Papaya Salad

This sparkling tangle of shredded unripe papaya, juicy tomatoes, shallots and garlic is infused with an incendiary combination of lime juice, palm sugar and chiles. Known by its Laotian name, som tum, *this rustic, intensely flavored dish is made from simple ingredients that epitomize the cuisine and spirit of northeastern Thailand. The classic companion is Laotian-style Sticky Rice (page 137) or Coconut Rice with Cilantro and Fresh Ginger (page 143).*

SERVES 4

Tip

If you do not have a heavy Thai-style mortar and pestle, here is a shortcut version: To crush and bruise shredded papaya, place in a big plastic bag on your cutting board, leaving the bag open. Pound with a cooking mallet or rolling pin, working it until all the shreds are limp and bruised. Transfer to a bowl. In a blender or mini processor, combine chile, garlic, shallots, sugar, salt and stock and blend until fairly smooth. Toss with papaya. Add green beans and pound to bruise. Add tomatoes and squeeze juice from lime quarters over salad, tossing in lime pieces when you are done. Using your hands, toss again, squeezing salad to crush tomatoes so they release some of their juice as you mix in the lime. Transfer to a deep serving platter and serve at once.

◆ Mortar and pestle (see Tip, left)

2	fresh green serrano chiles or 1 fresh green jalapeño	2
1 tbsp	coarsely chopped garlic (4 to 6 cloves)	15 mL
1 tbsp	coarsely chopped shallots	15 mL
1	small hard, green unripe papaya, peeled and finely shredded (about 2 cups/500 mL)	1
9	green beans, trimmed and cut into 2-inch (5 cm) lengths	9
2 tsp	palm sugar or brown sugar	10 mL
½ tsp	salt	2 mL
2 tbsp	Vegetable Stock (pages 189 and 190) or store-bought	30 mL
½	lime, quartered lengthwise	½
9	cherry tomatoes, quartered	9

1. In a large heavy mortar, combine chiles, garlic and shallots. Grind and pound with a pestle until everything is broken down but not completely mushy. Use a spoon to scrape down the sides occasionally and mix everything together well.

2. Add papaya and pound until the stiff shreds become limp and soft, about 3 minutes. Use the spoon to scrape and turn the mixture over as you work.

Variation

Green and Purple Cabbage Salad: If an unripe papaya is hard to come by, use a mix of shredded green and purple cabbage (a total of 2 cups/500 mL) spiked with a good sprinkling of shredded carrot.

3. Add green beans and pound to bruise. One at a time, add sugar, salt and stock, pounding a little after each addition. Squeeze in juice from each piece of lime and then add pieces of squeezed lime to the mortar as well. Add tomatoes and pound another minute, turning as before as the tomatoes release some of their liquid. Pound more gently so that you do not get splashed.

4. Taste sauce in bottom of the mortar and adjust the seasonings (there should be an interesting balance of sour, hot, salty and sweet). Using a slotted spoon, transfer salad to a small serving platter. Drizzle on some of the sauce remaining in the mortar and serve at once.

Muslim-Style Salad with Peanut Dressing

In Thailand, this dish is called salaht kaek, *the first word being the Thai pronunciation of salad and the second word meaning either "Indian" or "Muslim." Southern Thailand has a clear Indian influence due to centuries of seagoing trade with the subcontinent and to a significant number of Thais who follow the religion of Islam. Peanuts figure in most of the dishes considered* ah-hahn kaek *or "Indian-Muslim food," by Thais. Examples are satay, Indian noodles and mussamun curry.*

SERVES 4 TO 6

Tips

The dressing is thick and is usually enjoyed more as a dipping sauce than as a mixture for tossing with ingredients. If you want a tossed salad, thin the dressing with a little vegetable stock or water to the consistency you like.

The dressing will keep well for 2 to 3 days. It thickens as it stands and chills, so bring it to room temperature and thin with vegetable stock or water if needed before serving.

Dressing

¾ cup	unsweetened coconut milk	175 mL
1½ tsp	Red Curry Paste (page 180)	7 mL
½ cup	Vegetable Stock (pages 189 and 190) or store-bought	125 mL
2 tbsp	palm sugar or brown sugar	30 mL
2 tbsp	finely ground salted dry-roasted peanuts or peanut butter	30 mL
½ tsp	salt	2 mL
1 tbsp	freshly squeezed lime juice or lemon juice or vinegar	15 mL

Composed Salad

8 oz	leaf lettuce, torn into bite-size pieces (approx.)	250 g
1	small onion, preferably red, sliced crosswise into thin rings	1
1 cup	bean sprouts	250 mL
2 cups	potato chips (approx.)	500 mL
1	hothouse cucumber or about 8 oz (250 g) any variety cucumber, peeled and cut crosswise into thick rounds	1
3	hard-boiled eggs, quartered lengthwise	3
2	tomatoes, cut lengthwise into wedges, or 12 cherry tomatoes, halved lengthwise	2

Vegan Variation

Vegans can omit the hard-boiled eggs and add chunks of firm tofu fried to a crisp, golden brown.

1. *Dressing:* In a saucepan over medium heat, warm coconut milk to a gentle boil. Cook, stirring occasionally, until fragrant and thickened slightly, 2 to 3 minutes. Add curry paste and cook, mashing and scraping to dissolve curry paste and combine with coconut milk, 2 to 3 minutes. Add vegetable stock, sugar, peanuts and salt and stir well. Cook until sauce comes together and is thick and smooth, 3 to 5 minutes. Remove from heat, add lime juice and stir to mix well. Taste and add more lime juice, sugar or salt if needed for a pleasing balance of sour, sweet and salty flavors. Set aside and let cool to room temperature.

2. *Composed Salad:* Line a platter with lettuce leaves and sprinkle onion rings over lettuce. Place bean sprouts and potato chips in little mounds on one end of the platter, along with a small bowl containing the peanut sauce. Arrange cucumber rounds, eggs and tomatoes on and around the lettuce. Serve at once. Guests take portions of all the ingredients and a dollop or two of peanut sauce to use as a dip.

❀ Thai Tales

This southern Thai salad is satisfying enough to be a one-dish meal and it can also add a fresh note to a meal of rice and an array of savory dishes. You can vary the ingredients to suit yourself. Potatoes are widely available in Thailand, but they still remain a bit exotic to Thai cooks. The potato chips called for here were once freshly fried potato strips, but when potato chips came on the scene, Thai cooks spotted a shortcut to the rich, salty crunch called for here.

Kao Yum Rice Salad, Southern-Style

This salad is a crazy quilt of Thai flavors, with explosions of herbal freshness and sweet-sour crunch in every bite. I first tasted this terrific dish in the cool shadows of the marketplace in Nakorn Si Thammaraht, an old city that is rich with Buddhist history and the natural beauty of Thailand's enchanting southern provinces.

SERVES 6

Tips

Look for sataw beans in the freezer case in Asian markets. Simply let them thaw before adding them to the salad, as they would be used raw in Thailand.

Whatever citrus fruit you use, you want only the juicy pulp with none of the stringy membranes attached.

Dressing

5	stalks lemongrass	5
12	quarter-size slices fresh galanga or gingerroot or a handful of dried galanga pieces	12
10	wild lime leaves, optional	10
2½ cups	Vegetable Stock (pages 189 and 190) or store-bought	625 mL
1 cup	water	250 mL
1 cup	palm sugar or brown sugar	250 mL
1 tsp	Asian bean sauce	5 mL
1 tsp	salt	5 mL

Salad

6 cups	cooked Jasmine Rice (page 136), at room temperature	1.5 L
2	stalks lemongrass	2
25	wild lime leaves or 2 tbsp (30 mL) finely chopped lime zest	25
1 cup	Toasted Coconut (page 199)	250 mL
¼ cup	hot pepper flakes	60 mL
1 cup	thinly sliced winged beans or green beans, sliced crosswise	250 mL
1 cup	sataw beans or barely cooked fresh fava beans, snow peas or green peas (see Tips, left)	250 mL
3	small cucumbers or 1 hothouse cucumber, peeled, quartered lengthwise and cut crosswise into small triangles	3
1 cup	bean sprouts	250 mL
1 cup	peeled coarsely chopped pomelo, grapefruit or orange pulp	250 mL
1 cup	peeled slivered green unripe mango, chopped unpeeled green apple or chopped fresh or canned pineapple	250 mL

Tip

Make the rice and the dressing ahead of time so they will have time to cool to room temperature. If you are using rice that has been refrigerated, warm it gently in the microwave or on the stove with a little water and then let it cool down again.

Variation

Do not let the list of ingredients intimidate you. Use what you can find at the market, omitting the lemongrass or lime leaves or sataw beans if need be and adding whatever strikes you as being in the spirit of the dish.

1. *Dressing:* Prepare lemongrass by trimming away and discarding any hard, dried root portions, leaving a smooth, flat base just below the bulb. Trim away the tops, including any dried brown leaf portions (you should have handsome stalks about 6 inches/15 cm long, including the bulbous base). Slice these crosswise into paper-thin rounds. Place lemongrass in a saucepan and add galanga.

2. Cut lime leaves, if using, crosswise into strips and add to pot. Add vegetable stock, water, sugar, Asian bean sauce and salt. Bring to a rolling boil over high heat. Reduce heat to maintain a gentle boil and simmer, stirring occasionally, until sauce is dark and thickened, about 20 minutes. It should be as thick as real maple syrup, but thinner than pancake syrup or honey.

3. Remove from heat and let cool to room temperature. Strain, discarding solids and transfer to a jar and seal airtight. Set aside at room temperature until ready to serve. (The sauce will keep a day or two at room temperature or about 5 days in the refrigerator.)

4. *Salad:* Place rice in a large bowl. Prepare lemongrass as directed for the dressing. Set aside in a small bowl.

5. Shred lime leaves crosswise into hair-fine threads: Stack a few at a time and use a sawing motion to stay on the edge of the leaves. If you can figure out how to strip away the central vein of each leaf before you shred it, do so; if not, simply leave intact. Set aside in a small bowl.

6. Place coconut, pepper flakes, winged and sataw beans, cucumbers, bean sprouts, pomelo and mango into individual small bowls or arrange in heaps on a platter surrounding the rice.

7. To serve, toss rice in bowl with all the ingredients. Add dressing 2 tbsp (30 mL) at a time, using only enough dressing to season everything lightly; do not soak the ingredients. Serve at once.

continued on page 60

8. Alternatively, mound rice on a platter and surround with the accompaniments in small bowls or little heaps. Place dressing in a bowl on the side. Guests can serve themselves about 1 cup (250 mL) of the rice and several spoonfuls of each accompaniment, top it off with a dollop of dressing and then give everything a good toss.

❊ *Thai Tales*

The salad is a lunchtime standard in the cool, shaded corners of the marketplace near the main Buddhist temple. It is offered as a plate of room temperature rice and a rainbow of traditional accompaniments that you pile on as you like before giving it all a toss. I persuaded the smiling food vendor to fix mine up the way she liked it, as I was a greenhorn and wanted to try the standard version. You may want to toss it for your guests to keep things simple or offer everything a la carte and let folks put together their own combinations.

Sweet-and-Sour Cucumber Salad

Like the chutneys of India, this simple relish is a ideal counterpoint to the richness and fire of coconut milk-based curries. It is also always present alongside skewers of curry-kissed satay and spicy peanut sauce. Like the refrigerator pickles of my Southern childhood, these cool cucumbers are a good thing to have on hand, no matter what is on the menu.

½ cup	distilled white vinegar	125 mL
½ cup	water	125 mL
½ cup	granulated sugar	125 mL
1 tsp	salt	5 mL
1	large hothouse cucumber or other cucumber variety, about 12 oz (375 g)	1
¼ cup	coarsely chopped red onion	60 mL
3 tbsp	coarsely chopped fresh cilantro	45 mL
⅓ cup	finely chopped salted dry-roasted peanuts	75 mL
	A handful of cilantro leaves	

SERVES 4 TO 6

MAKES ABOUT 1¼ CUPS (300 ML)

Tips

If you have tender cucumbers from the garden or hothouse cucumbers with nice unwaxed skin, leave some of the skin on. If you are using a large cucumber with lots of seeds, halve it lengthwise, scoop out and discard the seeds with a spoon and then cut each half crosswise into crescent-moon slices.

I prefer these pickles crisp, so when preparing them in advance, I chill the dressing and mix it with the cucumbers about an hour before serving. Then I add the peanut and cilantro garnishes just before putting it on the table. But it is fine to mix them together in advance, stirring in the peanuts and cilantro leaves. Cover and refrigerate for 2 to 3 days.

1. In a small saucepan over medium heat, combine vinegar, water, sugar and salt and bring to a gentle boil, stirring occasionally to dissolve the sugar and salt. When syrup is clear and slightly thickened, after about 2 minutes, remove from heat. Let cool to room temperature.

2. Peel cucumber and quarter lengthwise to make 4 long strips. Slice strips crosswise into little triangles about ¼ inch (0.5 cm) thick. In a bowl, combine cucumber, cooled vinegar mixture, onion and chopped cilantro and stir well.

3. To serve, using a slotted spoon, scoop salad out of dressing into several small serving bowls. For a traditional presentation, add a little dressing to each bowl and then divide peanuts and cilantro leaves among the bowls. Sprinkle the garnishes over about half of each bowl, so that guests can see lots of cucumber with a burst of peanuts and cilantro leaves adorning one side. Or simply sprinkle evenly over the top. Either way, everything gets tossed together before eating.

Pickled Cabbage

This simple pickle goes beautifully with the sweet and spicy heat of Thailand's delicious coconut-milk curries. Add shredded or julienned carrots or thinly sliced green onions for a dash of color.

**MAKES ABOUT
3 CUPS (750 ML)**

1	small head green cabbage	1
¾ cup	distilled white vinegar	175 mL
½ cup	granulated sugar	125 mL
2 tsp	salt	10 mL

1. Fill a saucepan with water and bring to a rolling boil over high heat. Meanwhile, core cabbage and chop into large pieces about 2- by 1-inch (5 by 2.5 cm). (You will need about 4 cups/1 L.) Reserve remaining cabbage for another use. Place a colander in the sink.

2. When the water is boiling, add cabbage and press to submerge all the leaves. Cook for 30 seconds, then drain into the colander. Let cool to room temperature. When cool enough to handle, squeeze leaves to soften them and release some water.

3. Meanwhile, make the pickling brine: In a saucepan over medium heat, combine vinegar, sugar and salt and bring to a rolling boil, stirring to dissolve sugar and salt. Remove from heat, pour into a bowl large enough to accommodate cabbage and let cool to room temperature.

4. Add cabbage to brine and toss to coat well. Transfer cabbage and brine to a jar and seal with a tight-fitting lid. Refrigerate for 2 days, turning the jar occasionally to coat all the leaves with the brine.

5. Serve cold or at room temperature. The cabbage will keep refrigerated for about 3 weeks.

Green Salad with Spicy Thai Citrus Dressing

Here, Thai flavors jazz up a Western-style salad dressing that is bright in flavor and light in texture. If you want a hotter dressing, add more chiles; if you want a thicker dressing, add a little more oil. You can highlight the dressing's fruitiness by adding grapes, mandarin orange sections, chunks of apple or fresh strawberries to the salad.

SERVES 4

MAKES 1 CUP (250 ML) DRESSING (SEE TIP, BELOW)

Tip
This dressing makes more than needed for this salad. Store remaining dressing in the refrigerator for up to 3 days.

Dressing

½ cup	freshly squeezed orange juice	125 mL
½ cup	freshly squeezed lime juice	125 mL
¼ cup	palm sugar or brown sugar	60 mL
1 tsp	soy sauce	5 mL
¼ tsp	freshly ground black pepper	1 mL
1 tbsp	minced fresh green serrano or jalapeño chile	15 mL
1 tsp	minced garlic	5 mL
3 tbsp	vegetable oil	45 mL

Salad

6 oz	lettuce, torn into bite-size pieces (approx.)	175 g
1	ripe tomato or 3 plum tomatoes, cut into bite-size chunks	1
3	small cucumbers or 1 hothouse cucumber, peeled and cut crosswise into thick rounds	3
2	green onions, thinly sliced crosswise	2
	A handful of fresh cilantro leaves, coarsely chopped	

1. *Dressing:* In a jar with a tight-fitting lid, combine orange juice, lime juice, palm sugar, soy sauce and ground pepper. Cover and shake well until sugar is dissolved. Add chile, garlic and vegetable oil and shake again to combine well. You should have about 1 cup (250 mL).

2. *Salad:* In a large bowl, combine lettuce, tomatoes, cucumbers, green onions and cilantro. Drizzle on about ⅓ cup (75 mL) of the dressing. Toss well and serve at once.

Kale Salad with Thai Flavors

Although kale is not a traditional Thai ingredient, piquant, refreshing and intensely flavored salads are very traditional, as is the technique of mixing spicy and pungent dressing and seasoning ingredients into the salad by hand. This dish is called a yum, *a lovely unintentional pun in that it is indeed "yummy," using the English word.* Yum *means to mix, squeeze, incorporate and massage spicy hot and tangy ingredients into a room temperature dish using your hands. Kale salad or* yum pahk kale—*either way, you might take quite a liking to this dish.*

SERVES 4

Tips

For this recipe, purchase 1 bunch sturdy curly kale (8 oz/250 g) or 2 bunches slender lacinato kale (about 1 lb/500 g). To prepare, trim and discard stems and ribs. Tear remaining leaves into big, bite-sized pieces. Measure out 12 loosely packed cups (3L).

When massaging the kale, baby kale, with its young tender leaves, takes less time. Older tougher leaves take a little longer, but 3 minutes is a good basic time frame and longer won't hurt.

Variation

For a heartier version, add ¾ cup (175 mL) cooked quinoa to the chopped kale before adding the dressing and toss well. Or toss in ½ cup (125 mL) of any or all of these goodies: coarsely chopped dry-roasted salted peanuts, chopped fresh or drained canned pineapple or halved cherry tomatoes.

¼ cup	vegetable oil	60 mL
2 tbsp	freshly squeezed lime juice	30 mL
2 tsp	granulated sugar	10 mL
½ tsp	salt	2 mL
½ tsp	hot pepper flakes, optional	2 mL
¼ tsp	freshly ground black pepper	1 mL
1 tbsp	finely chopped green onion	15 mL
1 tsp	minced garlic	5 mL
12 cups	prepared kale (see Tips, left)	3 L

1. In a large bowl, combine vegetable oil, lime juice, sugar, salt, hot pepper flakes, if using, black pepper, green onion and garlic and whisk into a fairly smooth dressing.

2. Add kale and, using your hands, press, squeeze, mix and massage dressing into the sturdy green leaves until kale is darkened and becomes tender, 2 to 3 minutes (see Tips, left). Keep at it until most of the dressing is absorbed and the texture of the leathery kale leaves softens and wilts to a sturdy but pleasing tender state. Set aside to rest for 10 to 15 minutes. Serve at room temperature or chilled.

Crispy Spring Rolls with
Sweet and Hot Garlic Sauce (page 32)

Green Papaya Salad (page 54)

Wild lime leaves

Shallots

Galanga

Chiles

Straw mushrooms

Cilantro

**Tome Yum Soup with
Mushrooms and Tofu (page 72)**

Winter Vegetables Infused with
Coconut Milk and Cashews (page 91)

Yellow Curry with Pineapple and Peas (page 95)

Red Hot Vegetable
Stir-Fry (page 120)

Thai Fruit Salad

A platter of fresh fruit is the only traditional Thai dessert there is, so this beautiful cool salad would be right at home among the desserts at the end of this book. An ice-cold combo of plain ripe pineapple and watermelon is my sentimental favorite, but here I have expanded the palette with other fruits and a citrus dressing. This Thai-inspired fruit salad is at its best within a few hours of preparation, but it keeps surprisingly well in the refrigerator for a day or two.

SERVES 6

Variation

You can substitute other ripe fruits cut into bite-size chunks for those suggested here, planning on 10 cups (2.5 L) in all. Good candidates include honeydew melon, cantaloupe, orange sections, papaya, apple, peaches, nectarines and plums. You can also use berries. Add them closer to serving time if you are making the salad well in advance, however, so they keep their texture and shape.

1	pineapple, about 3½ lbs (1.75 kg), peeled and cut into bite-size chunks (about 4 cups/1 L)	1
3	large mangos, peeled, pitted and cut into bite-size chunks (about 2 cups/500 mL)	3
1	piece watermelon, about 1½ lbs (750 g), seeded and cut into bite-size chunks (about 3 cups/750 mL)	1
3	bananas, peeled and cut into 1-inch (2.5 cm) chunks	3
¼ cup	freshly squeezed lime or lemon juice	60 mL
3 tbsp	granulated sugar	45 mL

1. In a large bowl, combine pineapple, mangos, watermelon and bananas.

2. In a small bowl, combine lime juice and sugar and stir well until sugar dissolves. Pour over fruit and toss gently to coat the fruit well. Cover and refrigerate for at least 30 minutes before serving. Serve ice cold.

Orange Salad in Ginger Syrup with Fresh Mint

Like the Thai Fruit Salad on page 65, this simple dish would be enjoyed as a sweet snack in Thailand rather than as a salad. I like to serve it along with the carousel of sour, salty, sweet and fiery flavors that light up a traditional Thai menu. It can also round out a dessert course, served with an array of dainty cookies and a round of coffee or tea.

SERVES 4 TO 6

Tips

To chill the ginger syrup quickly, fill a large bowl with ice and nestle the syrup bowl in the ice. You can make the syrup in advance and hold it for several days before you combine it with the fruit and mint. You can also toss together oranges, room-temperature syrup and shredded mint, chill the lot for an hour or so and serve whenever you are ready.

If you do not have fresh mint, do not despair. In Thailand, this dish is *som loy gaew* or "orange jewels afloat," and it comes without mint or ginger and with a handful of crushed ice on top to cool it down on the spot.

For an express-lane version of this dish, toss the dressing with chunks of banana and well-drained mandarin oranges from a can.

1 cup	granulated sugar	250 mL
1 cup	water	250 mL
1	piece fresh gingerroot, about 3 inches (7.5 cm) long, peeled and sliced crosswise into ¼-inch (0.5 cm) thick coins	1
8	sweet oranges	8
	A handful of small fresh mint sprigs	

1. In a heavy saucepan, combine sugar, water and ginger and bring to a boil over high heat. Cook, stirring occasionally to dissolve sugar, until mixture becomes a medium syrup, 2 to 3 minutes. Remove from heat, pour into a bowl and let cool. Cover and chill until very cold (see Tips, left).

2. Meanwhile, section oranges: Working with 1 orange at a time, place on a cutting board and cut a thick slice off the top and bottom to expose the flesh. Stand orange on the cutting board and use a sharp knife to cut off the peel and all the white pith in thick strips, cutting downward and following the curve of the fruit. Repeat with remaining oranges. Then hold a peeled orange in the palm of one hand positioned over a bowl. Loosen the meat by running a knife between the segments and let them fall into the bowl as you work around the membrane. After you have removed all the segments, squeeze the core of membranes into the bowl to extract any remaining juice before you discard and continue with remaining peeled oranges.

3. Strain ginger coins from the chilled syrup and pour syrup into the bowl of orange sections. Discard ginger coins. Toss syrup and orange sections gently to combine well and cover and chill until serving time. Reserve a few mint sprigs for garnish. Remove remaining mint leaves from sprigs and shred leaves, cutting them crosswise into thin ribbons. Stir them into oranges. Serve salad very cold in small bowls. Garnish with mint sprigs.

Pink Grapefruit Salad with Toasted Coconut, Fresh Mint and Lime

In Thailand, this bright and flavorful dish is made with pomelo, a plump, thick-skinned first cousin of grapefruit with an intriguing combination of drier texture and sweeter flavor. This distinctive and delicious fruit can be found in Asian markets and some supermarkets during the winter. You can use grapefruit in place of pomelo as I have done here. Thai cooks shred coconut and toast it, and you can do the same. I love to make this with sweetened shredded coconut, because its long curly shape toasts up beautifully and its sweetness enhances the sweet-and-sour notes of this dish.

SERVES 4

Tip

If you can find ruby red grapefruit your dish will have an added appeal from its rosy hue. Since grapefruit is so much juicier than pomelo, you'll want to drain off some of the juice so that your salad is lightly dressed. (Sip this vibrantly flavored savory juice as a cook's treat.)

¼ cup	sweetened or unsweetened shredded coconut	60 mL
2 tbsp	freshly squeezed lime juice	30 mL
1 tbsp	granulated sugar	15 mL
½ tsp	soy sauce	2 mL
½ tsp	salt	2 mL
3 cups	bite-size chunks sectioned peeled grapefruit or pomelo (see Tip, left)	750 mL
1 tbsp	coarsely chopped shallots, purple onion or onion	15 mL
1 tsp	finely chopped fresh hot green chiles or hot pepper flakes or more to taste	5 mL
2 tbsp	coarsely chopped salted dry-roasted peanuts	30 mL
½ cup	coarsely chopped fresh mint or fresh cilantro	125 mL
	Leaves Boston or Bibb lettuce	

1. Set a small bowl by the stove to hold coconut when it has finished toasting. In a small, dry skillet over medium-high heat, toast coconut, stirring and tossing often, until lightly browned, 3 to 4 minutes. Transfer to bowl and let cool.

2. In a medium bowl, combine lime juice, sugar, soy sauce and salt and stir well to dissolve sugar and salt. Add grapefruit, shallots and chiles and toss gently to coat with dressing. Add peanuts, fresh mint and toasted coconut and toss gently just enough to mix and season everything evenly.

3. Arrange lettuce leaves on one side of a deep serving plate or small platter. Using a slotted spoon, scoop out grapefruit and mound on the plate. Serve immediately.

Soups

Tome Yum Soup with Mushrooms and Tofu. 72

Coconut Soup with Galanga and Butternut Squash . . . 74

Clear Soup with Spinach and Tofu. 76

Lemongrass Soup with Rice and Basil Chez Sovan . . . 77

Clear Soup with Roasted Portobello Mushrooms
and Bean Thread Noodles. 78

Rice Noodles with Spinach in Shiitake
Mushroom Soup. 80

Jasmine Rice Soup with Mushrooms,
Green Onions and Crispy Garlic 82

Sweet Potato Wonton Soup with Cilantro
and Crispy Garlic 84

Soups

IN THAILAND, SOUP IS AN ESSENTIAL COMPONENT OF ALMOST EVERY meal, served and savored along with rice and its accompanying dishes. In keeping with Thailand's Chinese culinary ancestry, soup functions as a beverage, a liquid refreshment that cleanses the palate between bites and makes way for further rides on the roller coaster of tastes that make up a classic Thai meal. Drinks come either before or after the rice, so soup gives diners something hot and delicious to sip throughout the meal. These soups work their magic in two ways, as a hot beverage and as another dish to spoon onto one's rice.

Many Thai restaurants in the West bow to Western habits and bring soup first, in tiny individual bowls and without a grain of rice, much less the remaining dishes that will make up the meal. This works with the co-queens of the Thai soup repertoire, *tome yum* and *tome kha,* because these classic soups are strongly flavored and spectacular enough to stand alone. But other soups, such as the less flashy representatives of the *gaeng jeute* category, never earn favor because they are what their name implies—plain soups created to support more dazzling dishes and contribute a nice, salty note to the sweet, sour and hot flavors on the Thai table.

Soup is woven into the heart of the Thai meal and is usually the last dish set before you. Most dishes, including curries, stews and stir-fries, are considered tastier when they have cooled off a little after removal from the heat. Soup is the exception, served steaming hot and right off the heat. I remember my Thai students calling our household to eat. We settled in on the straw mats covering the concrete kitchen floor where the meal had been laid out dish by dish as each one came off the two small charcoal stoves that fueled our cooking. One student piled our individual plates with rice, while another put finishing touches on the soup, fanning the charcoal to bring it to a boil, transferring it to a serving bowl and then finishing it off with a flourish of cilantro or a squeeze of lime. If company came, we passed out individual bowls, but if it was just us, we spooned the soup from the serving bowl onto our rice a few bites at a time, just as we did the other dishes.

However you eat your soup, you will find much pleasure in the recipes that make up this chapter. It opens with the aforementioned co-queens of Thai soup, *tome kha* and *tome yum*. *Tome* means "boiled," or "cooked in broth," and the former is a luxurious concoction of coconut milk, mushrooms and tofu infused with galanga, ginger's Siamese cousin known in Thailand as *kha*. The latter soup is a clear broth set on fire with chile paste and sharpened to a glorious edge with a final burst of freshly squeezed lime juice. If you like your food volcanic, add a few Thai chiles after bruising each one with the flat side of a chef's knife or cleaver to expose its fiery interior while leaving the chile intact.

Next come two versions of *gaeng jeute,* the plain soups. Incongruous as it may seem in a cuisine famed for fireworks and fancy presentation, Thai food has a cherished place for the chorus as well as the stars. A meal needs one or two hot and spicy dishes but not four or five, as that would be monotonous, albeit in a histrionic way. *Gaeng jeute* is comforting and satisfying, a boon companion to rice enjoyed with a rich coconut curry, a sweet-sour stir-fry and a salad-like dish with a sharp citrus tang.

The remaining soups in this chapter would be one-dish meals in Thailand, although you can serve them along with other dishes or as a warm, inviting option on a buffet. Jasmine Rice Soup is Thai comfort food made from yesterday's rice and is the classic cure for what ails you, simmered up for invalids, those with hangovers and the very old and the very young. The lemongrass soup is an herb-laced variation shared with me by my friend Sovan Boun Thuy, from her terrific Cambodian restaurant Chez Sovan in San Jose, California. Rice Noodles with Spinach in Shiitake Mushroom Soup is chopstick food, unlike most Thai dishes, although a soup spoon is always included so the tasty broth can be enjoyed.

Finally, there is my favorite, Sweet Potato Wonton Soup with Cilantro and Crispy Garlic. There is some work to making this, but what a fine feast when you are done. Try it with regular potatoes, pumpkin or any other winter squash and make enough wontons to tuck away in the freezer for a return engagement on a night when you need a treat. These last four dishes come to Thailand direct from her culinary godmother, China. In each case, however, the Thai touches are transcendent, creating dishes you will hunger for later and cook many times.

Tome Yum Soup with Mushrooms and Tofu

This classic soup is a one-bowl celebration of Thailand's sparkling cuisine. Spicy hot with Roasted Chile Paste and sharply fragrant with lemongrass, wild lime leaves and a squeeze of lime, tome yum *sounds an inviting reveille to your senses. Entice your guests with a glance at its gorgeous flame-colored broth studded with brilliant green herbs and then treat them to a whiff of its exotic citrus perfume as you serve it up Thai style, along with other dishes and a plate of jasmine rice.*

SERVES 4 TO 6

Tip

This soup should be intensely and wonderfully sour, salty and spicy hot. If you like, check the seasoning just before serving and fine-tune it to your liking with a little more lime juice, chile paste, sugar and/or salt.

4 cups	Vegetable Stock (pages 189 and 190) or store-bought	1 L
3	large stalks lemongrass	3
12	wild lime leaves, divided, optional	12
2½ tbsp	freshly squeezed lime juice	37 mL
3	green onions, cut crosswise into 1-inch (2.5 cm) lengths	3
1	fresh green jalapeño	1
8 oz	firm tofu, cut into 1-inch (2.5 cm) chunks	250 g
1 cup	well-drained, canned whole straw mushrooms or sliced fresh button mushrooms	250 mL
2 tbsp	Roasted Chile Paste (page 204) or store-bought	30 mL
2 tsp	granulated sugar	10 mL
½ tsp	soy sauce	2 mL
½ tsp	salt	2 mL

1. In a large saucepan, bring vegetable stock to a boil over medium heat. Meanwhile, trim lemongrass stalks: Cut away and discard any hard, dried root portions, leaving a smooth, flat base just below the bulb. Trim away the tops, including any dried brown leaf portions (you should have handsome stalks about 6 inches/15 cm long, including the bulbous base). Using the blunt edge of a cleaver blade or heavy knife or the side of an unopened can, bruise each stalk, whacking it firmly at 2-inch (5 cm) intervals and rolling over to bruise on all sides. Cut into 2-inch (5 cm) lengths.

Tips

To make this soup in advance, hold lime juice mixture aside until serving time and then gently reheat soup, combine with lime juice mixture and serve at once.

Except at banquets, Thai cooks serve soup along with rice and all the other dishes that make up a meal. If you prefer soup as a first course, you may want to offer small bowls of rice with it, so that your guests can savor it as Asian people traditionally do, both straight from the bowl and spooned over plain rice.

2. When stock is boiling, add bruised lemongrass stalks and half of the lime leaves, if using, and reduce heat to maintain a simmer. Cook until stock is fragrant and lemongrass has faded from bright green to a dull khaki, about 5 minutes.

3. While soup simmers, in a serving bowl large enough to accommodate the soup, combine lime juice, remaining lime leaves and green onions. Remove stem from jalapeño and cut crosswise into $1/4$-inch (0.5 cm) thick rounds. Add 2 or more of the rounds to the serving bowl (the amount depends on your love of chile heat). Reserve any leftover chile for another use.

4. Scoop out lemongrass from stock and discard. Increase heat to high and add tofu, mushrooms, chile paste, sugar, soy sauce and salt and stir well. When soup boils again, remove from heat and quickly pour into serving bowl. Stir to combine lime juice and herbs with the soup and serve at once.

> ### ❀ *Thai Tales*
>
> Thais value fresh lemongrass as a healing herb with particular power over fever and colds. If you are caring for an ailing friend who enjoys the chile pepper heat, this clear, sharp soup would be good medicine.

Coconut Soup with Galanga and Butternut Squash

This is my vegetarian version of the classic Thai soup tome kha, kha *meaning "galanga." Use shiitake, portobello or other exotic mushrooms in this extraordinary soup if you like or add a rainbow of bell peppers to the pot just before removing it from the heat.*

SERVES 6 TO 8

Tips

The lemongrass, galanga or ginger and lime leaves add flavor, but are too big and too tough to eat. Thais leave them in and eat around them, but if you prefer to remove them, use tongs as directed in the recipe. Or strain the soup into a large bowl, pick out and discard the flavorings and return the cooked squash and mushrooms to the soup.

Dried galanga works well in this dish, imparting lots of flavor and aroma. It keeps indefinitely on your pantry shelf, a plus since fresh galanga is not always available, even in Asian markets. Dried galanga does swell into enormous woody chunks as it cooks, so be sure to remove it prior to serving.

4	stalks lemongrass	4
2	cans (each 14 oz/400 mL) unsweetened coconut milk	2
1½ cups	Vegetable Stock (pages 189 and 190) or store-bought	375 mL
20	quarter-size slices fresh galanga or gingerroot or 10 large pieces dried galanga (see Tips, left)	20
10	peppercorns	10
20	wild lime leaves, divided, or 12 strips lime zest, each about 2 inches (5 cm) long by ½-inch (1 cm) wide	20
1	butternut squash, about 1½ lbs (750 g)	1
1	can (15 oz/450 g) straw mushrooms, rinsed and drained, or 6 oz (175 g) fresh mushrooms, sliced (about 1¼ cups/300 mL)	1
8 oz	firm tofu, cut into bite-size chunks	250 g
2 tbsp	freshly squeezed lime juice	30 mL
1 tbsp	soy sauce	15 mL
1 tsp	salt	5 mL
½ cup	coarsely chopped fresh cilantro	125 mL
3	green onions, thinly sliced crosswise	3

1. Trim lemongrass stalks: Cut away and discard any hard, dried root portions, leaving a smooth, flat base just below the bulb. Trim away the tops, including any dried, brown leaf portions (you should have handsome stalks about 6 inches/15 cm long, including the bulbous base). Using the blunt edge of a cleaver blade or heavy knife or the side of an unopened can, bruise each stalk, whacking it firmly at 2-inch (5 cm) intervals and rolling over to bruise on all sides. Cut into 2-inch (5 cm) lengths.

Variation

Use any winter squash or pumpkin instead of butternut, such as kabocha pumpkin or acorn squash, or use chunks of peeled sweet potato, which will cook a bit more quickly than the squash.

2. In a large saucepan over medium-high heat, combine coconut milk and vegetable stock and bring to a gentle boil. Stir in lemongrass, galanga, peppercorns and half of the lime leaves or all of the lime zest. Adjust heat to maintain an active simmer.

3. Meanwhile, cut butternut squash in half lengthwise. Scoop out and discard seeds, cut squash into large chunks, and, using a paring knife, peel chunks carefully. Cut peeled squash into generous bite-size pieces (you should have 3 to 4 cups/750 mL to 1 L). Add to the simmering soup along with mushrooms. Increase heat to medium-high and bring soup back to a gentle boil. Cook for 10 minutes.

4. Add tofu and cook until squash is tender but still firm and tofu is heated through, about 5 minutes.

5. Remove soup from heat and use tongs to remove and discard lemongrass, galanga and lime leaves or lime zest. Stir in lime juice, soy sauce, salt, cilantro, green onions and remaining lime leaves. Taste and add more salt, soy sauce or lime juice if you like. Transfer to a serving bowl and serve hot.

Clear Soup with Spinach and Tofu

This is the classic gaeng jeute *or "plain soup." Despite the usual Thai affection for over-the-top flavors, a bland soup is often welcomed as a soothing foil to the appealing cacophony of seasonings found in a traditional Thai meal. Serve with rice and pass a little hot sauce around if your guests crave a little drama.*

SERVES 4 TO 6		

4 cups	Vegetable Stock (pages 189 and 190) or store-bought	1 L
8 oz	firm tofu, cut into 1-inch (2.5 cm) chunks	250 g
½ tsp	freshly ground black pepper	2 mL
½ tsp	soy sauce	2 mL
¼ tsp	granulated sugar	1 mL
	A handful of small or large spinach leaves	
3	green onions, thinly sliced crosswise	3
	Salt to taste	
2 tbsp	Crispy Garlic in Oil (page 203)	30 mL

1. In a saucepan, bring stock to a gentle boil over medium heat. Add tofu, pepper, soy sauce and sugar and simmer until tofu is heated through, about 2 minutes.

2. If using small spinach leaves, stem and leave whole. If spinach leaves are large, tear into big bite-size pieces. Stir in spinach and green onions to pot and remove from heat.

3. Taste and add a little salt, if you like. Transfer to a serving bowl and top with Crispy Garlic in Oil.

❋ Thai Tales

In upcountry kitchens, Thai families keep alive the Chinese culinary legacy of serving soup as the sole beverage accompanying each meal. While many city-dwelling Thais have taken up the Western practice of sipping a cool beverage throughout the meal, the love of soup remains, and the question that arises when putting a Thai menu together is not whether to serve soup, but which soup to serve. Choose this one when you want satisfaction, simple and swift.

Lemongrass Soup with Rice and Basil Chez Sovan

Sovan Boun Thuy is chef-owner of Chez Sovan, a wonderful Cambodian restaurant in San Jose, California. She kindly shared her recipe for this delicate soup, called sgnor chhrok moin *in the Khmer language. It is soothing with a heavenly lemongrass perfume and bracing with a sunburst of citrus and lime. I have adapted it for vegetarian kitchens.*

SERVES 4 TO 6

Tip

If you would like some fireworks, dollop a little Roasted Chile Paste (page 204) onto each individual serving bowl. You can also add a few slices of fresh green jalapeño or smash several tiny Thai bird's eye chiles with the flat side of a knife and stir them into the soup just before serving.

Variation

Rice Soup with Mushrooms and Fresh Herbs: If you do not have fresh lemongrass, you can still enjoy a version of this soup. Skip the first step of simmering the lemongrass in the stock and begin by adding mushrooms, tofu and rice to boiling stock. Add a little extra lime juice and a bit of lime zest.

5	stalks lemongrass	5
3 cups	Vegetable Stock (pages 189 and 190) or store-bought	750 mL
2 cups	water	500 mL
1 tsp	granulated sugar	5 mL
¼ tsp	salt	1 mL
6	fresh button mushrooms, thinly sliced lengthwise (about ⅔ cup/ 150 mL)	6
8 oz	firm tofu, cut into 1-inch (2.5 cm) chunks	250 g
2 cups	cooked long-grain white rice	500 mL
3	plum tomatoes, stemmed and cut into big bite-size chunks, or 6 cherry tomatoes, halved lengthwise	3
3 to 4 tbsp	freshly squeezed lime juice	45 to 60 mL
2 tbsp	coarsely chopped fresh cilantro	30 mL
2 tbsp	coarsely chopped fresh basil	30 mL

1. Trim lemongrass, cutting away and discarding any withered outer leaves or roots. Cut stalks into 3-inch (7.5 cm) lengths and then split each piece in half lengthwise, to expose its fragrant core.

2. In a large saucepan over high heat, combine vegetable stock, water, lemongrass, sugar and salt and bring to a rolling boil. Reduce heat to maintain a gentle boil and simmer, stirring occasionally, for 5 minutes. Remove lemongrass with tongs or strain stock through a sieve and return to pan.

3. Add mushrooms, tofu and cooked rice and simmer only until soup returns to a boil, about 2 minutes. Remove from heat and stir in tomatoes and 3 tbsp (45 mL) of the lime juice. Taste and add a little more lime juice or salt if you need it for a pleasingly tart flavor. Stir in cilantro and basil, transfer to a serving bowl and serve at once.

Clear Soup with Roasted Portobello Mushrooms and Bean Thread Noodles

Here, a clear and shiny tangle of bean thread noodles and strips of roasted mushroom float in a garlic-and-pepper-laced broth. It is the perfect companion to a plate of jasmine rice, a feisty coconut milk curry and a plate of garlicky sautéed greens. If you do not have Roasted Chile Paste on hand, marinate the mushrooms in a little vegetable oil seasoned with minced garlic, a dash of soy sauce and a generous pinch of sugar.

SERVES 4 TO 6

Tip

This dish is a soup on its first serving, but if you should have some left over, it may well transform itself into a tasty noodle dish, with the bean thread noodles absorbing most of the broth. Covered and refrigerated, it will keep a day or so. Reheat it gently and serve it with forks and chopsticks instead of a spoon.

2 oz	bean thread noodles	60 g
6 oz	portobello mushrooms	175 g
3 tbsp	Roasted Chile Paste (page 204) or store-bought	45 mL
4 cups	Vegetable Stock (pages 189 and 190) or store-bought	1 L
1 tbsp	finely chopped garlic	15 mL
¾ tsp	freshly ground black pepper, divided	3 mL
½ tsp	soy sauce	2 mL
¼ tsp	granulated sugar	1 mL
3	green onions, thinly sliced crosswise	3
	A handful of fresh cilantro leaves, coarsely chopped	

1. Place bean thread noodles in a bowl, add warm water to cover and soak until softened and easily separated into threads, 15 to 20 minutes.

2. Meanwhile, trim away stems from mushrooms and cut lengthwise into strips about ¾ inch (2 cm) thick. Place in a bowl. Add chile paste and toss to coat evenly. Set mushrooms aside while you fire up a gas grill or broiler or preheat oven to 450°F (230°C). Grill or roast mushrooms, turning as needed, until tender and handsomely browned, 5 to 7 minutes. Set aside until cool enough to touch.

3. In a saucepan over medium heat, bring stock to a rolling boil. Meanwhile, drain noodles and dump the tangle onto your cutting board. Cut through the pile of noodles lengthwise and then crosswise. Cut cooled roasted mushrooms into big bite-size chunks and set aside with the noodles.

4. When stock boils, add noodles, mushrooms, garlic, $1/2$ tsp (2 mL) of the pepper, soy sauce and sugar and stir well. As soon as noodles are clear and curling into tendrils, add green onions. Remove soup from heat. Transfer to a serving bowl, spoon on remaining $1/4$ tsp (1 mL) of ground pepper and sprinkle with cilantro leaves. Serve at once.

❋ *Thai Tales*

Although this soup is filled with noodles, Thais consider it more a soup than a noodle dish, to be portioned out in small individual bowls and enjoyed with rice and other dishes. If you love Asian-style soup noodle dishes, served in gigantic individual bowls as a one-dish meal, try Rice Noodles with Spinach in Shiitake Mushroom Soup (page 80) and Sweet Potato Wonton Soup with Cilantro and Crispy Garlic (page 84).

Rice Noodles with Spinach in Shiitake Mushroom Soup

This is a meal in a bowl, perfect for a hearty supper. Thais have adopted the Chinese tradition of noodle soup, although since it is easy to find a noodle shop in even the tiniest Thai town, they seldom cook noodle dishes at home. Use fresh, soft rice noodles if you have access to an Asian market or use dried rice noodles or any cooked noodle with delicious results.

SERVES 6		

Variation

You can streamline this recipe by omitting the dried mushrooms and Crispy Garlic in Oil. You can enhance it by adding shredded carrots, bean sprouts, chunks of tofu, strips of omelet, slices of hard-boiled egg or any cooked vegetable.

3 oz	dried shiitake mushrooms or Chinese mushrooms	90 g
8 oz	dried rice noodles, preferably wide, flat ones, or 1 lb (500 g) fresh fettuccine or linguine	250 g
2 tbsp	vegetable oil	30 mL
1 tbsp	coarsely chopped garlic	15 mL
12 oz	fresh button mushrooms, sliced	375 g
½ tsp	salt	2 mL
6 cups	Vegetable Stock (pages 189 and 190) or store-bought	1.5 L
6 oz	spinach leaves (7 to 8 cups/ 1.75 to 2 L)	175 g
6	green onions, thinly sliced crosswise	6
2 tsp	freshly ground black pepper	10 mL
½ cup	chopped fresh cilantro, including some stems	125 mL
6 tbsp	Crispy Garlic in Oil (page 203)	90 mL

1. Place dried shiitake mushrooms in a small bowl and add hot water to cover. Let soften for 30 minutes, pressing occasionally to submerge.

2. Meanwhile, prepare noodles. For dried rice noodles, place in a large bowl. Add warm water to cover and soak until white and pliable, 15 to 20 minutes. To cook, bring a large pot of water to a rolling boil. Drain softened noodles, add to pot and cook, using chopsticks or forks to separate as they boil, until tender but still firm, about 3 minutes. If you are using fresh fettuccine or linguine, cook in the same way, then drain and set aside.

If you have Crispy Garlic in Oil made up in advance, this is a quick dish to put together. If you do not have it on hand, you can leave it out or increase the amount of garlic you sauté along with the mushrooms.

3. In a large skillet over high heat, warm oil until a bit of garlic dropped into the pan sizzles at once. Add garlic and fresh mushrooms and sprinkle with salt. Cook, tossing often, until softened and nicely browned, 4 to 5 minutes. Transfer to a bowl and set aside.

4. In a saucepan over medium heat, bring vegetable stock to a rolling boil. Meanwhile, over a bowl, strain softened shiitake mushrooms through a fine-mesh sieve or coffee filter. Add liquid to stock. Slice shiitakes into long, thin strips and set aside.

5. When stock is hot, divide noodles among 6 large bowls, one for each guest. Divide spinach, remembering that its volume will reduce greatly once it wilts in the hot soup. Garnish each serving with an equal portion of shiitake mushrooms, sautéed mushrooms and green onions. Ladle about 1 cup (250 mL) of hot stock into each bowl, sprinkle with ground pepper and cilantro leaves and top with a generous tbsp (15 mL) of Crispy Garlic in Oil. Serve at once.

Jasmine Rice Soup with Mushrooms, Green Onions and Crispy Garlic

Rice soup is comfort food in Thailand, simmered up from leftover rice to nourish a family member who is ill. It is also popular as a hearty breakfast or midnight snack. Colds, fevers, aches, hangovers and heartbreaks all seem to soften their edge just a little when a generous steaming bowl of kao tome *appears. I cannot make medical claims here, but I know this soup can boost your spirits and I love it even when all is well, especially on a blustery winter evening when I am hungry for a satisfying one-dish meal.*

Tips

You can use any cooked rice in this soup, including basmati, medium-grain rice, brown rice or a combination of wild and white rice.

The rice continues to absorb liquid, so when reheating the soup, thin with additional stock and season with salt.

◆ Blender

2 tbsp	coarsely chopped garlic	30 mL
½ tsp	freshly ground black pepper	2 mL
¼ cup	coarsely chopped fresh cilantro roots or stems	60 mL
5 cups	Vegetable Stock (pages 189 and 190) or store-bought, divided	1.25 L
1 tbsp	vegetable oil	15 mL
1 cup	thinly sliced fresh mushrooms (about 6 oz/175 g)	250 mL
1¼ tsp	salt, divided	6 mL
½	recipe Wheatballs (page 194) or 1 can (8 oz/250 g) wheat gluten, drained (about 1 cup/250 mL)	½
½ cup	shredded carrots	125 mL
½ tsp	granulated sugar	2 mL
1½ cups	cooked Jasmine Rice (page 136) (see Tips, left)	375 mL
2	green onions, thinly sliced crosswise	2
¼ cup	coarsely chopped fresh cilantro leaves	60 mL
¼ cup	Crispy Garlic in Oil (page 203)	60 mL

1. In a blender, combine garlic, pepper, cilantro roots and ½ cup (125 mL) of the vegetable stock and blend until fairly smooth, about 1 minute. In a saucepan over medium heat, combine remaining 4½ cups (1.125 L) of the vegetable stock and garlic-cilantro purée and bring to a boil. Reduce heat to maintain a simmer.

2. Meanwhile, in a skillet over medium-high heat, warm oil for 1 minute. Add mushrooms and cook, tossing often, until darkened and tender, about 5 minutes. Remove from heat and season with ¼ tsp (1 mL) of the salt.

3. Stir sautéed mushrooms, Wheatballs, carrots, remaining 1 tsp (5 mL) of salt and sugar into stock and cook for 5 minutes. Add rice and cook, stirring occasionally, for 5 minutes. Stir in green onions and remove from heat.

4. Serve hot or warm. Garnish serving bowl or individual bowls with cilantro leaves and Crispy Garlic in Oil just before serving.

❀ Thai Tales

Thais serve this with flavorful condiments to jump-start its mild flavor. Try Pickled Cabbage (page 62) or pickled garlic from an Asian market, sliced hard-boiled egg, chunks of cooked Salty Eggs (page 202), thinly sliced celery and celery leaves, chopped fresh or dried chiles, soy sauce and Asian sesame oil.

Sweet Potato Wonton Soup with Cilantro and Crispy Garlic

What a hearty soup you will have if you give this recipe a try! The wontons take a bit of work, but it is a breeze when there is a partner to share the tasks and pass the time. Once they are filled and shaped, you can have the soup on the table in minutes. Soup wontons are traditionally cooked in quantity in boiling water until tender, then portioned into individual bowls, doused with hot broth and crowned with herbs just before serving.

SERVES 10

Tip

The uncooked dumplings freeze well, so you can make only half a batch of the soup and freeze half of the dumplings. That way you will have the foundation of a future feast on hand. To freeze, arrange the dumplings, not touching, on a baking sheet and place in the freezer until frozen solid. Then transfer them to resealable bags or other airtight containers and freeze for up to 1 month. To cook, transfer them directly from the freezer to boiling water.

Wontons

1 cup	Mushroom Mince (page 192)	250 mL
1 cup	mashed cooked sweet potato	250 mL
½ cup	bread crumbs	125 mL
1	egg, lightly beaten	1
1 tsp	soy sauce	5 mL
¼ tsp	granulated sugar	1 mL
¼ tsp	salt	1 mL
3	green onions, finely chopped	3
¼ cup	finely chopped fresh cilantro leaves and stems	60 mL
2	packages (each 12 oz/375 g) wonton wrappers	2

Soup

12 cups	Vegetable Stock (pages 189 and 190) or store-bought	3 L
6	green onions, thinly sliced crosswise	6
⅔ cup	chopped fresh cilantro leaves	150 mL
¾ cup	Crispy Garlic in Oil (page 203)	175 mL
1 tbsp	salt	15 mL
	Vegetable oil, as needed	

1. *Wontons:* In a large bowl, combine Mushroom Mince, sweet potato, bread crumbs, egg, soy sauce, sugar, salt, green onions and cilantro. Mix until fully blended. Set up a work space with a clean, dry cutting board, a baking sheet, a small bowl of water, wonton wrappers and sweet potato filling.

2. Place a wonton wrapper before you on the cutting board and place about 1 tsp (5 mL) filling in center. Dip your finger in water and moisten edges of wrapper. Fold in half to form a small rectangle, enclosing the filling. Gently press out any air trapped inside and press edges to seal tight. With the flat, folded edge facing you, moisten the two sealed corners, pull in toward

You can also shape the wontons by folding them into triangles, pulling together the edges that are on the fold and then sealing them securely to each other. Or you can fold them into rectangles or triangles, press out the air, seal tightly and leave them as they are, with loose pasta "wings." If they burst, you can present them as open-face wontons, remembering that they will still taste great.

Vegan Variation

Vegan readers can omit the egg and add an extra 2 tbsp (30 mL) bread crumbs to sweet potato mixture. The filling will be quite soft, so take extra care in transferring the cooked dumplings from the cooking water to the soup.

each other and press to seal to each other well. This will make a plump dumpling. Place on the baking sheet. Continue shaping wontons until you have used up the filling, placing them without touching each other on baking sheet. You should have about 96. (You can refrigerate dumplings for 1 to 2 days if you prevent them from touching each other, as they tend to stick and tear. Place in a covered container with dry kitchen towels or plastic wrap between layers.)

3. To cook the wontons, fill a large pot with salted water (about 1 tbsp/15 mL salt), cover and bring to a rolling boil over medium heat. Have a teakettle or a pitcher filled with cold water handy. When water boils, uncover the pot and carefully add wontons. Stir gently to discourage the dumplings from sticking together and then let cook, uncovered, until pot returns to a boil. Add 1 cup (250 mL) or so of cold water, enough to stop water from boiling and then let return to the boil a second time. Again add enough cold water to quiet water and when it comes to a boil again, quickly drain dumplings into a colander, carefully transfer to a bowl and gently toss with a little oil to discourage them from sticking together. (You can set the wontons aside to let cool to room temperature, then cover and chill for up to 1 day before reheating them gently in the hot soup.)

4. *Soup:* In a large saucepan over medium heat, bring vegetable stock to a rolling boil. Meanwhile, place 8 wontons in each large, individual serving bowl. Pour about 1 cup (250 mL) of the hot stock into each bowl and then garnish each with some green onions, cilantro and a generous dollop of Crispy Garlic in Oil. Serve at once. Or you can prepare a single large serving bowl of wontons, garnished as directed and then ladle into individual bowls at the table.

❈ *Thai Tales*

I love this traditional method of cooking dumplings by adding cold water to the boiling water, because it solves questions of timing no matter how large or small your pot. Adding cold water paces the cooking process, so that the wrapper and its filling have time to cook evenly. That third return to the boil after you have added the wontons is the charm. Your wontons will be *sook laew!*—"ready, already!"

Curries

Red Curry with Red Sweet Peppers,
Snow Peas and Tofu. 90

Winter Vegetables Infused with Coconut Milk
and Cashews 91

Eggplant and Sweet Pepper–Studded Red Curry. 92

Hard-Boiled Eggs and Peas in Green Curry 93

Green Curry with Zucchini and Bamboo Shoots 94

Yellow Curry with Pineapple and Peas 95

Mussamun Curry with Peanuts, Potatoes
and Cardamom. 96

Burmese-Style Curry with Yams, Mushrooms
and Ginger 97

Panaeng Curry with Wheatballs and
Wild Lime Leaves 98

Choo Chee New Potatoes with Fresh Basil 99

Butternut Squash in Fresh Green Curry 100

Curries

THE CURRY DISHES OF THAILAND ARE THAI FOOD IN A NUTSHELL. They contain Thai trademarks galore: lemongrass, galanga, wild lime leaves and other aromatic Southeast Asian treasures; the juxtaposition of salty and sharp, tangy flavors against the luxurious sweetness of palm sugar and coconut milk; and the explosion of chile-pepper heat.

The Thai word *gaeng* is both a verb and a noun. As a verb, it refers to the cooking of a meat, vegetable or combination of the two with intense seasonings in abundant liquid, usually stock, water or coconut milk or a mixture. As a noun, it generally means a stew made with one of Thailand's signature curry pastes, but the same word can also mean a soup. *Gaeng jeute* is a mild, salty broth containing tofu, bean thread noodles and greens, and *gaeng liang* is a clear, delicate soup made with Chinese okra, fresh straw mushrooms, baby corn, lemony *maengluk* basil leaves and tender kabocha pumpkin vines, curly tendrils and all.

The most common Thai curries make up a delicious quartet. *Gaeng peht* means "spicy-hot curry," and is made from red curry paste. *Gaeng kiow wahn* means "green sweet curry," although it is not particularly sweet. *Gaeng mussamun* is made with what Thais call Muslim-style curry paste, a red curry paste spiced with cinnamon, cloves, nutmeg and cardamom and sharpened with a splash of tangy tamarind. *Gaeng kah-ree* means "curry curry," a red curry turned golden by turmeric and enlivened with curry powder, the latter known in Thailand as *pong kah-ree*. All curry pastes fall into one of two categories: green curry paste starts with fresh, ferociously hot green Thai chiles and red curry paste starts with dried, ferociously hot red chiles. All other curry pastes are variations on red curry paste, with turmeric adding a golden hue and an assortment of ground, toasted spices adding a sweet, complex note. The curries do not display their namesake colors; the names refer to the original chile color or the particular spice combination, rather than the resulting curry's hue.

The curry pastes used to work culinary magic are known as *krueng gaeng*. You could translate this as "curry essence" or "curry base," but *krueng* also means "engine" or "machine." This analogy delights me, that curry paste is the culinary equivalent of the key to the car, of the match that coaxes kindling into flames.

Krueng gaeng are part of Thailand's culinary legacy from India. Indian dishes defined in the West as curries include wet or dry *masalas*. *Masala* is a Hindi word denoting a concoction of herbs and spices ground together to breathe flavorful life into a dish. A dry *masala* would consist of whole dried spices such as cumin seeds, coriander seeds and peppercorns, often toasted to jumpstart their aroma and taste and then ground to a powder known in Thai as *pong*. In India, a wet *masala* might include onion, cilantro, fresh ginger and garlic ground with powdered spices to a glorious purée. Thai cooks adapted the wet *masala* to their own culinary repertoire, adding a profusion of herbs that thrive in the Southeast Asian countryside: lemongrass, galanga and wild lime peel, along with fresh or dried chiles and the sturdy little roots of cilantro plants. Home cooks in Thailand pound their own curry pastes from scratch in the large, heavy mortars that are standard equipment in any Thai kitchen. But most Thai people will gladly purchase a meal's worth of ready-made curry paste from the curry vendors who set up shop in every marketplace, enjoying a shortcut when they lack time to make their own.

Thai-style curries are among the easiest of Thai dishes to cook at home once you have the elements for creating them. These include curry paste and coconut milk, both of which are available in most Asian markets and many supermarkets or are easily ordered through the mail (page 230). You can also make your own curry pastes from scratch, using recipes in the Basic Recipes chapter. You may find it essential to do so despite the work involved, since shrimp paste is a common ingredient in traditional Thai curry pastes, both those made commercially and in Thai homes.

Coconut milk is the most common base for Thai curries, but it is not the only one. If you use water or stock, you will have a traditional *gaeng bah*. This means "country-style curry," with the literal translation of *bah* meaning the "forest" or even the "jungle." In a remote village, coconut milk is a special-occasion ingredient, prepared for celebrations and honored guests. City folks can buy freshly ground coconut grated to a delicate floss by machine in the market and squeeze out a batch of coconut milk in a few minutes' time. Country folks must usually go to the trouble to hack open a hairy brown coconut or two, grate it up laboriously by hand, soak the bright white confetti of coconut in rainwater and then squeeze it through a wicker sieve into fresh coconut milk. This is a lot of trouble on a weeknight when family members are tired and are hungry for rice.

Red Curry with Red Sweet Peppers, Snow Peas and Tofu

Think of this recipe as the basic game plan for a Thai curry and vary it according to the produce you have on hand when you yearn for a Thai curry's appealing flavors. Use tempeh instead of tofu if you like and change the vegetables, keeping in mind that firm vegetables like carrots, potatoes and winter squash go in along with the tofu. Softer vegetables like zucchini need only a few minutes' cooking time and delicate vegetables like snow peas and sugar snap peas go in when you are ready to remove the curry from direct heat.

SERVES 4 TO 6

Tip

Use a wooden spoon to stir the curry so that tofu chunks stay whole rather than break up or crumble.

Variation

A nontraditional alternative to coconut milk is to substitute soy milk or another nondairy milk or a range of dairy milk products, including evaporated skim milk, for the coconut milk called for in these recipes. The choice depends on your culinary practices and the texture of sauce you prefer. You will notice that most curry recipes instruct you to begin by cooking the curry paste in a little coconut milk, to release its aroma. If you substitute another liquid for coconut milk, simply sauté the curry paste gently in a few tbsp (30 mL) of oil first and then continue, adding the liquid of your choice along with the vegetables or tofu and seasonings.

1	can (14 oz/400 mL) unsweetened coconut milk (about 1¾ cups/ 425 mL), divided	1
1 tbsp	Red Curry Paste (page 180) or more to taste	15 mL
8 oz	tofu, cut into ½-inch (1 cm) chunks	250 g
¼ cup	Vegetable Stock (pages 189 and 190) or store-bought	60 mL
1 tbsp	palm sugar or brown sugar	15 mL
½ tsp	soy sauce	2 mL
½ tsp	salt	2 mL
1	red bell pepper, cut into long, thin strips	1
4 oz	snow peas, trimmed	125 g

1. Shake coconut milk can well. Spoon out ⅓ cup (75 mL) into a medium saucepan and bring to a gentle boil over medium heat. Cook, stirring occasionally, until thickened and fragrant, about 3 minutes.

2. Add curry paste and cook, mashing and stirring often to soften paste and combine with coconut milk, about 3 minutes. Add tofu and stir gently to coat with curry paste. Add remaining coconut milk, vegetable stock, sugar, soy sauce and salt and stir well. Bring to an active boil. Reduce heat to maintain a gentle boil and simmer, stirring occasionally, for 15 minutes.

3. Add bell pepper and snow peas and stir gently. Remove from heat. Serve hot or warm.

Winter Vegetables Infused with Coconut Milk and Cashews

Here is a pleasing pot full of harvest gold, perfect for a winter night's feast. If you have time to prepare this curry in advance, do so, as its flavors will blossom as it stands. Keep the cashews and cilantro by the stove and add them after you have gently reheated the curry, to get the most pleasure from their crunch and color.

Tips

The most typical Thai curry has a texture closer to that of milk or soy milk, rather than that of thick gravy or cream soup. The reliance on thick coconut milk, frozen or from cans, has influenced the way curries are made in many Thai restaurants in the West, as has our affection for rich, thick, creamy sauces. You can adjust the texture of the curries you make to your liking, by thinning the coconut milk with vegetable stock and adjusting the seasonings to keep the flavors robust.

You can use any combination of root vegetables—parsnips add a pleasing sweet note—or members of the pumpkin family.

1	can (14 oz/400 mL) unsweetened coconut milk (about 1¾ cups/425 mL), divided	1
2 tbsp	Red Curry Paste (page 180) or more to taste	30 mL
1	onion, thinly sliced lengthwise	1
1 cup	wheat gluten, Wheatballs (page 194), seitan or tofu, cut into bite-size chunks	250 mL
1 lb	assorted winter vegetables such as parsnips, carrots, sweet potatoes and winter squash, in any combination (see Tips, left)	500 g
1 cup	Vegetable Stock (pages 189 and 190) or store-bought	250 mL
1 tbsp	palm sugar or brown sugar	15 mL
1 tsp	each soy sauce and salt	5 mL
¾ cup	salted, dry-roasted cashews	175 mL
¼ cup	chopped or whole cilantro	60 mL

1. Shake coconut milk can well. Spoon out ⅓ cup (75 mL) into a medium saucepan and bring to a gentle boil over medium heat. Cook, stirring occasionally, until thickened and fragrant, about 3 minutes.

2. Add curry paste and cook, mashing and stirring often to soften paste and combine with coconut milk, about 3 minutes. Add onion and wheat gluten and stir gently to coat with curry paste.

3. Peel and cut winter vegetables into 2-inch (5 cm) chunks. Add remaining coconut milk, stock, vegetables, sugar, soy sauce and salt and stir well. Bring to an active boil. Reduce heat to maintain a gentle boil and simmer, stirring occasionally, until vegetables are tender but not mushy, 15 minutes.

4. Add cashews and stir gently. Remove from heat. Transfer to a serving dish, sprinkle with cilantro and serve hot or warm.

Eggplant and Sweet Pepper–Studded Red Curry

This recipe makes a generous pot of curry, enough for a crowd of your favorite Thai food fans with a little left over for your next day's lunch.

SERVES 8 TO 10

Tips

You can use any type of eggplant, including large globe, slender Japanese or the golf ball-sized Thai variety called *makeuah poh*.

Use a wooden spoon to stir the curry so that the tofu chunks stay whole rather than break up or crumble.

2	cans (each 14 oz/400 mL) unsweetened coconut milk (about 3½ cups/875 mL), divided	2
2 tbsp	Red Curry Paste (page 180) or more to taste	30 mL
1 lb	eggplant, cut into bite-size chunks (about 3 cups/750 mL) (see Tips, left)	500 g
12	wild lime leaves, torn in half lengthwise, divided, optional	12
2 cups	Vegetable Stock (pages 189 and 190) or store-bought	500 mL
1 tbsp	palm sugar or brown sugar	15 mL
2 tsp	soy sauce	10 mL
1½ tsp	salt	7 mL
1 lb	firm tofu, cut into ½-inch (1 cm) chunks	500 g
½	red bell pepper, cut into 2-inch (5 cm) strips	½
½	green bell pepper, cut into 2-inch (5 cm) strips	½
½ cup	fresh cilantro leaves	125 mL

1. Shake coconut milk can well. Spoon out ⅓ cup (75 mL) into a medium saucepan and bring to a gentle boil over medium heat. Cook, stirring occasionally, until thickened and fragrant, about 3 minutes.

2. Add curry paste and cook, mashing and stirring often to soften and combine with coconut milk, about 3 minutes. Add eggplant and stir gently to coat with paste. Add remaining coconut milk, half of the lime leaves, if using, stock, sugar, soy sauce and salt and stir well. Bring to an active boil. Reduce heat to maintain a gentle boil and simmer, stirring occasionally, just until eggplant is tender, 10 to 15 minutes.

3. Add tofu, red and green bell peppers and remaining lime leaves and stir gently. Return to a boil and then remove from heat. Transfer to a serving dish, sprinkle with cilantro leaves and serve hot or warm.

Hard-Boiled Eggs and Peas in Green Curry

What a satisfying dinner this makes. Frozen green peas are added at the end of cooking since they only need to be heated until fully thawed. But if you have fresh green peas, add them after the curry has simmered for about 10 minutes. When they are tender, add the eggs and remove from the heat.

SERVES 6 TO 8

Vegan Variation

Vegan readers could substitute 8 oz (250 g) firm tofu, cut into 1-inch (2.5 cm) chunks, for the eggs or add about 1 cup (250 mL) potato and carrot chunks when the curry begins its 15-minute simmer.

1	can (14 oz/400 mL) unsweetened coconut milk (about 1¾ cups/ 425 mL), divided	1
2 tbsp	Green Curry Paste (page 182) or more to taste	30 mL
1	onion, thinly sliced lengthwise	1
¾ cup	Vegetable Stock (pages 189 and 190) or store-bought	175 mL
1 tbsp	palm sugar or brown sugar	15 mL
1 tsp	soy sauce	5 mL
½ tsp	salt	2 mL
5	hard-boiled eggs, peeled and halved lengthwise	5
1 cup	frozen green peas	250 mL
¼ cup	coarsely chopped fresh cilantro	60 mL

1. Shake coconut milk can well. Spoon out ⅓ cup (75 mL) into a medium saucepan and bring to a gentle boil over medium heat. Cook, stirring occasionally, until thickened and fragrant, about 3 minutes.

2. Add curry paste and cook, mashing and stirring often to soften paste and combine with coconut milk, about 3 minutes. Add onion and stir gently to coat with curry paste. Add remaining coconut milk, vegetable stock, sugar, soy sauce and salt and stir well. Bring to an active boil. Reduce heat to maintain a gentle boil and simmer, stirring occasionally, until onion is tender and the curry thickens slightly, about 15 minutes.

3. Add hard-boiled eggs and peas and stir gently. Remove from heat. Transfer to a serving dish, sprinkle with cilantro and serve hot or warm.

Green Curry with Zucchini and Bamboo Shoots

Green curry paste gets its fire from fresh green chile peppers, rather than dried red ones. If you can get fresh wild lime leaves toss in a handful when you add the vegetable stock and seasonings and add a few more just before serving. These add a lovely citrus note in fragrance and flavor. Think of them as equivalent to a bay leaf, added to impart their scent and taste but not to be eaten. If you can't find them, simply omit them. It will still be a great curry.

1	can (14 oz/400 mL) unsweetened coconut milk (about 1¾ cups/ 425 mL), divided	1
1 tbsp	Green Curry Paste (page 182) or more to taste	15 mL
1	can (8 oz/250 g) sliced bamboo shoots, rinsed and drained (see Tip, left)	1
1	onion, coarsely chopped	1
½ cup	Vegetable Stock (pages 189 and 190) or store-bought	125 mL
1 tbsp	palm sugar or brown sugar	15 mL
½ tsp	soy sauce	2 mL
½ tsp	salt	2 mL
2	zucchini, sliced crosswise (about 1 cup/250 mL)	2
½	bunch fresh cilantro, coarsely chopped	½

1. Shake coconut milk can well. Spoon out ⅓ cup (75 mL) into a medium saucepan and bring to a gentle boil over medium heat. Cook, stirring occasionally, until thickened and fragrant, about 3 minutes.

2. Add curry paste and cook, mashing and stirring often to soften paste and combine with coconut milk, about 3 minutes. Add bamboo shoots and chopped onion and stir gently to coat well with curry paste. Add remaining coconut milk, vegetable stock, sugar, soy sauce and salt and stir well. Bring to an active boil. Reduce heat to maintain a gentle boil and simmer, stirring occasionally, until onion is tender and curry thickens slightly, about 15 minutes.

3. Stir in zucchini, cook for 1 minute and remove from heat. Transfer to a serving bowl, sprinkle with cilantro and serve hot or warm.

Yellow Curry with Pineapple and Peas

Here is a scrumptious curry with spicy notes and moderate chile heat. Green peas punctuate its sun-colored sauce, drawing everyone to the table. If you like, add a little of the Indian spice mixture called garam masala or a mixture of freshly ground black pepper and ground cinnamon and cloves, along with the curry paste. For more chile heat, cut a few fresh serrano chiles in half lengthwise and add them along with the pineapple and seasonings.

SERVES 4 TO 6

Tip
Use a wooden spoon to stir the curry so that the tofu chunks stay whole rather than break or crumble.

1	can (14 oz/400 mL) unsweetened coconut milk (about 1¾ cups/ 425 mL), divided	1
1 tbsp	Yellow Curry Paste (page 184) or more to taste	15 mL
12 oz	potatoes, peeled and cut into bite-size chunks	375 g
1	can (8 oz/250 g) pineapple chunks, drained	1
½ cup	Vegetable Stock (pages 189 and 190) or store-bought	125 mL
1 tbsp	palm sugar or brown sugar	15 mL
½ tsp	soy sauce	2 mL
1 tsp	salt	5 mL
8 oz	firm tofu, cut into ½-inch (1 cm) cubes	250 g
1	red bell pepper, cut into long, thin strips	1
4 oz	snow peas, trimmed	125 g
¾ cup	frozen green peas	175 mL

1. Shake coconut milk can well. Spoon out ⅓ cup (75 mL) into a medium saucepan and bring to a gentle boil over medium heat. Cook, stirring occasionally, until thickened and fragrant, about 3 minutes.

2. Add curry paste and cook, mashing and stirring often to soften paste and combine with coconut milk, about 3 minutes. Add potatoes and pineapple chunks and stir gently to coat with curry paste. Add remaining coconut milk, vegetable stock, sugar, soy sauce and salt and stir well. Bring to an active boil. Reduce heat to maintain a gentle boil and simmer, stirring occasionally, until potatoes are tender, about 15 minutes.

3. Add tofu, pepper and peas and stir gently. Return to a boil and remove from heat. Transfer to a serving bowl and serve hot or warm.

Mussamun Curry with Peanuts, Potatoes and Cardamom

This delicious curry is a culinary legacy of Muslim traders from India, who traveled the sea coasts of Southeast Asia in centuries past. The use of peanuts, potatoes and whole cardamom in a curry are unusual in most of Thailand, but not in the southern provinces where this curry originated and where Islam is a major religion.

SERVES 4 TO 6

Tips

Mussamun curry paste is a red curry paste that includes not only the standard cumin, coriander and peppercorns, but also an aromatic array of sweet spices, including cinnamon, cloves, nutmeg and cardamom.

I like Thai curries thick, thin and in between. I like them ferociously hot, medium spicy or mellow and sweet like *gaeng* mussamun. I like them with tofu and with wheat gluten, with sweet peppers and with gnarly purple-skinned yams. I like them because they are easy to make and I like them because their flavor improves with time. I like them because I can buy ready-made paste for a quick supper or create my own incredibly delicious paste by hand. I like them because despite their simplicity they remind me of all that is delightful and unique about Thailand and Thai food.

1	can (14 oz/400 mL) unsweetened coconut milk (about 1¾ cups/ 425 mL), divided	1
1 tbsp	Mussamun Curry Paste (page 186) or more to taste (see Tips, left)	15 mL
1	can (8 oz/250 g) wheat gluten, drained, or 2 cups (500 mL) Wheatballs (page 194)	1
1	small onion, coarsely chopped	1
1	potato, peeled and cut into 1-inch (2.5 cm) chunks	1
1	sweet potato, peeled and cut into 1-inch (2.5 cm) chunks	1
¾ cup	Vegetable Stock (pages 189 and 190) or store-bought	175 mL
1 tbsp	palm sugar or brown sugar	15 mL
½ tsp	soy sauce	2 mL
1 tsp	salt	5 mL
25	whole green or white cardamom pods	25
1 cup	unsalted, dry-roasted peanuts	250 mL

1. Shake coconut milk can well. Spoon out ⅓ cup (75 mL) into a medium saucepan and bring to a gentle boil over medium heat. Cook, stirring occasionally, until thickened and fragrant, about 3 minutes.

2. Add curry paste and cook, mashing and stirring often to soften paste and combine with coconut milk, about 3 minutes. Add wheat gluten and onion and stir gently to coat with curry paste. Add remaining coconut milk, white potato, sweet potato, vegetable stock, sugar, soy sauce, salt and cardamom pods and stir well. Bring to an active boil. Reduce heat to maintain a gentle boil and simmer, stirring occasionally, until sweet potato is tender, about 15 minutes.

3. Add peanuts and stir gently. Remove from heat. Transfer to a serving bowl and serve hot or warm.

Burmese-Style Curry with Yams, Mushrooms and Ginger

Northern Thai cooks long ago adopted this deliciously earthy curry that originated in Burma. Its Thai name is gaeng hahng ley *and it provides a beautiful balance of spicy red-chile heat, sour tamarind punch and sweet notes of brown sugar. Make it in advance and reheat it gently, as its flavors deepen in a pleasing way.*

SERVES 6

Tip

The classic two- to three-quart saucepan of Thailand is known as *maw gaeng*, with *maw* meaning "cooking pot" and *gaeng* denoting the size and shape suitable for making a curry.

Variation

You can use freshly squeezed lime juice in place of the tamarind liquid.

¼ cup	slivered peeled fresh gingerroot	60 mL
2 tbsp	Red Curry Paste (page 180)	30 mL
¼ cup	packed brown sugar	60 mL
2 tsp	ground turmeric	10 mL
2½ cups	Vegetable Stock (pages 189 and 190) or store-bought	625 mL
1 tsp	dark soy sauce or 2 tsp (10 mL) regular soy sauce	5 mL
½ tsp	salt	2 mL
2 lbs	yams or sweet potatoes, peeled and cut into 2-inch (5 cm) chunks	1 kg
8 oz	small fresh button mushrooms, cut into ½-inch (1 cm) thick slices	250 g
¼ cup	thinly sliced shallots	60 mL
2 tbsp	minced garlic	30 mL
2 tbsp	Tamarind Liquid (page 191)	30 mL
2 tbsp	chopped fresh cilantro	30 mL

1. Place slivered ginger in a small bowl, add warm water to cover and set aside.

2. In a large, heavy saucepan or Dutch oven (see Tip, left), combine curry paste, brown sugar and turmeric. Mash with a spoon to mix together well. Add vegetable stock, soy sauce and salt and stir well. Bring to a rolling boil over medium heat and add yams. Reduce heat to maintain a gentle boil and cook, uncovered, until yams are tender and sauce has cooked down and thickened slightly, about 20 minutes.

3. Drain ginger and add soaking water to curry. Place ginger in a mortar and pound lightly with a pestle to soften fibers and release flavor. Or place on your cutting board and use the dull edge of your knife to bruise it.

4. Add ginger, mushrooms, shallots, garlic and tamarind, stir well and continue cooking for 10 minutes. Transfer to a serving bowl, sprinkle with cilantro and serve hot or warm.

Panaeng Curry with Wheatballs and Wild Lime Leaves

Panaeng dishes are thick, rich red-hot curries made with less coconut milk than most other Thai curries and enriched with coarsely ground peanuts. Traditionally, they are made with meat alone, rather than a combination of meat and vegetables.

SERVES 4

Tip

To slice wild lime leaves, stack several leaves and cut them crosswise into extremely thin threads, using a sawing motion and a very sharp knife. If possible, without tearing the leaf in half, strip away and discard the center vein running lengthwise along each leaf. Wild lime leaves are too tough to eat whole, but cutting them into wire-thin strips allows them to impart their bright citrus flavor while making them fine enough to eat.

Variations

In place of the Wheatballs or wheat gluten, add firm tofu, fresh mushrooms (whole or sliced), chunks of cooked kabocha pumpkin or potato or a mix of pineapple and zucchini.

Instead of the 2 *chee fah* chiles, use ¼ of a red bell pepper, cut into long, thin strips.

1	can (14 oz/400 mL) unsweetened coconut milk, divided	1
3 tbsp	Red Curry Paste (page 180)	45 mL
2 cups	Wheatballs (page 194) or 1 can (8 oz/250 g) wheat gluten, drained	500 mL
2 tbsp	Vegetable Stock (pages 189 and 190) or store-bought	30 mL
1 tbsp	brown sugar	15 mL
1 tsp	salt	5 mL
½ tsp	soy sauce	2 mL
10	fresh horapah basil leaves (page 220) or any other basil leaves	10
¼ cup	coarsely ground or chopped salted dry-roasted peanuts	60 mL
9	wild lime leaves, sliced crosswise into wire-thin threads, optional	9
2	fresh red *chee fah chiles*, cut crosswise on the diagonal into ovals ¼ inch (0.5 cm) thick	2

1. Scoop out about ¼ cup (60 mL) of the coconut milk from the top of the can and set aside to garnish the finished curry. In a skillet over medium heat, bring ½ cup (125 mL) of coconut milk to a gentle boil. Cook, stirring occasionally, until thickened slightly and fragrant, about 3 minutes.

2. Add paste and cook, mashing and stirring often to soften and combine with coconut milk, about 3 minutes. Add Wheatballs and toss to coat with paste. Add remaining coconut milk, stock, sugar, salt and soy sauce and stir well. Bring to a gentle boil and cook, stirring occasionally, until sauce is smooth and heated through, about 5 minutes. Tear all but a few of the basil leaves in half crosswise and add to curry along with peanuts and most of the lime leaf threads, if using.

3. Transfer to a serving platter. Pour reserved coconut milk on top and sprinkle on remaining lime leaf threads, chiles and reserved whole basil leaves. Serve hot or warm.

Choo Chee New Potatoes with Fresh Basil

Choo chee curries, which are traditionally made with seafood, are thick and rich. They call for less coconut milk than most Thai curries and use lots of pungent herbs. Panaeng curries (page 98) are similar, but they include ground peanuts. Choo chee curries are flavored with krueng gaeng kua, a red curry paste made without the toasted cumin, coriander seeds and peppercorns used in most Thai curry pastes (see Tips, left).

SERVES 4

Tips

You can make your curry paste by using the Red Curry Paste recipe (page 180) and omitting the spices. Or you can use any curry paste you like and be assured of a delicious result.

This dish traditionally calls for fresh horapah basil, but you can use any variety of fresh basil instead. Even if you omit the fresh basil and wild lime leaves altogether, you'll still have a wonderful Thai dish. Dried basil and dried lime have too little fragrance and flavor, so I never use them, even if they are all I can find.

1	can (14 oz/400 mL) unsweetened coconut milk, divided	1
2 tbsp	Red Curry Paste (page 180), made without coriander, cumin and peppercorns (see Tips, left)	30 mL
1 lb	new potatoes, halved or quartered, cooked in boiling water for about 5 minutes and drained	500 g
¼ cup	Vegetable Stock (pages 189 and 190) or store-bought	60 mL
2 tbsp	palm sugar, light brown or white sugar	30 mL
1 tsp	salt	5 mL
½ tsp	soy sauce	2 mL
½ cup	loosely packed fresh horapah basil leaves (see Tips, left)	125 mL
12	wild lime leaves, sliced crosswise into wire-thin threads, optional	12

1. Shake coconut milk can well. Spoon out about ½ cup (125 mL) into a medium saucepan and bring to a gentle boil over medium heat. Adjust heat to maintain a gentle boil and cook, stirring occasionally, 6 to 8 minutes. The coconut milk will become fragrant as it thickens. When you see tiny pools of oil glistening on the surface, add curry paste and continue cooking, stirring to dissolve paste into coconut milk, 1 to 2 minutes.

2. Add potatoes, remaining coconut milk, vegetable stock, sugar, salt and soy sauce and stir well. Bring to an active boil, adjust heat to maintain a gentle boil and cook, stirring occasionally, until curry is thickened and potatoes are cooked, about 10 minutes.

3. Cut all but a few of the basil leaves into thin strips and stir into curry along with lime leaves, if using. Remove from heat and transfer to a serving dish. Garnish with reserved basil leaves and serve hot or warm.

Butternut Squash in Fresh Green Curry

This simple fresh curry paste takes only minutes to prepare. It envelops sweet, golden chunks of butternut squash with a beautiful and savory green sauce in the time it takes the accompanying rice to cook. Try making it with any prepared curry paste for an even simpler dish (see Tips, right).

SERVES 4 TO 6

Tip

Butternut squash and other hard winter squash are a challenge to peel. Use a chef's knife or a Chinese cleaver if you are handy with either one of these tools or use a good paring knife, holding each chunk steady on your cutting board and cutting down along its side to remove the peel.

◆ Mini food processor or blender

1	small butternut squash, about 1½ lbs (750 g) (see Tips, left)	1
2 tbsp	coarsely chopped shallot or onion	30 mL
1 tbsp	coarsely chopped garlic	15 mL
1 tsp	coarsely chopped, peeled fresh gingerroot	5 mL
2	fresh green jalapeños or 1 fresh green serrano chile (see Tips, right)	2
¾ cup	coarsely chopped cilantro leaves and stems, divided	175 mL
1	can (14 oz/400 mL) unsweetened coconut milk (about 1¾ cups/ 425 mL), divided	1
1 tsp	granulated sugar	5 mL
1 tsp	salt	5 mL
¼ cup	fresh basil leaves	60 mL

1. Trim off stem and blossom end of butternut squash. Halve lengthwise and scoop out and discard seeds and fibers. Cut into large chunks and carefully peel each chunk. Cut peeled chunks into 1-inch (2.5 cm) pieces. You will have about 4 cups (1 L). Set aside.

2. In a mini food processor or blender, combine shallot, garlic, ginger, chiles, 3 tbsp (45 mL) water and ½ cup (125 mL) of the cilantro and grind, pulsing and stopping often to scrape sides of container, until a fairly smooth paste. You will have about ¼ cup (60 mL) bright green paste. Set aside.

3. Shake coconut milk can well. Spoon out ½ cup (125 mL) into a medium saucepan and bring to a gentle boil over medium heat. Cook, stirring occasionally, until thickened and fragrant, about 3 minutes.

This recipe makes a moderately hot curry. If you like your curries very hot, increase the amount of fresh chiles to suit your palate.

Variation

To substitute prepared curry paste (any type will do; see Basic Recipes chapter), omit the shallot or onion, garlic, ginger, chile peppers, water and cilantro and begin by cooking 2 tbsp (30 mL) prepared curry paste in the ½ cup (125 mL) coconut milk.

4. Add curry paste and cook, mashing and stirring until paste is dissolved into coconut milk and heated through, 1 to 2 minutes. Add remaining coconut milk, ½ cup (125 mL) water, sugar, salt and butternut squash. Increase heat to high and bring curry to a rolling boil. Stir well, reduce heat to maintain a gentle boil and continue cooking until squash is tender and sauce is smooth and evenly colored a soothing green, about 15 minutes.

5. Meanwhile, cut all but a few of the basil leaves crosswise into thin strips. When curry is cooked, stir in basil strips and the remaining ¼ cup (60 mL) of cilantro. Remove from heat and transfer to a serving bowl. Garnish with the reserved basil leaves and serve hot or warm.

❋ *Thai Tales*

Traditional curries are easy to find in Thailand, although if you try to order a curry at just any upcountry restaurant you will probably be disappointed. Restaurants tend to specialize, doing one thing or a certain category of things repeatedly and consequently very well. At the café near the train station or bus depot you can feast on noodles, fried rice and other one-dish specials. Here is where you take a load off after a hot, dusty journey, nursing a wonderfully tall Thai iced coffee as you cool your palms on the tiny pearls of cool water beading your glass in the heat of the day. If you are celebrating your birthday or otherwise feeling swell due to a burst of good fortune, you will host your friends at *rahn ahahn jeen*, the Chinese restaurant with that soupçon of uptown ambience, where the chef-owner cooks up seafood, Cantonese-style stir-fries, memorable soups, *yum*-style salads and other fancy dishes. No curries here, but remember the national motto, *mai pen rai* or "never you mind." Walk on, for even the smallest town upcountry supports at least one curry shop, whose proprietor cooks up a dozen or so curries first thing in the morning and sets them out on display to entice you in. Here, customers can order a splash of curry over a mountain of rice for a quick one-plate lunch or buy a family meal's worth for breakfast or supper, toting it home in a little plastic bag, which seems too full to survive the journey but invariably does.

Stir-Fries and Other Main Dishes

Mixed Grill 106

Oyster Mushrooms with Red Sweet Peppers
and Ginger 108

Baby Corn and Tofu with Cashews . . . 109

Mushrooms and Tofu with Fresh Mint 110

Sweet-and-Sour Tempeh with Cucumber
and Cauliflower 111

Triple Mushroom Feast. 112

Bean Sprout Toss-Up 113

Garlicky Brussels Sprouts 114

Spinach in Sweet-Sour Tamarind Sauce 115

Chinese Cabbage with Black Pepper and Garlic 116

Butternut Squash and Spinach in
Roasted Chile Paste. 117

Eggplant and Red Sweet Peppers
in Roasted Chile Paste 118

Zucchini and Tofu in Roasted Chile Paste 119

Red Hot Vegetable Stir-Fry 120

Golden Cabbage with Mushrooms and Peas 121

Eggplant Paht Peht 122

Firecracker Broccoli 123

Son-in-Law Eggs 124

Five-Spice Hard-Boiled Eggs in Sweet Soy Stew 126

Steamed Eggs with Cilantro and Crispy Garlic 128

Thai Omelet with Sriracha Sauce 129

Minced Mushrooms and Tofu with Chiles
and Holy Basil 130

Stir-Fried Spinach with Garlic and Pepper 131

Stir-Fries and Other Main Dishes

THIS IS THE CATCH-ALL CHAPTER FOR THE THAI DISHES THAT I have lassoed together because they share the distinction of not fitting in anywhere else in the book. If this cataloging decision suggests to you that the recipes to follow are ordinary, minor or otherwise relegated to supporting roles, take another look. Along with the preceding chapters of Salads, Soups and Curries, these recipes offer you plenty of options for Thai-style vegetarian feasts, anchored by an abundance of jasmine rice or sticky rice.

The Mixed Grill included here is perfect for days when cooking outdoors is appealing and possible. If you were using an upcountry kitchen in Thailand, this would be an everyday dish, since a traditional kitchen like the one I had during my Peace Corps days becomes almost a patio when the wooden shutters and door are thrown open to greet the dawn. My Thai kitchen included a pair of bucket-sized charcoal stoves that we used for the grilling technique known charmingly as *ping*.

Most of the following recipes are for traditional stir-fries, the Chinese cooking method Thais call *paht* and use at almost every meal. Whenever you stir-fry, set the scene to make your work easier when it's time to cook. Prepare the main ingredients, such as vegetables and tofu, washing and chopping as necessary and setting them near the stove. In a small bowl, combine any liquid ingredients, such as water, stock and soy sauce. In another small bowl, combine any dry ingredients such as sugar, salt and spices. Set these bowls near the stove, along with any herbs or garnishes. Then you are ready for the demands of a stir-fry, cooking through from start to finish without a pause.

There is a quartet of hearty classics, all fortified with tofu but each with its own special spark. Oyster Mushrooms with Red Sweet Peppers and Ginger is *paht king,* lit up with a shower of shredded ginger and studded with fresh mushrooms. You can throw in softened, shredded cloud ear mushrooms if you want to give it a traditional spin. Following is Baby Corn and Tofu with Cashews. Its Thai name is *paht meht mamuang Himapahn,* with the three enchanting but unwieldy modifying words adding up to the concise English word cashew. *Meht* is "seed" or "nut," *mamuang* is "mango" and *Himapahn* is an enchanted forest locale in the *jataka* tales of Theravada Buddhist tradition. In Thai, cashews are "mangos of the forest of Himapahn," a poetic reference probably springing from the fact that the nuts are shaped like the incomparable mangos of Southeast Asia.

Completing this classic quartet are *paht briow-wahn,* the pleasing Thai version of Chinese sweet-and-sour dishes and *paht bai graprao.* The latter is a stir-fry with holy basil, a delicious and delicate herb for which you can substitute any variety of its first cousins, fresh basil and fresh mint. Each of these classic stir-fry recipes calls for tofu, but you could substitute other protein-rich ingredients such as wheat gluten, seitan or tempeh, with tasty results.

Next come recipes in which successive vegetables deliciously take a bow in the spotlight, including Bean Sprout Toss-Up, Chinese Cabbage with Black Pepper and Garlic and Triple Mushroom Feast. Following are *paht* dishes jazzed up with some of the voluptuous sauces you will find in the Basic Recipes chapter. If you lay in a supply of these concoctions, you will have the short, high road to incredible flavor in remarkably little time. Start with my favorite, Butternut Squash and Spinach in Roasted Chile Paste and progress and work your way through tasty dishes spiked with curry paste to the deceptively simple Firecracker Broccoli, a gorgeous sparkler fueled by Sweet and Hot Garlic Sauce.

All the previous dishes are vegan, but this *gahp kao*—"with rice"—parade concludes with four traditional Thai egg dishes, beginning with two unique Asian ways with hard-boiled eggs and ending with a savory custard and a simple omelet served with fiery Sriracha Sauce. Vegans can adapt the first two dishes by substituting crisp-fried tofu or wheat gluten for the hard-boiled eggs.

Mixed Grill

This spectacular rainbow of vegetables, seasoned with the traditional Thai combination of cilantro, garlic and peppercorns, makes a fine companion to a pot of curry, a simple green salad and a mountain of jasmine rice. If you can grill outdoors on a summer afternoon, add a pitcher of lemonade and make Sticky Rice (page 137) rather than jasmine; the former is finger food and perfect for picnics. Cook up a double batch of grilled vegetables, as you can turn the leftovers into instant feasts galore. Pile the garlicky morsels onto a veggie burger, stack them on crusty peasant bread for a sensational sandwich or toss with noodles.

SERVES 4

Tip

For the vegetables use any combination of portobello mushrooms, zucchini, yellow summer squash, eggplants, onions, large green onions, whole heads of garlic, firm small to medium tomatoes, asparagus spears, or peppers such as red, yellow or green bell peppers, or New Mexico, Anaheim or Hungarian wax peppers.

• Food processor or blender

1½ cups	coarsely chopped fresh cilantro leaves and stems	375 mL
2 tbsp	coarsely chopped garlic (8 to 12 cloves)	30 mL
2 tbsp	soy sauce	15 mL
2 tbsp	Vegetable Stock (pages 189 and 190) or store-bought	15 mL
1 tsp	freshly ground black pepper	5 mL
½ cup	vegetable oil	125 mL
3 lbs	vegetables, in any combination (approx.) (see Tip, left)	1.5 kg

1. In a food processor fitted with metal blade, combine cilantro, garlic, soy sauce, stock and pepper and pulse to mince and combine well. With machine running, pour in oil and process to a fairly smooth marinade. If using a blender, combine cilantro, garlic, soy sauce, stock, pepper and oil and blend to a fairly smooth marinade, pulsing and scraping down sides as needed. Transfer marinade to a large, shallow baking dish and set aside.

2. Prepare vegetables for grill or broiler: Rinse mushrooms and pat dry. Remove stems and make 3 shallow diagonal slashes on the dark side of each cap. Or slice whole mushrooms through the stem about ¾ inch (2 cm) thick. Trim ends of zucchini or yellow squash and halve lengthwise. Trim ends of a large globe eggplant and slice crosswise into rounds 1 inch (2.5 cm) thick. For long, slender Asian eggplant, trim ends and halve lengthwise.

Tip

If you like, line the grill rack with foil to minimize flare-ups and discourage vegetables from slipping through the grate onto the coals.

3. Cut onions crosswise into 1-inch (2.5 cm) thick slices or cut in half lengthwise. Trim green onions, slicing off roots and any fading tips or greens. Leave garlic heads whole or cut crosswise just below the pointed tip, exposing the cloves.

4. Cut tomatoes in half crosswise. Snap off and discard woody base of each asparagus stem. Cut peppers in half lengthwise and remove stems, seeds and ribs. Leave in halves or cut pepper halves lengthwise into wide strips.

5. Place prepared vegetables in a baking dish with marinade and toss to coat well. Let stand at room temperature, tossing occasionally, 30 minutes to 1 hour.

6. Preheat greased gas or charcoal grill to medium heat or preheat broiler. Grill or broil vegetables until tender and nicely browned, using tongs to turn often and transferring to a plate as they are ready. Serve hot, warm or at room temperature.

Oyster Mushrooms with Red Sweet Peppers and Ginger

This flavorful stir-fry marries velvety mushrooms with flame-colored peppers and a shower of piquant ginger shreds. This dish goes beautifully with a creamy curry and steamed broccoli or a simple green salad, all to be savored over a plate or two of jasmine or basmati rice.

SERVES 4

Tips

Beautiful gray clusters of oyster mushrooms can be found in Asian grocery stores and some supermarkets. You can leave them whole or cut them lengthwise into thick strips. The cloud ear mushrooms add a handsome note of color and crunch, but omit them if they are difficult to find.

To prepare fresh ginger, select plump, shiny chunks that are heavy and firm for their size. Peel away the skin using a paring knife. Alternatively, use the tip of a spoon to peel it: Holding the ginger chunk in one hand and an ordinary spoon, bowl up, in the other, place the bowl of the spoon face down over the ginger and press the tip into the ginger, pulling down toward you and scraping away the peel. Cut peeled ginger into very thin slices and then stack and cut these slices into delicate strips.

4	large pieces dried cloud ears or black tree fungus, optional (see Tips, left)	4
8 oz	firm tofu, cut into ¼-inch (0.5 cm) cubes	250 g
2 tbsp	vegetable oil	30 mL
1 tbsp	coarsely chopped garlic	15 mL
½ cup	long, thin peeled strips fresh gingerroot (see Tips, left)	125 mL
1	onion, cut lengthwise into thick wedges	1
2 cups	fresh oyster mushrooms or any other sliced mushrooms	500 mL
2 tbsp	soy sauce	30 mL
1 tbsp	granulated sugar	15 mL
1 tsp	salt	5 mL
½	red bell pepper, cut into 2-inch (5 cm) long strips	½

1. Place cloud ears, if using, in a bowl, add warm water to cover and soak until softened, about 30 minutes.

2. Meanwhile, in a saucepan over high heat, bring 4 cups (1 L) water to a rolling boil. Gently add tofu and cook for 1 minute. Drain and place near stove along with oil. When cloud ears have softened, drain and cut away any tough stem ends. Slice into thin strips and set near stove.

3. Heat a wok or a large, deep skillet over medium-high heat for 30 seconds. Add oil and swirl to coat the surface. Add garlic and toss for 10 seconds. Add ginger and toss for 1 minute. Add onion and toss for 1 minute.

4. Add mushrooms and cloud ears and toss until mushrooms are shiny and softened, about 2 minutes. Add tofu, 1 tbsp (15 mL) water and soy sauce and toss gently to coat everything well while keeping tofu pieces whole. Add sugar, salt and bell pepper strips, toss gently to combine and cook until everything is heated through, 1 to 2 minutes. Transfer to a serving platter and serve hot or warm.

Baby Corn and Tofu with Cashews

You will love this tumble of petite, crunchy corn cobs and luscious cashews. Look for large, dark red New Mexico and California chiles wherever ingredients for Mexican cooking are sold. They add a subtle, smoky heat. You can, however, use a handful of small, fiery chiles if you prefer a volcanic note. In the summer, make this dish with fresh corn, shaving the kernels off the cob.

SERVES 4

4	large, mild dried red chiles such as New Mexico or California chiles	4
8 oz	firm tofu, cut into 1-inch (2.5 cm) cubes	250 g
3 tbsp	vegetable oil	45 mL
1	onion, sliced lengthwise into thick wedges	1
1 tbsp	soy sauce	15 mL
1	can (14 oz/400 g) baby corn, rinsed and drained	1
1 tsp	granulated sugar	5 mL
½ tsp	salt	2 mL
½ cup	salted, dry-roasted cashews	125 mL
3	green onions, cut into 2-inch (5 cm) lengths	3

1. Cut off chile stems and shake out most of the seeds. Cut chiles into quarters lengthwise and set aside.

2. In a saucepan over high heat, bring 4 cups (1 L) water to a rolling boil. Gently add tofu and cook for 1 minute. Drain and place near the stove along with a serving platter for the finished dish.

3. Heat a wok or a large, deep skillet over medium-high heat for 30 seconds. Add oil and swirl to coat surface. Add chiles, toss for 1 minute and transfer to serving platter, leaving oil in wok. Add onion and toss until shiny and softened, 1 to 2 minutes.

4. Add tofu, 2 tbsp (30 mL) water and soy sauce and cook, tossing gently, for 1 minute. Add corn, sugar and salt and toss gently. Return chiles to pan and add cashews and green onions. Toss gently and cook until heated through, about 1 minute. Transfer to serving platter and serve hot or warm.

Mushrooms and Tofu with Fresh Mint

I learned this delicious stir-fry recipe from Mrs. Wongkiow, a great home cook in northern Thailand's Chiang Rai province. She used fresh straw mushrooms and lots of pepper and cooked up an array of other dishes to go with mountains of sticky rice. This vegetarian version of her recipe works beautifully with almost any fresh mushroom (see Tips, below).

SERVES 4

Tips

If you can find small button mushrooms, trim stems and leave whole. Halve regular button mushrooms lengthwise or cut into thick slices. Leave oyster mushrooms whole and cut portobellos or other large mushrooms into bite-size pieces.

If you do not have dark soy sauce, you can leave it out; its main culinary role here is to add a handsome caramel color to the dish.

8 oz	firm tofu, cut into ¼-inch (0.5 cm) cubes	250 g
1 tbsp	vegetable oil	15 mL
1 tbsp	coarsely chopped garlic (4 to 6 cloves)	15 mL
1 or 2	fresh green serrano chiles, stemmed and minced	1 or 2
8 oz	fresh mushrooms (see Tips, left)	250 g
1 tsp	regular soy sauce	5 mL
1 tsp	dark soy sauce (see Tips, left)	5 mL
1 tbsp	granulated sugar	15 mL
1 tsp	salt	5 mL
½	red bell pepper, cut into 2-inch (5 cm) long strips	½
1 cup	lightly packed fresh mint leaves	250 mL

1. In a medium saucepan over high heat, bring 4 cups (1 L) water to a rolling boil. Gently add tofu and cook for 1 minute. Drain and place near the stove.

2. Heat a wok or a large, deep skillet over medium-high heat for 30 seconds. Add oil and swirl to coat surface. Add garlic and chiles and toss for 10 seconds. Add mushrooms and cook until shiny and softened, about 2 minutes. Add tofu, 1 tbsp (15 mL) water and regular and dark soy sauces and toss for 1 minute. Add sugar and salt, toss well and add bell pepper and mint. Toss until heated through, about 1 minute. Transfer to a serving platter. Serve hot or warm.

Sweet-and-Sour Tempeh with Cucumber and Cauliflower

The Thai take on sweet-and-sour dishes is light and crunchy. Here, a chorus of tomatoes, cauliflowers and cucumbers is bathed in a tangy sauce. Cucumber, a sturdy member of the melon family, is much appreciated in the Thai pantry, where it is cooked in soups and stir-fries as well as used raw in salads. Chinese stir-fry dishes are often thickened with cornstarch, tapioca starch, arrowroot powder or other flours, but Thai cooks prefer to leave the sauce in its natural state and use it as a flavorful juice perfect for seasoning a plate of rice.

SERVES 4

Variation

You can substitute broccoli florets or chunks of fresh or canned pineapple for the cauliflower.

2 tbsp	vegetable oil	30 mL
1 tbsp	coarsely chopped garlic (4 to 6 cloves)	15 mL
8 oz	tempeh, cut into bite-size pieces	250 g
1½ cups	small cauliflower florets	375 mL
½ cup	Vegetable Stock (pages 189 and 190) or store-bought	125 mL
1	onion, cut lengthwise into thick wedges	1
1 tbsp	soy sauce	15 mL
2 tbsp	distilled white vinegar	30 mL
3 tbsp	granulated sugar	45 mL
1 tsp	salt	5 mL
½	hothouse cucumber, peeled, halved lengthwise and cut crosswise into thick slices	½
8	cherry tomatoes, halved lengthwise	8

1. Heat a wok or large deep skillet over medium-high heat for 30 seconds. Add oil and swirl to coat pan. Add garlic and toss for about 10 seconds. Add tempeh, toss well, and spread out in a single layer. Cook, turning once, until lightly browned, about 1 minute per side.

2. Add cauliflower and toss well to coat with the other ingredients. Add stock and cook, tossing occasionally, until cauliflower is tender, 2 to 3 minutes. Add onion, soy sauce, vinegar, sugar and salt and toss well. Cook for 3 minutes.

3. Add cucumber and cook, tossing once, for 1 minute. Add cherry tomatoes, toss well, and cook until heated through, about 1 minute. Transfer to a serving platter and serve hot or warm.

Triple Mushroom Feast

For this simple stir-fry, you can splurge on exotic mushrooms such as shiitake, oyster or cremini, or make it with familiar button mushrooms. Either way you will have a tasty dish with lots of flavorful broth for seasoning a steaming plate of jasmine rice. The dish can be served hot, warm or at room temperature, and it reheats nicely. Its flavor note is salty, so accompany it with a fiery curry and a soup or salad with the sharp edge of freshly squeezed lime juice. A wok is best here for ease in tossing the mushrooms as they cook, but you can use a large skillet and turn them carefully.

SERVES 4

Tip

You can use a total of about 1 lb (500 g) button mushrooms in place of the combination suggested with good results. You can also make this dish with whole oyster mushrooms, which are often available in Asian markets at reasonable prices.

3 oz	fresh shiitake mushrooms (see Tip, left)	90 g
3 oz	fresh oyster mushrooms	90 g
8 oz	fresh button mushrooms	250 g
2 tbsp	vegetable oil	30 mL
6	large cloves garlic, thinly sliced crosswise	6
2	small shallots, thinly sliced lengthwise	2
1 tsp	granulated sugar	5 mL
½ tsp	salt	2 mL
¼ cup	water	60 mL
3	green onions, thinly sliced crosswise	3
½ tsp	freshly ground black pepper	2 mL

1. Remove and discard stems from shiitakes and separate any clusters of oyster mushrooms into individual mushrooms. Score the dark cap of each shiitake with an X. In a large bowl, combine shiitake and oyster mushrooms. Slice button mushrooms and add to bowl. Set aside.

2. Heat a wok or a large deep skillet with a tight-fitting lid over medium-high heat for 30 seconds. Add oil and swirl to coat pan. Add garlic and shallots and cook, tossing occasionally, until fragrant and coated with oil, about 1 minute. Add mushrooms and toss until shiny and beginning to soften, about 1 minute. Add sugar, salt and water and toss well. Reduce heat to medium, cover, and cook for 2 minutes.

3. Uncover and toss well. Stir in green onions and ground pepper, toss to mix. Transfer contents of pan, including liquid, to a serving dish. Serve hot, warm or at room temperature.

Bean Sprout Toss-Up

Thais adore fresh mung bean sprouts and use them in abundance, both raw and cooked. In a classic Paht Thai (page 150), the cook tosses a handful of sprouts in with the noodles to wilt them in the sauce. The finished dish is then garnished with another handful of raw bean sprouts as a cool, crunchy foil to the tasty, tangy noodles. Here is a simple symphony in homage to beans: tofu from soybeans, green beans from the garden and a confetti of crisp sprouts from the tiny green mung bean.

SERVES 4

Tip
If you do not have dark soy sauce, you can leave it out; its main culinary role here is to add a handsome caramel color to the dish.

2 tbsp	vegetable oil	30 mL
2 tbsp	coarsely chopped garlic (8 to 12 cloves)	30 mL
10	green beans, trimmed and thinly sliced crosswise	10
8 oz	firm tofu, cut into 1-inch (2.5 cm) cubes	250 g
¼ cup	Vegetable Stock (pages 189 and 190) or store-bought	60 mL
1 tbsp	granulated sugar	15 mL
1 tsp	salt	5 mL
1 tsp	regular soy sauce	5 mL
½ tsp	dark soy sauce (see Tip, left)	2 mL
8 oz	fresh mung bean sprouts (about 4 cups/1 L)	250 g
2 or 3	plum tomatoes, cut into bite-size chunks	2 or 3

1. Heat a wok or a large, deep skillet over medium-high heat for 30 seconds. Add oil and swirl to coat pan. Add garlic and toss until fragrant and coated with oil, about 1 minute. Add green beans and toss until tender and bright green, about 2 minutes. Add tofu, vegetable stock, sugar, salt and regular and dark soy sauces and toss gently. Spread tofu in a single layer and cook, tossing gently occasionally to coat with sauce, until heated through, about 2 minutes.

2. Increase heat to high and add bean sprouts and tomatoes. Cook, tossing often, until hot and beginning to wilt, about 1 minute. Transfer to a deep serving platter and serve hot or warm.

Garlicky Brussels Sprouts

Vegetarian oyster sauce, made from mushrooms, is a commercially made substitute for oyster sauce, the classic Asian condiment made from dried oysters, sold in Asian markets and some supermarkets with extensive Asian food selections. Dried shiitake mushrooms give it its deep, rich flavor, and its thick, rich texture gives a boost to the simplest stir-fry. Thais use traditional oyster sauce often, particularly with broccoli, bok choy and other members of the cabbage family. Brussels sprouts are not common in Thailand, but they take beautifully to this Thai way of cooking sturdy greens. This is a salty stir-fry, made to go with a spicy or sweet-and-sour dish and a plateful of grains.

SERVES 4

Tip

Look for small, tightly furled Brussels sprouts that are bright green. Yellow or brown leaves indicate aging, so avoid them.

Variation

Garlicky Cabbage or Broccoli: Substitute 2½ cups (625 mL) shredded cabbage or florets of broccoli and cauliflower for the Brussels sprouts if they are not in season.

1 lb	Brussels sprouts, trimmed and halved lengthwise (about 3 cups/750 mL) (see Tip, left)	500 g
½ tsp	salt	2 mL
¾ cup	water	175 mL
1 tbsp	vegetarian oyster sauce	15 mL
2 tsp	soy sauce	10 mL
1 tsp	granulated sugar	5 mL
½ tsp	freshly ground black pepper	2 mL
2 tbsp	vegetable oil	30 mL
1 tbsp	chopped garlic	15 mL

1. In a saucepan over medium heat, combine Brussels sprouts, salt and ½ cup (125 mL) water and bring to a rolling boil. Reduce heat to maintain a simmer, cover and cook until tender and bright green, 7 to 9 minutes.

2. Meanwhile, in a small bowl, combine vegetarian oyster sauce, soy sauce, sugar, pepper and ¼ cup (60 mL) water. Stir well and set aside.

3. When sprouts are tender, remove from heat and set aside. Heat a wok or large, deep skillet with a tight-fitting lid over medium-high heat. Add oil and swirl to coat pan. Add garlic and cook, tossing often, for 30 seconds. Add braised Brussels sprouts and cook, tossing often, until sprouts are shiny, about 1 minute.

4. Quickly stir sauce mixture to combine and add to pan. Cook, tossing to coat well with sauce, until heated through, about 1 minute. Transfer to a serving dish and serve hot, warm or at room temperature.

Spinach in Sweet-Sour Tamarind Sauce

Thais gladly eat their greens, which is no surprise given their brilliant touch in cooking them to create lots of flavor with little time and effort. Serve this dish Thai-style, with plenty of rice and remember to spoon on lots of the thin, vitamin-packed pan sauce, known in my home of North Carolina as pot liquor, where it is treasured along with the greens from which it came.

SERVES 4

Tips

This is a salty dish, so you may want to serve it with a sweet dish such as Mee Grop (page 147), a crispy, tangy noodle dish and a hot, spicy curry.

If you have some left over, sautéed spinach is quite tasty the next day, although it will lose much of its sparkle in the presentation department. Reheat gently, as more actual cooking will tire it out rather than wake it up.

A wok is ideal here because of the sheer volume of this much spinach in the raw. A wokful of unwieldy leaves swiftly sizzles down into a tidy tender platter for four, but if a big, deep skillet is all you have to work with, that's fine, too. Simply ease the spinach into the pan in batches, adding fresh leaves as soon as the previous batch wilts down to make room for more.

1½ tbsp	palm sugar or brown sugar	22 mL
1½ tbsp	Tamarind Liquid (page 191)	22 mL
2 tsp	soy sauce	10 mL
½ tsp	salt	2 mL
¼ tsp	freshly ground black pepper	1 mL
2 tbsp	vegetable oil	30 mL
1 tbsp	coarsely chopped garlic (4 to 6 cloves)	15 mL
12 oz	baby spinach (18 to 20 loosely packed cups/4.5 to 5 L)	375 g

1. In a small bowl, combine sugar, tamarind, soy sauce, salt and pepper. Stir well and place near stove.

2. Heat a wok or a large, deep skillet with a tight-fitting lid over medium-high heat for 30 seconds. Add oil and swirl to coat pan. Add garlic and toss until fragrant and shiny, about 1 minute. Add spinach and toss to begin coating with oil. You may need to add spinach in batches, tossing and turning until it all fits into the pan (see Tips, left).

3. When all of the spinach has been touched by oil, reduce heat to medium. Quickly stir sauce mixture to combine and add to pan. Toss well and cover immediately. Cook until spinach is wilted but still bright green, 1 to 2 minutes. Transfer spinach, including its cooking liquid, to a deep serving platter and serve hot, warm or at room temperature.

Chinese Cabbage with Black Pepper and Garlic

This quick-and-easy stir-fry of healthful greens spiked with garlic and pepper is destined to become a standard whenever your menu centers on rice. This is my version of pahk boong fai daeng *or "water spinach on fire." The dish is wonderfully salty, so serve it with mountains of rice and something sweet, perhaps Son-in-Law Eggs (page 124) and something hot and spicy, such as Tome Yum Soup with Mushrooms and Tofu (page 72).*

SERVES 4 TO 6

Tip

Pahk boong, a broccoli-green Asian vegetable, has delicate, arrowhead-shaped leaves attached to long, slender, hollow stalks. It is available seasonally in Asian markets, but you can enjoy this dish made with other greens as well (see Variation, below).

Variation

Kale with Black Pepper and Garlic: You can use this same recipe with kale or other sturdy winter greens such as collards, mustard greens or chard. For best results, separate the leaves and stems. Cut the stems on the diagonal into bite-size spears and cut leaves into generous 2- to 3-inch (5 to 7.5 cm) pieces. Blanch for 1 to 3 minutes in boiling water until tender, then drain well and proceed as directed, adding to oil and garlic. You can also use spinach, which needs no blanching or use half napa cabbage and half bok choy for a gorgeous display of shades of green.

1¼ lbs	napa cabbage, bok choy or other leafy Asian cabbage (about 2 cups/500 mL loosely chopped pieces)	625 g
1 tbsp	Vegetable Stock (pages 189 and 190) or store-bought or water	15 mL
2 tsp	granulated sugar	10 mL
½ tsp	soy sauce	2 mL
½ tsp	salt	2 mL
¼ tsp	freshly ground black pepper	1 mL
2 tbsp	vegetable oil	30 mL
2 tbsp	coarsely chopped garlic (8 to 12 cloves)	30 mL

1. Trim napa cabbage or bok choy, cutting away and discarding the core end and cutting remaining leaves crosswise into 1-inch (2.5 cm) wide pieces. Place in a large bowl, add cold water, swish around with your fingers and then drain well, allowing some water to cling to the leaves. Set aside.

2. In a small bowl, combine vegetable stock, sugar, soy sauce, salt and pepper and stir well. Set aside near the stove.

3. Heat a wok or a large, deep skillet with a tight-fitting lid over high heat for 30 seconds. Add oil and swirl to coat pan. Add garlic and toss until fragrant and beginning to brown, about 30 seconds. Add greens and toss (2 slotted spoons work well) until coated with oil and begin to wilt, about 1 minute. Quickly stir sauce mixture to combine and add to pan. Toss well and cover immediately. Cook until greens are somewhat wilted and tender but still bright green, 1 to 2 minutes. Transfer greens, including cooking liquid, to a deep serving platter and serve hot or warm.

Butternut Squash and Spinach in Roasted Chile Paste

Roasted chile paste, a sensational combination of sweetness and heat, complements the pairing of butternut squash and spinach. You can make your own paste or buy it prepared in Asian groceries. If you bake the butternut squash in advance and have chile paste on hand, this dish goes together in a flash.

SERVES 4

Tip

Avoid baking the butternut squash too long, as you want it sturdy enough to cut into chunks that will hold their shape when cooked on the stove top. You can bake it several hours in advance, let cool to room temperature and then cover and chill until cooking time.

♦ Preheat oven to 400°F (200°C)

1	small butternut squash, about 1 lb (500 g) (see Tip, left)	1
2 tbsp	vegetable oil	30 mL
1 tbsp	coarsely chopped garlic (4 to 6 cloves)	15 mL
1	onion, cut lengthwise into thin strips	1
6 oz	spinach leaves (7 to 8 loosely packed cups/1.75 to 2 L)	175 g
2 tbsp	Roasted Chile Paste (page 204) or store-bought	30 mL
1 tbsp	water	15 mL
1 tsp	soy sauce	5 mL
½ tsp	salt	2 mL

1. Cut butternut squash in half lengthwise, scoop out and discard seeds and place cut side down on a baking sheet. Bake in preheated oven until tender, about 30 minutes. Remove from oven and set aside until squash is cool enough to handle. Peel and cut into 1-inch (2.5 cm) chunks.

2. Heat a wok or large, deep skillet over medium-high heat. Add oil and swirl to coat pan. Add garlic and onion and cook, tossing often, until onion is shiny and softened, 1 to 2 minutes. Add squash and spinach and cook, turning so spinach leaves begin to wilt, for 1 minute. Add chile paste, water, soy sauce and salt and toss well. Cook until spinach is tender and brilliant green and squash is heated through, 1 to 2 minutes. Transfer to a serving dish and serve hot or warm.

Eggplant and Red Sweet Peppers in Roasted Chile Paste

In this dish, eggplant's slightly bitter note is softened by the pepper's sweetness and the tangy explosion of the extraordinary chile sauce.

SERVES 4 TO 6		

Tip

The slender, deep purple Japanese eggplants are ideal here, but chunks cut from a large globe eggplant or golf ball-size Thai eggplants halved lengthwise would work as well.

1¼ lbs	eggplant (see Tip, left), cut into 1-inch (2.5 cm) chunks (about 7 cups/1.75 L)	625 g
3 tbsp	vegetable oil	45 mL
1 tbsp	coarsely chopped garlic (4 to 6 cloves)	15 mL
1	red onion, cut lengthwise into thin strips	1
2 tbsp	Roasted Chile Paste (page 204) or store-bought	30 mL
1 tbsp	palm sugar or brown sugar	15 mL
1 tbsp	water	15 mL
1 tsp	soy sauce	5 mL
½ tsp	salt	2 mL
1	red bell pepper, cut into long, thin strips	1

1. Trim off stems from eggplants. If using Japanese eggplants, cut each one in half lengthwise and then cut each half crosswise into 1-inch (2.5 cm) pieces. If using Thai eggplants, quarter lengthwise. If using one or more globe eggplants, cut into 1-inch (2.5 cm) chunks.

2. Heat a wok or a large, deep skillet over medium-high heat. Add oil and swirl to coat pan. Add garlic and red onion and cook, tossing often, until onion is shiny and softened, 1 to 2 minutes. Add eggplant pieces and cook, tossing often, until tender but still holding their shape, 5 to 7 minutes. Add chile paste, sugar, water, soy sauce and salt and toss well. Add bell pepper and cook, tossing often, until shiny and beginning to wilt, about 2 minutes. Transfer to a serving dish and serve hot or warm.

Zucchini and Tofu
in Roasted Chile Paste

Make a double batch of Roasted Chile Paste so that you can use it often in this satisfying dish. You can switch the vegetables to suit your whim or your garden's bounty or merely to make supper out of what you have on hand. Use yellow squash or pattypan squash instead of the zucchini and add a handful of halved cherry tomatoes at the end for a burst of color.

SERVES 4		
4 cups	water	1 L
8 oz	firm tofu, cut into 1-inch (2.5 cm) cubes	250 g
2 tbsp	vegetable oil	30 mL
1 tbsp	coarsely chopped garlic (4 to 6 cloves)	15 mL
1	onion, cut lengthwise into thick strips	1
3	zucchini, cut into ¼-inch (0.5 cm) thick rounds	3
3 tbsp	Roasted Chile Paste (page 204) or store-bought	45 mL
¼ cup	Vegetable Stock (pages 189 and 190) or store-bought	60 mL
1 tsp	soy sauce	5 mL
½ tsp	salt	2 mL

1. In a saucepan over high heat, bring water to a rolling boil. Gently add tofu and cook for 1 minute. Drain and place near the stove.

2. Heat a wok or a large, deep skillet over medium-high heat. Add oil and swirl to coat pan. Add garlic and onion and cook until fragrant and softened, about 1 minute. Add zucchini and cook, tossing occasionally, until tender and a brilliant green, about 2 minutes.

3. Reduce heat to medium and add chile paste, vegetable stock, soy sauce and salt. Toss well. Add tofu and cook, gently tossing occasionally, until heated through and evenly coated with sauce, about 1 minute. Transfer to a serving dish and serve hot or warm.

Red Hot Vegetable Stir-Fry

Put your homemade Thai curry paste to work when your hunger for curry heat and flavor insists on instant satisfaction. When you request this paht peht *or "red-hot stir-fry dish" from a Thai cook, you will generally be asked, "Peht towrai kah?" or, in other words, "Just how much fire are we looking for here?" This is hot stuff to my palate, but you can increase the amount of curry paste if you crave food at what my friend Jim O'Connor calls "the core temperature of the sun."*

SERVES 4

Tip

Use green, yellow or mussamun curry paste (pages 182 to 186) instead of red.

Variation

Vary the vegetables to suit your fancy, adding longer-cooking vegetables early on and delicate ones toward the end of cooking time.

8 oz	firm tofu, cut into ½-inch (1 cm) chunks	250 g
4 oz	green beans, trimmed and cut into 2-inch (5 cm) lengths	125 g
3 tbsp	vegetable oil	45 mL
3 tbsp	Red Curry Paste (page 180)	45 mL
2	Japanese eggplants, cut crosswise on the diagonal into thick slices	2
1½ cups	chopped peeled butternut squash (¼-inch/0.5 cm wedges)	375 mL
⅓ cup	Vegetable Stock (pages 189 and 190) or store-bought	75 mL
2 tsp	granulated sugar	10 mL
1 tsp	each soy sauce and salt	5 mL
½ cup	loosely packed fresh basil leaves	125 mL
¼	red bell pepper, cut into 2-inch (5 cm) long strips	¼

1. Fill a large saucepan with water and bring to a rolling boil over high heat. Gently add tofu and cook for 1 minute. Using a slotted spoon, transfer to a plate. Add green beans to the same water and cook for 2 minutes. Drain and transfer to plate.

2. In a wok or skillet over medium-low heat, warm oil until very warm but not hot. Add curry paste and cook, mashing and scraping to mix it with the oil, until it is well-blended and fragrant, about 2 minutes.

3. Add green beans, eggplant, squash, vegetable stock, sugar, soy sauce and salt and toss well. Cook, tossing occasionally, for 5 minutes. Add tofu and continue cooking, tossing gently, until vegetables are tender and tofu is heated through, about 2 minutes.

4. Meanwhile, set a few of the basil leaves aside. Stack the remaining leaves and cut crosswise into thin ribbons. When vegetables are ready, toss in basil ribbons and bell pepper. Transfer to a serving platter. Garnish with reserved basil leaves and serve hot or warm.

Golden Cabbage with Mushrooms and Peas

Cabbages are popular year-round in Thailand, where cooks stir-fry them quickly in a hot wok to preserve their flavor and crunch. Make this satisfying winter vegetable braise on a blustery day while dreaming of a rainbow of produce in your garden next summer.

SERVES 4 TO 6			
1	small head cabbage, about 1 lb (500 g)	1
2 tbsp	vegetable oil	30 mL
2 tbsp	coarsely chopped garlic	30 mL
1	onion, cut lengthwise into thin strips	1
1 cup	sliced fresh mushrooms (about 6 oz/175 g)	250 mL
2 tsp	Yellow Curry Paste (page 184) or more to taste	10 mL
¼ cup	water	60 mL
1 tsp	soy sauce	5 mL
1 tsp	salt	5 mL
1 tsp	granulated sugar	5 mL
1 cup	green peas	250 mL

1. Trim cabbage, removing and discarding hard core and outer leaves. Quarter lengthwise and cut into thin shreds. You will have 5 to 6 cups (1.25 to 1.5 L). Set aside.

2. Heat a wok or a large, deep skillet with a tight-fitting lid over medium-high heat. Add oil and swirl to coat pan. Add garlic and onion and toss until shiny and fragrant, about 1 minute. Add mushrooms and cook, tossing often, until darkened and tender, about 5 minutes.

3. Add cabbage and toss until shiny and beginning to wilt, about 1 minute. Add curry paste, water, soy sauce, salt and sugar and toss well. Cover and cook, tossing occasionally, until cabbage is shiny and tender but still crisp, about 5 minutes. Add peas, toss well and remove from heat. Transfer to a deep serving platter and serve hot or warm.

Eggplant Paht Peht

If you adore the fiery flavors of Thai curries but want a quicker, lighter dish, try this one. Paht means "to stir-fry in a wok" and peht means "chile-pepper hot." Here, curry paste is softened in oil and then tossed with vegetables and kissed with a bouquet of Asian herbs. The resulting dish is served up with plain rice, untempered by the velvety sweetness of coconut milk that would extinguish a bit of a curry paste's fire. This is Thai home cooking at its delicious best.

SERVES 4

Tips

Eggplant is part of the classic *paht peht* and the standard choice is the golf ball-size Thai eggplant known as *makeuah poh*. It is hard and seedy and you will find it with green, purple or white skin in Asian markets. This dish is also delicious made with everyday globe eggplants or long, slender Japanese eggplants.

The final cooking time will depend on the type of eggplant you use, with Japanese eggplant cooking the quickest, small, round Thai eggplant taking the longest and friendly globe eggplant in between.

If you do not have wild lime leaves or fresh basil, leave them out. You can even omit the ginger, if it calls for a trip to the store. These traditional ingredients inarguably enhance the dish, but it is delicious even without them.

3 tbsp	vegetable oil	45 mL
3 tbsp	Red Curry Paste (page 180)	45 mL
1	onion, cut lengthwise into thick strips	1
1¼ lbs	eggplant (see Tips, left), cut into 1-inch (2.5 cm) chunks (about 7 cups/1.75 L)	625 g
¾ cup	Vegetable Stock (pages 189 and 190) or store-bought	175 mL
1 tbsp	palm sugar or brown sugar	15 mL
1 tsp	salt	5 mL
½ tsp	soy sauce	2 mL
2 tbsp	finely shredded peeled fresh gingerroot	30 mL
¼ cup	fresh basil leaves	60 mL
12	wild lime leaves, optional (see Tips, left)	12

1. Heat a wok or a large, deep skillet over medium heat. Add oil and swirl to coat pan. Add curry paste and mash and scrape paste against pan to soften and combine with oil. Adjust heat so paste and oil sizzle pleasantly without a lot of popping, sticking or burning. Cook, stirring occasionally, until fragrant and well mixed with oil, about 2 minutes.

2. Add onion and toss to coat with paste. Add eggplant, toss well and cook, tossing occasionally, for 2 minutes. Add vegetable stock, sugar, salt, soy sauce and ginger, toss well and cook until eggplant is tender and everything is well combined, 5 to 7 minutes.

3. Add basil and wild lime leaves, if using, toss well and turn out onto a serving platter. Serve hot or warm.

Firecracker Broccoli

Charlisa Cato of Arkansas became famous last Christmas by making my diabolically delicious Sweet and Hot Garlic Sauce (page 206) by the gallon to share with her friends. She was kind enough to pass along her recipe for broccoli. This makes broccoli taste so good so fast that you will put on your cha-cha heels and dance around the kitchen.

SERVES 4

Variation

With adjustments to the timing and amount of liquid, you can enjoy this quick fix with other gifts from the garden, including asparagus, carrots, cauliflower, snow peas and sugar snap peas. It can be covered and stored in the refrigerator for up to 2 days.

1 tbsp	vegetable oil	15 mL
8 oz	broccoli florets (about 4 cups/1 L)	250 g
¼ cup	Vegetable Stock (pages 189 and 190) or store-bought	60 mL
Pinch	salt	Pinch
1 tbsp	Sweet and Hot Garlic Sauce (page 206)	15 mL

1. In a skillet with a tight-fitting lid over medium-high heat, warm oil for about 1 minute or until a bit of broccoli tip sizzles at once. Add broccoli florets and toss until bright green and beginning to shine, about 1 minute. Add vegetable stock and salt, cover, reduce heat to medium and cook until tender but still crisp, 1 to 2 minutes.

2. Uncover, add Sweet and Hot Garlic Sauce, toss well and remove from heat. Transfer to a serving dish and serve hot, warm, at room temperature or cold.

Son-in-Law Eggs

This unique dish is hearty and delicious, with its combination of golden hard-boiled eggs napped with a pungent tamarind sauce and enlivened with crispy garlic and shallots. It is one of my favorites, perhaps because I often enjoyed it as part of a banquet menu in Thailand when friends were celebrating a wedding, a birth, the ordination of a family member as a Buddhist monk or some other auspicious occasion. These eggs have a chewy-crisp texture, which is unusual by Western standards but prized in Asian cuisines. Try them with lots of jasmine rice, or serve the halved or quartered eggs in lettuce cups with a dollop of sauce and toppings as an exotic starter to offer as guests arrive.

SERVES 6 TO 8

Tips

It is frustratingly easy to burn the garlic and shallots. To get them all out fast, position a large fine-mesh strainer over a large deep saucepan placed near the stove. When the garlic and shallots are nearly ready, simply empty the oil into the saucepan through the sieve. Then turn the contents of the sieve onto the towel-lined baking sheet.

You can prepare the sauce an hour or so in advance and let it stand, covered, at room temperature. Reheat gently over low head just before serving. You can also fry the shallots and garlic several hours in advance and set them aside at room temperature until serving time.

- ◆ Mini food processor or blender
- ◆ Baking sheet, lined with double thickness of paper towels
- ◆ Candy/deep-fry thermometer

Sauce

½ cup	Vegetable Stock (pages 189 and 190) or store-bought, divided	125 mL
1 tbsp	Asian bean sauce	15 mL
⅓ cup	Tamarind Liquid (page 191)	75 mL
¼ cup	palm sugar or brown sugar	60 mL
1 tsp	soy sauce	5 mL
½ tsp	salt	2 mL

Eggs

8	small shallots or 3 medium shallots (about ½ cup/125 mL)	8
20	cloves garlic, thinly sliced lengthwise (about ½ cup/125 mL)	20
8	hard-boiled eggs, peeled	8
	Vegetable oil for deep-frying	
1 to 2 tsp	hot pepper flakes	5 to 10 mL
	Handful of fresh cilantro leaves, coarsely chopped	

1. *Sauce:* In mini food processor or blender, combine ¼ cup (60 mL) of the stock and bean sauce and blend until smooth. Pour into a saucepan and add remaining ¼ cup (60 mL) of stock, tamarind, sugar, soy sauce and salt. Place over medium heat and bring to a rolling boil. Stir well and reduce heat to maintain a gentle but active boil. Simmer until sugar is dissolved and sauce is smooth and slightly thickened, 10 minutes. Remove from heat and let cool to room temperature.

Variation

If you long to try this but have neither tamarind nor Asian bean sauce on hand, improvise a tangy sauce using hoisin sauce, sugar, salt, vegetable stock and freshly squeezed lime juice.

Vegan Variation

Vegans can enjoy this fabulous sauce and its accompaniments on large chunks of tempeh sautéed with garlic, soy sauce and a little sugar and salt, or with chunks of pressed tofu (purchased or homemade, see page 200), fried to golden crispiness in hot oil.

Serving suggestions

For a traditional presentation, leave the eggs whole. Coat a deep serving platter with about half the sauce and place eggs on the sauce. Pour remaining sauce over eggs and sprinkle with shallots, garlic, pepper flakes and cilantro.

You can serve these as an appetizer to be eaten out of hand. Cut eggs in half lengthwise, place each half on a lettuce leaf and sprinkle with shallots, garlic, pepper flakes and cilantro. Serve the sauce on the side to be added at serving time by each guest.

2. *Eggs:* Place prepared baking sheet next to the stove along with a slotted spoon, sliced shallots, garlic and eggs. Fill a wok or large deep skillet with vegetable oil to a depth of 3 inches (7.5 cm). Heat oil over medium heat until a bit of garlic dropped into the pan sizzles at once. The oil should register 350° to 375°F (180° to 190°C) on the thermometer.

3. Sprinkle shallots into oil and cook until golden brown but not burned, 1 to 2 minutes. Using the slotted spoon, transfer to prepared baking sheet to drain. Sprinkle sliced garlic into oil and cook until golden brown but not burned, about 1 minute. Transfer with slotted spoon to baking sheet.

4. Pat eggs dry with paper towels and gently add 3 eggs to oil, sliding them gently down the side of the wok or lowering them into oil with the slotted spoon. Cook, using the spoon to turn them occasionally and to keep them from settling on bottom of pan, until evenly colored, golden brown and crisp, 5 to 7 minutes. Using the spoon, transfer eggs to baking sheet. Repeat with remaining eggs.

5. *To serve:* Cut eggs in half lengthwise. Coat a deep serving platter with sauce. Place eggs on the sauce and sprinkle with shallots and garlic, some pepper flakes and cilantro. Serve hot, warm or at room temperature.

Five-Spice Hard-Boiled Eggs in Sweet Soy Stew

This is kai pa-loh, *a direct Chinese import, combining the sweetness of cinnamon, cloves and star anise with the richness of* si-yu wahn, *the dark sweet soy sauce found in every Thai pantry. Like curry powder, five-spice powder is widely available in Thai kitchens, although its use is limited to stews similar to this one. This dish comes together quickly once the eggs are cooked and peeled and it keeps beautifully, blossoming to a deeper, richer flavor in the refrigerator overnight. Offer lots of rice to savor with this luxurious mahogany sauce.*

SERVES 6 TO 8

Tip

I like to remove the eggs, halve them lengthwise and return them to the sauce just before serving to add color, but you can also serve them whole, the traditional way.

♦ Mini food processor or blender

2 tbsp	coarsely chopped garlic (8 to 12 cloves)	30 mL
2 tbsp	coarsely chopped cilantro roots or cilantro leaves and stems	30 mL
½ tsp	freshly ground black pepper	2 mL
2 tbsp	water	30 mL
2 tbsp	vegetable oil	30 mL
1	onion, sliced lengthwise into thick wedges	1
2 tsp	five-spice powder (see Tip, right)	10 mL
3 cups	Vegetable Stock (pages 189 and 190) or store-bought	750 mL
⅓ cup	dark sweet soy sauce or 3 tbsp (45 mL) dark soy sauce and 2 tbsp (30 mL) molasses or honey	75 mL
3 tbsp	brown sugar	45 mL
1 tbsp	soy sauce	15 mL
1 tsp	salt	5 mL
7	hard-boiled eggs, peeled	7
8 oz	firm tofu, cut into 1-inch (2.5 cm) chunks	250 g
⅓ cup	coarsely chopped fresh cilantro	75 mL

Tip

You can substitute cinnamon, cloves and star anise, whole or ground, for the five-spice powder. If using whole spices, add 3 cinnamon sticks, 12 whole cloves, ¼ tsp (1 mL) whole fennel seeds and 3 whole star anise. If using ground spices, add ½ tsp (2 mL) cinnamon, ¼ tsp (1 mL) cloves, ¼ tsp (1 mL) fennel and ½ tsp (2 mL) star anise.

Vegan Variation

Vegans can omit eggs and add 2 cups (500 mL) Wheatballs (page 194) or wheat gluten or a combination of potatoes and sweet potatoes, totaling about 2 cups (500 mL) peeled, bite-size chunks.

1. In mini food processor or blender, combine garlic, cilantro root, pepper and water and grind to a fairly smooth paste. Heat vegetable oil in a saucepan over medium heat for about 30 seconds. Add garlic-cilantro paste and cook, stirring and scraping, for 1 minute. Add onion wedges and cook, tossing often, until shiny and fragrant, about 2 minutes.

2. Add five-spice powder and toss to mix with onions. Add vegetable stock, dark sweet soy sauce, sugar, soy sauce and salt and stir well. Add eggs and tofu and bring to a boil. Adjust heat to maintain an active simmer and cook, stirring occasionally, until eggs and tofu are a rich, deep brown and sauce is a smooth, pleasing blend of soy sauce, sugar, salt and spice, about 25 minutes.

3. Transfer eggs, tofu and a generous pool of sauce to a serving bowl. Sprinkle with cilantro and serve hot or warm. Or let cool to room temperature, cover and refrigerate for up to 2 days.

Steamed Eggs with Cilantro and Crispy Garlic

This classic dish, called kai toon, *fortified me many a night during the two years I lived in the small northeastern Thai town of Thatoom. My students used duck eggs for everyday and chicken eggs if we had guests and we never found out about the keeping properties of this old favorite, since we always ate up every bite. As with rice soup, it is often on the menu for a family member who is ailing and it is a traditional favorite of children. Thais eat this egg dish plain, but if you like a bit of fire, enjoy it with a little Sriracha Sauce (page 210) or store-bought.*

SERVES 4 TO 6

Tips

If you do not have a steaming rack, you can use the standard Asian shortcut: two long, sturdy chopsticks laid in an X in the bottom of the wok. Place the bowl of eggs on the spot where the chopsticks intersect and steam away. Be sure to use blunt-tipped Chinese-style chopsticks, rather than pointed-tipped Japanese-style ones for this job, as their extra length is needed.

You will probably need to add water at least once during the steaming process, so have a kettle simmering. If you add boiling or very hot water to the pan, you will avoid losing cooking time while the steaming water pokes its way back to a boil. Do your best to prevent the water inside the lid from dripping into the custard. And take great care to avoid burning your hands as you check on the progress of your eggs.

♦ Wok or steaming rack (see Tips, left)

3	eggs	3
½ cup	Vegetable Stock (pages 189 and 190) or store-bought	125 mL
½ tsp	soy sauce	2 mL
¼ tsp	each salt and ground black pepper	1 mL
1	small shallot, minced	1
1	green onion, minced	1
1 tbsp	coarsely chopped fresh cilantro	15 mL
2 tbsp	Crispy Garlic in Oil (page 203)	30 mL

1. Place a wok or the base of a large steaming rack on the stove and add 3 to 4 inches (7.5 to 10 cm) of water. Place a steaming rack over water, cover and bring to a rolling boil over high heat.

2. Meanwhile, in a bowl, beat eggs with a fork until frothy. Add vegetable stock, soy sauce, salt, pepper, shallot and green onion and beat to combine well. Pour into a shallow, heatproof bowl and set aside.

3. When you have a strong, steady flow of steam, uncover and carefully place bowl of eggs on steaming rack. Place a paper towel on top of bowl to prevent condensing steam from dripping onto eggs. Cover wok or steaming rack and reduce heat slightly to maintain a steady flow of steam without the water boiling away. Check often to be sure that the water level remains high and the steam is flowing, adding very hot or boiling water as needed if the level drops.

4. Steam eggs until firm and a little puffed up, 25 to 45 minutes. They are ready when a fork inserted near the center comes out clean. Uncover, turn off heat and let stand for 5 minutes while the steam subsides. Carefully remove bowl from steamer. Sprinkle with cilantro and pour Crispy Garlic in Oil over top. Serve hot, warm or at room temperature.

Limes

Lemongrass

Star anise

Son-in-Law Eggs (page 124)

Red Curry Paste (page 180) and Green Curry Paste (page 182)

Dried shiitake mushrooms

Sataw beans

Sticky Rice (page 137)

Mee Grop (page 147)

Paht Thai (page 150)

Coconut Ice Cream (page 164)

Thai Iced Tea (page 173)

Thai Omelet with Sriracha Sauce

Plates of this homey dish appeared as a last course when the principal of the secondary school where I taught English took his staff out for a dinner banquet. We gathered at Thatoom's finest eatery, officially called Thatoom Pochanah, but known affectionately around town as rahn ahahn jeen, *the "Chinese restaurant." After a parade of delicious dishes, including volcanic* tome yum *soup, stir-fried water spinach with brown bean sauce and an array of Cantonese-style stir-fries, we knew the omelets were a gentle and satisfying signal that it was time to finish up the feast and stroll home surrounded by a chorus of crickets, bullfrogs, radio music and children's laughter decorating the dark.*

SERVES 4 TO 6

Tips

The green onions and cilantro are my addition to the Thai classic. For a truly Thai version, omit green onions and cilantro and increase the oil to 3 to 4 tbsp (45 to 60 mL). Be sure that it is very hot before you add the eggs. The extra oil makes the omelet puff up beautifully and brown in a pleasing, tasty manner.

Use any hot chile sauce if you do not have sriracha sauce, or mix up a bowl of ripe tomato salsa spiked with onion, cilantro, serrano chiles and freshly squeezed lime juice.

I serve this omelet almost every time I cook Thai food for a crowd because it is easy to prepare at the last minute and is a hit with children and other guests who may be new to Thai food and are looking for something familiar.

4	eggs	4
2 tbsp	Vegetable Stock (pages 189 and 190) or store-bought or water	30 mL
½ tsp	soy sauce	2 mL
½ tsp	salt	2 mL
2	green onions, thinly sliced crosswise	2
2 tbsp	finely chopped fresh cilantro	30 mL
2 tbsp	vegetable oil	30 mL
	Sriracha Sauce (page 210) or other hot chile sauce (see Tips, left)	

1. In a bowl, combine eggs, vegetable stock, soy sauce, salt, green onions and cilantro and beat to mix well. Heat vegetable oil in a skillet over medium heat until very hot. When a drop of the egg mixture sizzles and blooms at once, the oil is ready.

2. Add eggs and tilt pan to spread evenly. Using a spatula, pull the puffy edges in toward the center, working around the edges to coax any liquid pooling in the center to seep out and extend the borders of the omelet. Cook until edges are golden and top is opaque and nearly set, about 2 minutes. Gently flip omelet over and brown top for about 1 minute.

3. Turn omelet out onto a plate and serve hot or warm with a small saucer of chile sauce.

Minced Mushrooms and Tofu with Chiles and Holy Basil

Bright notes of fresh hot green chiles and aromatic leaves of holy basil (bai graprao) give this classic Thai stir-fry an irresistible and satisfying flavor. Holy basil has oval leaves with a matte finish and sometimes a serrated edge, and I adore its scent and flavor. It wilts quickly, so when you find it, use it as soon as possible. The more commonly available Asian basil (bai horapah) makes a great substitute, and I love this dish with Italian basil and fresh mint as well.

SERVES 4

Tips

You can use other types of mushrooms for this dish, including shiitakes, oyster mushrooms, cremini, in combination, or just one type.

Fresh green Thai bird's eye chiles are traditional, but you could use serranos or jalapeños instead, or 1 tsp (5 mL) hot pepper flakes.

1 tsp	granulated sugar	5 mL
1 tsp	salt	5 mL
¼ tsp	freshly ground black pepper	1 mL
2 tsp	water	10 mL
2 tsp	soy sauce	10 mL
2 tbsp	vegetable oil	30 mL
⅓ cup	chopped onion	75 mL
1 tbsp	chopped fresh garlic	15 mL
8 oz	fresh button mushrooms, finely chopped (see Tips, left)	250 g
4 oz	firm tofu, finely chopped	125 g
1 tbsp	chopped fresh hot green chiles (see Tips, left)	15 mL
1 cup	fresh holy basil leaves or any other fresh basil	250 mL

1. In a small bowl, combine sugar, salt, pepper, water and soy sauce and stir together well. Place by the stove with a spoon to have handy for a final stir.

2. Heat a wok or a large, deep skillet over medium-high heat for 30 seconds. Add oil and swirl to coat surface. Add onion and toss for 10 seconds. Add garlic and toss well. Add mushrooms and cook, tossing often, until they release their liquid and become shiny and softened, about 3 minutes. Add tofu and cook, tossing often, for 30 seconds.

3. Stir soy sauce mixture and then add to wok and toss well. Cook, tossing occasionally, for 1 minute. Add green chiles and fresh basil leaves. Toss until heated through, about 30 seconds. Transfer to a serving platter. Serve hot or warm.

Stir-Fried Spinach with Garlic and Pepper

We need no coaxing to eat our vegetables when they appear on the table in the form of this bright green, pleasing dish. Simple to make and wonderful paired with a plate of rice, which takes on the clear sauce nicely, this dish is part of my standard party menu: a curry, rice, omelet with Sriracha sauce and spinach. You may think there's too much spinach but it shrinks down profoundly; and we never find we have too much of this dish.

SERVES 4

2 tbsp	vegetable oil	30 mL
1 tbsp	coarsely chopped garlic	15 mL
12 oz	baby spinach (18 to 20 loosely packed cups/4.5 to 5 L)	375 g
½ tsp	granulated sugar	2 mL
½ tsp	salt	2 mL
½ tsp	freshly ground black pepper	2 mL
1 tbsp	water	15 mL

1. Heat a large, deep skillet or a wok over medium-high heat and add oil. Swirl to coat pan. Add garlic and toss and cook until fragrant. Add spinach and cook for about 15 seconds. Then carefully turn the pile of leaves so that all the spinach wilts a little.

2. Add sugar, salt and pepper and toss well. Add water and cook, until spinach has softened and formed a thin sauce, about 1 minute more. Turn out into a deep plate or small platter and serve hot or warm.

Rice and Noodles

Jasmine Rice 136

Sticky Rice 137

Sticky Rice with Coconut Sauce 138

Everyday Fried Rice with Shiitakes 139

Brown Rice 140

Pineapple Fried Rice 141

Yellow Curry Fried Rice with Crispy Potatoes
and Peas 142

Coconut Rice with Cilantro and Fresh Ginger. 143

Tofu and Shiitakes Hidden in Curried Rice
with Crispy Shallots. 144

Mee Grop 147

Paht Thai 150

Rice Noodles with Eggs, Broccoli and Dark
Sweet Soy Sauce 152

Mee Ga-ti Rice Noodles with
Coconut-Bean Sauce 154

Rice and Noodles

NO MATTER HOW MUCH YOU CHERISH CHILES, SAVOR SATAY OR plow through platters of *paht Thai,* you will be missing the essential nature of Thai food unless you learn to love rice. Plain white rice, cooked in water without seasoning—not even salt—is the heart of Thai cooking, the field on which all the intense flavors and dishes of Thai cuisine come together to play. To Thai people, rice is what fills them up, what comforts them, what makes them feel they are living an abundant life. This holds true even when the dishes that come with the rice are simple and few and the surroundings in which they are eaten are equally plain.

Thais eat long-grain white rice morning, noon and night, plates and plates of it, spooned up in the presence of family and friends to make it taste even better. When I lived in Thatoom, in a teacher's house with four students from the middle school where I taught English, supper began with a yell from the kitchen, *"Cheun mah kin kao!"* ("Y'all come and get it, the rice is ready!") One or two of the students had cooked dinner, using whatever I had brought home from the morning market to make a soup, a curry, an egg dish and *nahm prik,* a chile-hot, tangy dipping sauce with raw vegetables. Five or six such dishes were placed in the center of a hand-woven straw mat spread out over the concrete floor of our kitchen, ringed by five plates mounded with steaming jasmine rice and stainless-steel spoons shaped like porcelain soup spoons used at Chinese banquets. In the course of our meal, each of us had at least a second plateful of rice and it was not uncommon to request a third helping if we were especially hungry or the dishes were particularly good.

The category of dishes that are served with rice has a Thai name that perfectly expresses the elevated status of rice in Asian cuisines. All the dishes are lumped together as *gahp kao,* literally "with rice." This phrase acts as a noun, rounding up what Westerners would separate into main courses, side dishes, salads, sauces, dips, omelets and even soups in a bundle defined as accompaniments to rice. "What's for dinner?" in Thai becomes *"Dai arai gahp kao?"* ("What have you got with the rice tonight?"). This in no way implies that Thai people are indifferent to the quality and variety of the dishes that go with rice. They are in fact quite passionate about them in every detail, from shopping for the ingredients through cooking them, devouring them and reminiscing about them at a later date. What they do not do is see rice as a starch that stands by to round out the meal or soak up the extra sauce. Rice sustains life and tasty *gahp kao* make the human task of taking in the nourishment given by the rice a delight rather than a chore.

I learned to love rice effortlessly by eating Thai home cooking with my students at breakfast, lunch and dinner for two years. It was not my intention to open a new door, but this happened because I had the good fortune to eat Thai food in its traditional context over time. I urge you to put rice at the center of your Thai menus, not to convert you to a particular way of eating, but because rice explains and enhances the intense seasonings and textures present in Thai dishes.

In this chapter you will find basic rice recipes, as well as seasoned rice dishes. The first recipe is for jasmine rice, the aromatic long-grain rice Thais grow in the green checkerboard of paddy fields that quilt the Central Plain and the Korat Plateau of the northeastern region.

The second recipe is for sticky rice, a long-grained white rice that the people of Laos eat at every meal instead of jasmine rice. Sticky rice contains prodigious amounts of a starch that causes it to cling together in a most pleasing, chewy manner. Due to northern and northeastern Thailand's strong historical and cultural ties to Laos, sticky rice is preferred there, too.

There are also several recipes for special-occasion rice dishes, special in that they are particularly handsome and delicious, but not so special that you could not enjoy them on short notice for a quick weeknight supper. These include two recipes for rice in coconut milk and three versions of the beloved Thai dish, fried rice.

The chapter ends with a few noodle favorites, including the spectacular crispy-sweet confection called *mee grop,* an appealing broccoli-soy sauce stir-fry and my version of *paht Thai.*

Jasmine Rice

Jasmine rice is a treasure of Thailand's fertile fields, naturally endowed with a delicate nutty flavor and toasty aroma that gently draws everyone within olfactory range right to your table. The rice thrives in Thailand's seemingly infinite paddy fields, which stretch from the lush central plain to the vast northeastern plateau. In Asian markets, jasmine rice is sold for a song in very large sacks, but it is also increasingly available in supermarkets and specialty stores in smaller packages. If you have storage space for a large quantity, buy yourself a great sack, as it is a lovely everyday rice and keeps well for many months.

**MAKES ABOUT
5 CUPS (1.25 L)**

SERVES 3 OR 4

Tips

If you have a rice cooker, you can place it on your countertop and make great rice without using the stove. I like to add a little less water than the cooker directions call for, since the ones imported from Asia tend to be designed for making Japanese- or Chinese-style rice. They prefer shorter-grained rice that needs to be moist enough to eat with chopsticks from a rice bowl.

The label "new crop" on your rice sack tells you that the contents are from a recent harvest and therefore retain more moisture than rice from a few crops back. This alerts you to use less water for cooking, to avoid mushy rice. Try 2¾ (675 mL) cups water to start with and adjust as needed to cook up firm, fluffy, distinctively separate grains.

- ◆ Rice cooker, optional

2 cups	jasmine rice or other long-grain white rice	500 mL
3 cups	cold water	750 mL

1. Place rice in a medium saucepan that has a tight-fitting lid and rinse several times with cold water. Drain well and add 3 cups (750 mL) water to saucepan. Bring to a rolling boil over medium heat and stir well. Reduce heat to low, cover and cook until rice kernels are tender and liquid is absorbed, for 20 minutes.

2. Remove saucepan from heat without lifting the lid and let stand, covered, for 10 minutes. Uncover, fluff gently with a fork and serve hot or warm.

> ### ❀ *Thai Tales*
>
> Thai people eat rice from plates using a spoon and often using a fork to help mix the flavors and push food onto the spoon. They cook it in the South Asian manner, so that it comes out fluffy and separate, rather than moist and clinging together as is preferred in East Asian countries.

Sticky Rice

Allow plenty of time to prepare sticky rice, as it needs at least 3 hours to soak before you steam it. Sticky rice is finger food, so each diner should pull off a fist-size hunk and place it on his or her plate. Then eat it by pinching off a walnut-size lump, rounding it off quickly with fingers and either dipping it into a sauce, using it as a means to pick up chunks of vegetables or simply enjoying it neat.

Sticky rice, a flat-white, long-grain rice, often called glutinous rice or sweet rice, is the daily bread of the people of Laos. It is also the staple grain of northern and northeastern Thailand, the two regions that border Laos and consequently share with it an abundance of cultural and culinary traditions. Asian markets sell it in large sacks imported from Thailand labeled "sweet rice." They often sell it in smaller quantities sealed in plastic bags. Look for long-grain rice with a startlingly flat, whitewashed color, labeled sweet rice or sticky rice.

**MAKES ABOUT
5 CUPS (1.25 L)**

SERVES 3 OR 4

Tips

Laotian-style bamboo steaming basket and steamer base are widely available in Southeast Asian markets. The base is a tall, shiny aluminum or tin pot without handles and with a 3-inch (7.5 cm) high slanted rim around the opening. The steaming basket, shaped like an enormous straw ice cream cone, fits snugly into the opening of the pot, holding a quantity of water well away from the soaked rice.

Traditional cooks avoid using a metal lid to hold in the steam, as it traps too much steam that drips back onto the cooking rice. Using a damp cloth (or a folded banana leaf) traps enough of the steam for cooking without the drips.

- ◆ Bamboo steaming basket
- ◆ Rice cooker, optional

| 2 cups | long-grain sticky rice | 500 mL |

1. Soak rice in cold water to cover by 2 inches (5 cm) for at least 3 hours or for as long as overnight.

2. Drain rice and transfer to a bamboo steaming basket specifically designed for steaming sticky rice or to another steaming vessel such as a colander or a sieve that can be suspended above boiling water.

3. Fill a wok or bottom of a steamer pan with 3 inches (7.5 cm) of water. Place steaming basket or other container inside the wok or steamer pan so holds the soaked rice at least 1 inch (2.5 cm) above the water level. Bring water to a rolling boil over high heat. When steam is rising steadily through rice, place a damp kitchen towel over rice, folded to cover rice fully and to slow the escape of steam from the pan. Reduce heat to maintain a steady flow of steam and cook until rice swells and becomes sticky enough to be easily shaped into little balls, 30 to 45 minutes. Keep a teakettle filled with simmering water handy to add to the wok or pan as needed to maintain the original water level.

4. As soon as rice is ready, turn out onto a large tray or a baking sheet. Dampen a wooden spoon with water and quickly and gently spread rice into a shallow layer to release some of the steam and moisture. As soon as it is cool enough to touch, gently gather rice into a large lump and place it in a sticky-rice basket or on a serving platter. Serve hot, warm or at room temperature.

Sticky Rice with Coconut Sauce

This rich, salty-sweet rice is a velvety foil to both sweet and savory dishes, notably ripe sweet mangos as a dessert (page 163) and the hot and garlicky green papaya slaw known as som tum (page 54). Allow lots of time to fix this luxurious grain dish, as you will need about 4 hours to soak and steam the rice, season it with coconut cream and let it cool to room temperature.

MAKES ABOUT 3 CUPS (750 ML)

SERVES 4

Tip

The rice will keep at room temperature for 6 to 8 hours. While it is best freshly made, you can keep it for 1 to 2 days and reheat it gently in a steamer or microwave. Aim to warm and soften it rather than to make it hot.

Variation

You can use black sticky rice in this recipe, cooking it as directed or simply soaking it for an hour and cooking it on the stove as you would cook jasmine rice (page 136). It is less sticky than white long-grain sticky rice and when cooked, it develops a magnificent purple hue.

- ◆ Rice cooker, optional

1½ cups	long-grain sticky rice	375 mL
2 cups	unsweetened coconut milk	500 mL
1 cup	granulated sugar	250 mL
2 tsp	salt	10 mL

1. Cook sticky rice as directed on page 137. While it steams, combine coconut milk, sugar and salt in a saucepan. Stir to combine well and then bring to a gentle boil over medium heat. Stir well, remove from heat and set aside.

2. When rice is soft, swollen and shiny and can be easily shaped into a small ball, transfer 3 cups (750 mL) to a large bowl. Pour coconut milk mixture over rice and stir well. Cover and set aside for 30 minutes to 1 hour to allow rice to absorb most of the sauce. Serve at room temperature with ripe fruit or with savory dishes.

> ❀ *Thai Tales*
>
> Unlike the Western practice of loading a full portion of each dish onto a plate of rice before eating, we ate Thai style, spooning a bite or two of one dish at a time onto the rice and savoring it before moving on to the next. This kept the meal at a graceful pace and we dawdled along, indulging our culinary whims as we visited and unwound from the cares of the day. The meal ended with a big bowl of rainwater placed in the center, into which we dipped our cups to cleanse our palates and satisfy the thirst created by the roller coaster of flavors that decorated the evening's rice.

Everyday Fried Rice with Shiitakes

In upcountry households and small cafés, this dish is the simplest one-dish meal offered. You can serve it instead of plain rice with curries and other main dishes, but if you need a quick hot supper, this is a winner.

Tip

Thais toss in a squeeze or two of lime juice just before eating. Some Thais spike it with chopped fresh or dried chiles as well.

Vegan Variation

You can add firm tofu, tempeh or wheat gluten for protein and omit the eggs.

4 cups	cooked long-grain rice (page 136), preferably jasmine rice, chilled	1 L
3 tbsp	vegetable oil, divided	45 mL
1 tbsp	coarsely chopped garlic	15 mL
1	onion, coarsely chopped	1
1 cup	sliced fresh shiitakes or button mushrooms (about 6 oz/175 g)	250 mL
2	eggs, beaten	2
1 tsp	salt	5 mL
½ tsp	granulated sugar	2 mL
2	plum tomatoes, coarsely chopped, or 9 cherry tomatoes, halved lengthwise	2
½ cup	coarsely chopped fresh cilantro	125 mL
1	hothouse cucumber, peeled and sliced into ¼-inch (0.5 cm) thick rounds	1
1	lime, quartered lengthwise	1
	A few fresh cilantro sprigs	

1. Using your hands, crumble rice gently between your fingers to separate into individual grains. Set aside.

2. In a wok or a large, deep skillet, heat 2 tbsp (30 mL) of the oil over medium-high heat, swirling to coat pan, about 1 minute. Add garlic and onion and toss until fragrant and softened, 1 to 2 minutes. Add mushrooms and cook, tossing often, until tender, 3 to 4 minutes.

3. Push onion and mushrooms to edges of pan and add eggs to the center. Cook until set and then scramble, breaking into small pieces.

4. Add remaining 1 tbsp (15 mL) oil, heat for about 1 minute and then add rice. Toss, breaking up any lumps and mixing with onion, mushrooms and eggs, about 1 minute. Add salt, sugar and tomatoes and toss until ingredients are well combined and rice is softened and heated through, 2 to 3 minutes.

5. Remove from heat, add cilantro and toss well. Transfer to a platter and garnish with cucumber, lime and cilantro. Or squeeze limes over individual portions before eating. Serve hot or warm.

Brown Rice

Thai people eat long-grain rice and sticky rice all day, at nearly every meal, but in traditional cooking, brown rice has had only a small following. One major factor in white rice's traditional presence is that it keeps indefinitely, since the fragile oils present in unprocessed rice will spoil after six months or so, whereas processed white rice will last for years. I love brown rice—long and short grain—though long is my favorite and I cook it with Thai dishes. Curries and stir-fried greens pair with it especially well. I cook it in my rice cooker as well as on the stove, and love its nutty, substantial quality as well as its nutritional benefits.

**MAKES ABOUT
5 CUPS (1.25 L)**

SERVES 3 OR 4

Tip

If you have a rice cooker, you can place it on your countertop and make great rice without using the stove. I like to add a little less water than the cooker directions call for, since the ones imported from Asia tend to be designed for making Japanese- or Chinese-style rice. They prefer shorter-grained rice that needs to be moist enough to eat with chopsticks from a rice bowl.

- Saucepan with tight-fitting lid
- Rice cooker, optional

| 2 cups | long-grain brown rice | 500 mL |
| 3 cups | cold water | 750 mL |

1. Place rice in a medium saucepan that has a tight-fitting lid and rinse several times with cold water. Drain well and add 3 cups (750 mL) water to saucepan. Bring to a rolling boil over medium heat and stir well. Reduce heat to low. Cover and cook until rice kernels are tender and liquid is absorbed, 30 to 40 minutes.

2. Remove saucepan from heat and let stand, covered, for 10 minutes. Uncover, fluff gently with a fork and serve hot or warm.

Pineapple Fried Rice

This dish is yummy, pretty and quick. Serve as is as a foil for a stir-fry, a curry or a platter of grilled vegetables or add small cubes of firm tofu at the end and serve as a hearty main dish.

SERVES 4

Tip

If a smashing presentation is in order, use a fresh pineapple for serving: Halve a ripe pineapple lengthwise, cutting through its leafy top as well as the fruit. Hollow out each half, reserving 1 cup (250 mL) of the fruit for the rice and some extra for a garnish; set aside the remainder for other uses. Make a small slice on the outside of each half to create a flat base to hold the hollow pineapple steady on its side. Fill each half with the warm rice, mounding it high and garnishing the top with a flourish of cilantro leaves and chunks of pineapple.

4 cups	cooked long-grain rice (page 136), preferably jasmine rice, chilled	1 L
3 tbsp	vegetable oil, divided	45 mL
1 tbsp	coarsely chopped garlic (4 to 6 cloves)	15 mL
1	onion, coarsely chopped	1
1 cup	shredded carrots	250 mL
1	can (8 oz/250 g) crushed pineapple, with juice, or 1 cup (250 mL) finely chopped fresh pineapple	1
1 tsp	salt	5 mL
½ tsp	granulated sugar	2 mL
3	green onions, thinly sliced crosswise	3

1. Using your hands, crumble cold rice gently between your fingers to separate into individual grains. Set aside.

2. In a wok or a large, deep skillet, heat 2 tbsp (30 mL) of the oil over medium-high heat, swirling to coat pan, until a bit of garlic added to pan sizzles at once, about 1 minute. Add garlic and onion and toss until fragrant and softened, 1 to 2 minutes.

3. Add remaining 1 tbsp (15 mL) oil, heat for about 1 minute and then add rice. Toss, breaking up any lumps and mixing with garlic and onion, about 1 minute. Add carrots, pineapple, salt and sugar and toss until ingredients are well combined and rice is softened and heated through, 2 to 3 minutes. Add green onions, toss well and remove from heat. Transfer to a serving platter and serve hot or warm.

Yellow Curry Fried Rice with Crispy Potatoes and Peas

Fried rice works best with leftover rice that has been chilled until its grains are firm and dry. Make extra the next time you cook rice and then turn it into a quick meal the following day.

Tips

For this recipe you will also need leftover baked or boiled potatoes. If you do not have any on hand, boil 2 cups (500 mL) diced peeled potato until tender, drain well and then proceed as directed in the recipe.

You can substitute any Thai-style curry paste for the Yellow Curry Paste.

4 cups	cooked long-grain rice (page 136), preferably jasmine rice, chilled	1 L
3 tbsp	vegetable oil, divided	45 mL
1 tbsp	chopped garlic (4 to 6 cloves)	15 mL
2 cups	peeled, cooked and diced potatoes (see Tips, left)	500 mL
1 cup	chopped onion	250 mL
2 tbsp	Yellow Curry Paste (page 184) (see Tips, left)	30 mL
1½ cups	frozen green peas	375 mL
1 tsp	salt	5 mL
¼ cup	chopped fresh cilantro leaves and stems	60 mL

1. Using your hands, crumble cold rice gently between your fingers to separate into individual grains. Set aside.

2. Line a plate with paper towels and place near the stove. In a wok or a large, deep skillet, heat 2 tbsp (30 mL) of the oil over medium-high heat, swirling to coat pan, until a bit of garlic added to pan sizzles at once, about 1 minute. Add potatoes and cook, tossing occasionally, until golden brown and crisp, 4 to 5 minutes. Using a slotted spoon, transfer potatoes to prepared plate.

3. Add remaining 1 tbsp (15 mL) of oil to the wok along with garlic and onion. Reduce heat to medium and toss until shiny and slightly softened, about 1 minute. Add curry paste and cook, mashing and scraping often to soften and mix with onions, until paste is fragrant and mixture is well combined, about 1½ minutes.

4. Add rice and toss well. Return potatoes to wok along with peas and salt and cook, tossing occasionally, until rice is softened, mixed with curry paste and heated through, 2 to 3 minutes. Transfer to serving platter, garnish with cilantro and serve hot or warm.

Coconut Rice with Cilantro and Fresh Ginger

Pair this luscious alternative to plain jasmine rice with grilled vegetables or your favorite Thai curry. Thais serve it with som tum, *sharp and spicy Green Papaya Salad (page 54).*

Tip

You can use basmati rice or any long-grain white rice if you are out of jasmine rice.

• Saucepan with tight-fitting lid

1	can (14 oz/400 mL) coconut milk	1
1¾ cups	water	425 mL
6	quarter-size slices peeled fresh gingerroot	6
1 tsp	salt	5 mL
2 cups	jasmine rice (see Tip, left)	500 mL
½ cup	coarsely chopped fresh cilantro	125 mL

1. In a saucepan with a tight-fitting lid over medium heat, combine coconut milk, water, ginger and salt and bring to a rolling boil. Add rice and stir well. When liquid boils again, cover, reduce heat to low and cook for 25 minutes. The rice kernels will be tender and the liquid will be absorbed.

2. Remove saucepan from heat and let stand, covered, for 10 minutes. Uncover and remove and discard ginger. Add cilantro and, using a fork, toss gently to distribute cilantro evenly. Fluff rice kernels and serve hot or warm.

Tofu and Shiitakes Hidden in Curried Rice with Crispy Shallots

This handsomely colored, vividly seasoned pot of rice is a meal in itself, rather than a foundation for an array of dishes comprising a rice meal. Known in Thailand as kao moke, *this beloved dish varies from the traditional Thai way of cooking rice, in water and without any seasonings at all. Like biryani dishes of India and South Asia,* kao moke *begins with onions and spices sizzled in hot oil. (Kao means "rice" in Thai, while* moke *means "to hide" or "tuck away.") Mounded onto a platter, topped with crispy shallots and cilantro leaves and served with a light, tangy sauce on the side, it makes a lovely and satisfying party dish.*

<table>
<tr><td colspan="2">SERVES 6</td></tr>
</table>

Tip

If you want to get this cooked more quickly, simply toss the shiitake-tofu mixture with the partially cooked rice before covering the pot to cook it through. Or mix everything together after cooking, instead of trying to keep the curried tofu-mushrooms separate.

- Rice cooker, optional
- Slotted spoon or Asian-style wire strainer

8 oz	fresh shiitakes or button mushrooms	250 g

Spice Mixture

1 tsp	cayenne pepper	5 mL
1 tsp	ground cumin	5 mL
1 tsp	coriander powder	5 mL
½ tsp	ground turmeric	2 mL
½ tsp	freshly ground black pepper	2 mL
2 tsp	salt, divided	10 mL

Curried Rice

3 tbsp	vegetable oil, divided	45 mL
8 oz	extra-firm or firm tofu, chopped into ½-inch (1 cm) cubes	250 g
1 cup	edamame beans, fresh or frozen	250 mL
8	slices fresh gingerroot	8
½ cup	coarsely chopped onion	125 mL
1 tbsp	coarsely chopped garlic	15 mL
2 cups	jasmine rice or other long-grain white rice	500 mL
2¾ cups	water	675 mL

Crispy Shallots

	Vegetable oil	
½ cup	shallot, thinly sliced crosswise	125 mL

Tangy Chile Sauce

½ cup	distilled white vinegar	125 mL
¼ cup	granulated sugar	60 mL
3	fresh hot green chiles, such as Thai bird's eye chiles, serranos or jalapeños, thinly sliced crosswise	3

Garnishes

4	small cucumbers, peeled and sliced	4
	Fresh cilantro leaves	

1. Slice shiitake caps crosswise into ¼-inch (0.5 cm) thick pieces, discarding stems.

2. *Spice Mixture:* In a small bowl, combine cayenne, cumin, coriander, turmeric, pepper and ½ tsp (2 mL) of the salt and mix well.

3. *Curried Rice:* In a large saucepan or Dutch oven, heat 2 tbsp (30 mL) of the oil over medium-high heat until hot. Add shiitakes and tofu and cook, tossing often, until browned and softened, 6 to 8 minutes. Add about half the spice mixture and toss well. Scoop out mushrooms and tofu, leaving as much oil behind as possible, and transfer to a medium bowl. Stir in edamame beans and set aside.

4. Reheat oil and when hot, scatter in ginger slices and cook, tossing and pressing into oil, for 30 seconds. Add onion and garlic, toss well, and cook until onion has begun to wilt, about 2 minutes. Add remaining spice mixture, toss well, and cook until onion is tender and evenly spiced, and spices are fragrant, about 1 minute. Add rice and toss until coated with spiced oil and starting to become translucent, about 2 minutes.

5. Add water and 1 tsp (5 mL) of salt to rice. Bring to a boil over high heat, stirring occasionally, until grains begin to swell, 5 to 7 minutes.

continued on page 146

6. Reduce heat to low. Scoop out about two-thirds of the rice into a medium bowl. Spoon half shiitake-tofu mixture over rice in pan and cover with a layer of reserved rice. Repeat, spooning remaining shiitake mixture over rice, and then cover with remaining reserved rice. Smooth surface of rice. Cover pan and cook over low heat until rice is tender, fragrant and fluffy, about 30 minutes. When rice is cooked, remove from heat and let stand, covered, for about 15 minutes.

7. Meanwhile, prepare *Crispy Shallots:* In a small skillet or saucepan, pour in oil to a depth of 2 inches (5 cm). Heat over medium-high heat until hot but not smoking (to test, drop a piece of shallot in oil; if it sizzles right away, oil is ready). Sprinkle sliced shallots over hot oil and, with a fork, separate rings and turn over quickly. When most of shallots are golden brown, remove with a slotted spoon to paper towels to drain. When cool enough to touch, spread out on a small plate and set aside, uncovered.

8. *Tangy Chile Sauce:* In a small mixing bowl, combine vinegar, sugar and remaining $\frac{1}{2}$ tsp (2 mL) salt, stirring until dissolved and thickened. Sprinkle chile slices over sauce and transfer to a small serving bowl.

9. To serve, uncover rice and scoop onto a serving platter, endeavoring to keep shiitake-tofu mixture intact, rather than mixing everything together. Garnish with cucumber slices, cilantro leaves and crispy shallots. Serve warm or room temperature along with the Tangy Chile Sauce.

Mee Grop

In this spectacular dish, wiry rice noodles are deep-fried to a light, crisp tangle and tossed in a piquant chile sauce. The resulting dish is unique in its juxtaposition of textures and in its classic Thai explosions of flavor. Served at room temperature, it makes a grand centerpiece for a celebration meal. Thais prepare it in large quantities for the feasts that accompany weddings, Buddhist ordinations or welcoming a baby to the world.

SERVES 6 TO 8

Tip

You can purchase Thai pickled garlic in Asian markets. What you buy will be petite whole heads, with papery sheaths still in place, packed in their brine. These should be drained and then sliced crosswise into ¼-inch (0.5 cm) thick rounds that display a pleasing mosaic of round cloves clustered into a large circle. These delicate slices are placed decoratively on the mountain of noodles just before serving.

- Candy/deep-fry thermometer
- Large long-handled Asian wire strainer
- 2 long-handled metal slotted spoons
- Large tray or 2 baking sheets, lined with paper towels

8 oz	wire-thin dried rice noodles	250 g
	Vegetable oil	
4 oz	firm tofu, cut into slender 1-inch (2.5 cm) long rods	125 g
¼ cup	finely chopped garlic, divided	60 mL
8 oz	fresh button mushrooms, thinly sliced	250 g
1¼ tsp	salt, divided	6 mL
2 tbsp	coarsely chopped shallots	30 mL
½ cup	Vegetable Stock (pages 189 and 190) or store-bought	125 mL
2 tbsp	distilled white vinegar	30 mL
1 tbsp	Asian bean sauce	15 mL
½ tsp	soy sauce	2 mL
1 tsp	hot pepper flakes	5 mL
½ cup	palm sugar or brown sugar	125 mL
¼ cup	granulated sugar	60 mL
¼ cup	Tamarind Liquid (page 191)	60 mL
2 tbsp	freshly squeezed lime juice	30 mL
1	bunch fresh garlic chives or 9 green onions, cut into 1-inch (2.5 cm) lengths	1
1 cup	coarsely chopped fresh cilantro	250 mL

continued on page 148

Garnishes

3 cups	bean sprouts	750 mL
5	heads Thai pickled garlic, cut crosswise into ¼-inch (0.5 cm) thick rounds, or 24 cloves pickled garlic (see Tip, page 147)	5
1	red bell pepper, cut into long thin strips	1
	Handful of cilantro leaves	

1. Gently pull noodles apart, breaking into small handfuls about 3 inches (7.5 cm) long. Set aside in a heap (see Tip, left). Place prepared baking sheets near stove to hold the fried noodles. Have handy a large serving platter or large deep bowl and 2 long-handled spoons or pasta forks for tossing the puffed noodles with the sauce.

2. Pour oil into a wok or large deep skillet to a depth of about 3 inches (7.5 cm). Place over medium heat and heat to 325° to 350°F (160° to 180°C). Drop a piece of rice noodle into pan. If it sinks and then floats and puffs immediately, the oil is ready.

3. Drop a small handful of noodles into oil. Turn once and remove as soon as they swell and turn a very faint golden brown. This takes only seconds. Using the wire strainer, scoop out puffed noodles, holding them over the pan briefly to drain. Transfer to prepared baking sheet. Repeat until all noodles are cooked.

4. In same hot oil, cook tofu, in small batches, turning to cook evenly, until crispy and golden, 1 to 2 minutes. Remove as quickly as you did the noodles, draining briefly. Then transfer to prepared baking sheet and let cool.

5. In a medium skillet, heat 2 tbsp (30 mL) vegetable over medium heat until a bit of garlic added to the pan sizzles at once. Add half of the garlic and toss until fragrant and shiny, about 1 minute. Add mushrooms and cook, tossing occasionally, for 1 minute. Add ¼ tsp (1 mL) of the salt, toss well, and then cook, tossing often, until mushrooms are softened and browned, about 5 minutes. Transfer to the plate and set aside.

6. Add 2 tbsp (30 mL) more oil to skillet and heat over medium-high heat until a bit of garlic added to the pan sizzles at once. Add remaining garlic and shallots and cook, tossing often, until shiny and tender, about 2 minutes. Add remaining 1 tsp (5 mL) of salt, vegetable stock, vinegar, bean sauce, soy sauce, pepper flakes, palm and granulated sugars and tamarind and bring to a gentle boil. Stir to dissolve the sugars, mixing well. Reduce heat to medium and cook gently until sauce is a thin, shiny syrup, 5 to 7 minutes.

7. Add lime juice. Taste and adjust seasoning for a pleasing balance of sweet, salty and sour flavors.

8. Transfer sauce to a large bowl, add noodles and mushrooms and toss gently, thoroughly, and patiently to coax apart the clumps, distributing sauce and coating noodles evenly. Add garlic chives or green onion and cilantro and toss again to mix well.

9. Mound noodles on the serving platter. Arrange bean sprouts attractively on the plate. Garnish with pickled garlic, red pepper strips and cilantro leaves. Serve at room temperature.

❁ Thai Tales

Although I have given you a somewhat-simplified recipe, this classic Thai celebration dish nonetheless calls for a considerable amount of work, from deep-frying the noodles to making their tangy sauce and tossing them in it. You can turn its preparation into a pleasure doing as Thai cooks do when preparing for a special occasion: Call in some culinary reinforcements! Have a friend or two come over to provide good company along with extra hands under your instruction and the time will sail by, leaving you all with a small, glorious mountain of scrumptious Thai noodles to enjoy.

Paht Thai

In Thailand, most noodle dishes have clear Chinese origins and have been adapted very little, since they please Thais just the way they are. This is the exception, a Thai invention, with the basic technique of stir-frying applied to seasonings that marry sweet with sour and salty with hot in a way Thais adore. The full name for this dish is kwaytiow paht Thai. *The first word means rice noodles and* paht *means to stir-fry in a wok or shallow skillet. The word* Thai *says that the use of tamarind, sugar, peanuts, bean sprouts and lime in this dish is a signature of Thai ingenuity in the kitchen. Noodle chefs in Thailand freely include their own touches to create a signature version, so use your ingenuity once you get the hang of cooking the noodles.*

Tips

This makes only one or two portions, which is the best I can do with a wok on a Western stove. In Thailand, expert cooks do only a batch or two at a time, too, even when a tableful of diners orders *paht Thai*. A wok can only do justice to so many noodles at one time.

My recipe instructs you to squeeze the lime juice over the noodles just before serving. This is because I have found that if I present the dish Thai style, with a lime wedge on the side, it is left behind like a parsley garnish on a dinner plate at a banquet. Thais always squeeze on lime juice, so I like to include some and then offer extra lime wedges to those who like an extra sour hit.

- Asian-style wire strainer or slotted spoon

4 oz	dried rice noodles, the width of linguine or fettuccine	125 g
	Vegetable oil	
8 oz	firm tofu, cut into slender 1-inch (2.5 cm) long rods	250 g
1 tbsp	coarsely chopped garlic (4 to 6 cloves)	15 mL
1	egg, lightly beaten	1
¼ cup	Vegetable Stock (pages 189 and 190) or store-bought	60 mL
2 tbsp	Tamarind Liquid (page 191) or freshly squeezed lime juice	30 mL
1 tbsp	Asian bean sauce	15 mL
1 tbsp	granulated sugar	15 mL
2 tsp	soy sauce	10 mL
1 tsp	salt	5 mL
½ tsp	hot pepper flakes	2 mL
½ cup	finely chopped salted dry-roasted peanuts, divided	125 mL
2 cups	bean sprouts, divided	500 mL
3	green onions, whites thinly sliced crosswise and tender green tops cut into 1-inch (2.5 cm) lengths	3
1	lime, quartered lengthwise	1

1. Place dried rice noodles in warm water to soak for 15 to 20 minutes.

2. Meanwhile, pour vegetable oil into a medium skillet to a depth of about 2 inches (5 cm). Place over medium heat until a bit of tofu added to pan sizzles at once. Line a plate with paper towels and place near the stove. When oil is ready, add tofu in small batches to discourage them from sticking together.

Vegan Variation

Vegans can omit the egg.

Fry, turning to cook evenly, until crispy and golden, about 2 minutes. Using a long-handled wire strainer or a slotted spoon, remove from oil, draining over pan briefly and transfer to prepared plate.

3. When noodles are very limp and white, drain and measure out 2½ cups (625 mL). Set near the stove.

4. Heat a wok or a large, deep skillet over medium-high heat. Add 1 tbsp (15 mL) oil and swirl to coat pan. Add garlic and toss until golden, about 1 minute. Add egg and tilt pan to coat surface in a thin sheet. As soon as egg is opaque and beginning to set, scramble well and transfer to a serving platter.

5. Add 2 more tbsp (30 mL) oil to pan and heat for 30 seconds. Add softened noodles and, using a spatula, spread and pull noodles into a thin layer covering surface of pan. Then scrape down into a clump again and gently turn over.

6. Add vegetable stock, tamarind, bean sauce, sugar, soy sauce and salt and toss well. Hook loops of noodles with edge of spatula and pull up the sides, spreading out into a layer again. Repeat this process several times as the stiff, white noodles soften and curl into ivory ringlets. Add pepper flakes and about half of the peanuts and turn noodles a few more times.

7. Set aside a little less than half of the bean sprouts for garnish. Add remainder to pan along with green onions and cooked egg. Toss well and cook until bean sprouts and green onion tops are shiny and beginning to wilt, 1 to 2 minutes more. Transfer to serving platter and squeeze lime wedges over top. Garnish with remaining peanuts and bean sprouts on one side and serve at once.

❀ Thai Tales

The classic version of *paht Thai* includes crispy little tofu rods, minced pickled turnip (known as *tay-po*) and a handful of little salty dried shrimp. Raw bean sprouts and a wedge of purple-and-yellow banana flower (if it can be found) always garnish the plate, as these two add a cool, raw crunch. The addition of fresh seafood and meat is a modern one, as is the inclusion of tomato paste or ketchup. The latter is common in Thai restaurants in the West, probably added more for color than for flavor.

Rice Noodles with Eggs, Broccoli and Dark Sweet Soy Sauce

In Thailand, this classic dish is almost as popular as paht Thai, *plus it is a boon for home cooks because it is easier to prepare. The dark sweet soy sauce, known as* si-yu, *bestows a gorgeous mahogany color to the noodles, while the broccoli turns a brilliant green. Check the menu at your favorite Thai restaurant for this one, which may be listed under its Thai name,* paht si-yu. *Widely available in the West, it is easily adapted for vegetarian diners since it is always cooked to order. If you want an authentic dish, be sure to doctor up your portion with a little extra sugar, salt and chiles and then dollop on a little Chile-Vinegar Sauce before you dig in.*

SERVES 4

Tip

Instead of fresh, soft rice noodles, you can use dried rice noodles, soaked in warm water for about 20 minutes until softened. Or even cooked fettuccine or linguine with tasty results.

2 tbsp	dark sweet soy sauce or 2 tbsp (30 mL) dark soy sauce and 1 tbsp (15 mL) molasses or brown sugar	30 mL
2 tbsp	Vegetable Stock (pages 189 and 190) or store-bought	30 mL
1 tbsp	soy sauce	15 mL
1 tsp	salt	5 mL
½ tsp	freshly ground black pepper	2 mL
3 tbsp	vegetable oil, divided	45 mL
1 tbsp	coarsely chopped garlic (4 to 6 cloves)	15 mL
8 oz	fresh mushrooms, sliced	250 g
3 cups	bite-size broccoli florets	750 mL
1 lb	soft, fresh flat rice noodles (see Tip, left)	500 mL
2	eggs, lightly beaten	2

Condiments

Chile-Vinegar Sauce (page 208)

Granulated sugar

Hot pepper flakes

1. In a small bowl, combine dark soy sauce, vegetable stock, regular soy sauce, salt and pepper. Stir well and place near the stove along with a serving platter.

Tip

Thai cooks make this noodle dish with the sturdy dark green cabbage cousin called *pahk ka-nah*, rather than broccoli. You could use any member of the healthful family known as cruciferous vegetables, all of which have a cross-shaped formation of leafy stem at the base. Cabbage, such as napa, winter greens (kale, collards or Swiss chard), broccoli and cauliflower are part of this group and any of them would work nicely in this recipe. Be sure to cut them on the diagonal into thin, bite-size pieces so they will cook quickly. You can also use bok choy or any of the Asian greens Cantonese speakers refer to as choy. You could also use spinach if you stir in just before the dish is ready and cook only long enough for it to wilt.

Vegan Variation

Vegans can omit the eggs and add about a cupful of crumbled firm tofu in their place.

2. Heat a wok or a large, deep skillet over medium-high heat. Add 1 tbsp (15 mL) of the oil and swirl to coat pan. Add garlic and toss until fragrant and just beginning to brown, about 1 minute. Add mushrooms and cook, tossing often, until dark and softened, about 3 minutes. Add broccoli and cook, tossing often, until shiny and bright green, about 2 minutes. Scoop out mushrooms and broccoli and place on serving platter. Set aside.

3. Add remaining 2 tbsp (30 mL) of oil to pan and heat for about 30 seconds. Add noodles and toss until separated and heated through. Push noodles to one side of wok and add eggs. Swirl to spread out the eggs and let cook for about 30 seconds. Then scoop and toss everything together gently, scrambling eggs and mixing well.

4. Quickly stir soy sauce mixture to combine and then pour over noodles. Add reserved broccoli and mushrooms and their juices and toss until noodles are handsomely colored and evenly coated with sauce, about 1 minute. Transfer to serving platter and serve at once, offering condiments in small bowls on the side.

Mee Ga-ti Rice Noodles with Coconut-Bean Sauce

Try this terrific noodle dish when you crave noodles but find stir-frying them too much work. The noodles are tossed with the sauce and then enjoyed warm or at room temperature, so it makes a good choice for serving on a buffet. Like Paht Thai (page 150), this delicious sweet-and-tangy rice noodle classic is traditionally garnished with raw bean sprouts and chunks of fresh banana flower. These flourishes provide what Thais call rote faht-faht, *a cool, raw taste and texture that are welcome counterpoints to the lush, sweet, salty and sour flavors of many Thai dishes.*

SERVES 4

Tips

Asian bean sauce is the flavor note here, a sharp, salty concoction of salted fermented soybeans that is a terrific foil for the richness of *ga-ti* (coconut milk).

If you have a heavy Thai-style mortar and pestle, do not mince the shallots. Instead, chop the shallots coarsely and then pound them to a coarse mush to release their flavor and juice.

8 oz	dried rice noodles, either wire-thin or about the width of linguine or fettuccine	250 g
1 tbsp	vegetable oil	15 mL
2	eggs, beaten	2
3 cups	unsweetened coconut milk	750 mL
½ cup	minced shallots	125 mL
⅓ cup	Asian bean sauce (see Tips, left)	75 mL
8 oz	firm tofu, cut into slender 1-inch (2.5 cm) long rods	250 g
2	zucchini, halved lengthwise and cut crosswise into thin half-moons or cut into slender 2-inch (5 cm) long rods	2
2 tbsp	Tamarind Liquid (page 191) or freshly squeezed lime juice	30 mL
2 tbsp	Vegetable Stock (pages 189 and 190) or store-bought	30 mL
2 tbsp	granulated sugar	30 mL
1 tsp	salt	5 mL
1 tsp	freshly ground black pepper	5 mL
1 tsp	hot pepper flakes	5 mL
	A handful of fresh garlic chives, cut into 2-inch (5 cm) lengths, or 3 green onions, white part thinly sliced crosswise and green part cut into 2-inch (5 cm) lengths	
2 cups	bean sprouts	500 mL
½ cup	coarsely chopped fresh cilantro	125 mL
1	lime, cut lengthwise into 6 wedges	1

Tip

This dish is also served with the cooked noodles served up in small heaps and the sauce on the side, to be added by each diner along with the garnishes. You could do this on individual plates or offer the noodles on a platter with the bowl of sauce alongside.

Vegan Variation

Vegans can omit the eggs. Add a handful of shredded carrots to the coconut milk along with the shallots, if you like.

1. Place dried rice noodles in a bowl, add warm water to cover and let stand until limp and pliable, 15 to 20 minutes. Put a large pot of water on to boil.

2. Meanwhile, heat vegetable oil in a medium skillet over medium-high heat until a drop of egg added to the pan sizzles at once, about 1 minute. Add only enough of the eggs to coat pan, swirling to make a thin sheet. Cook until egg sets, about 30 seconds. Flip to warm other side and then turn onto a cutting board to cool. Repeat with remaining egg. When egg sheets are cool, shred into fine strips and set aside.

3. Drain noodles and add to boiling water. Cook until tender but still firm, 1 to 2 minutes. Drain well and set aside.

4. Pour coconut milk into a medium skillet over medium heat and bring to a gentle boil. Adjust heat to maintain an active simmer and cook, stirring occasionally, until fragrant and thickened slightly, 3 to 5 minutes. Add shallots, bean sauce, tofu and zucchini and cook, stirring occasionally, for 3 minutes. Add tamarind, vegetable stock, sugar, salt, pepper and pepper flakes. Stir well and cook for 2 minutes.

5. Add noodles, garlic chives and most of the bean sprouts, reserving a handful for garnish. Toss well to coat everything with sauce. Transfer to a serving platter and sprinkle with cilantro. Garnish with reserved bean sprouts and lime wedges and serve warm or at room temperature.

✿ *Thai Tales*

Should you be fortunate enough to be cooking this in a tropical clime, find a teardrop-shaped banana flower, quarter it lengthwise and offer it to diners to nibble along with the noodles. Or pull off some delicate and colorful portions, slice them and use to garnish the platter.

Sweets and Drinks

Cool, Crisp Rubies in Coconut Milk 160

Maengluk Basil Seeds in Coconut Milk 162

Sticky Rice with Mangos 163

Coconut Ice Cream 164

Thai Coffee Ice Cream 165

Thai Ice Cream Sandwiches 166

Thai Tea Ice Cream 167

Lemongrass Ginger Sorbet 168

Wild Lime Leaf Sorbet 169

Speedy Mango Sorbet 170

Coconut Rice Pudding 171

Thai Iced Coffee 172

Thai Iced Tea 173

Maengluk Basil Seed Drink with Fresh Fruit
and Honey 174

Fresh Lemongrass Lemonade 175

Sweets and Drinks

THAI PEOPLE HAVE AN UNDENIABLE SWEET TOOTH, BUT SWEETNESS plays a different role in Thailand than it does in Western food. Thais consider sweetness one of the four essential flavors that make eating a pleasure, along with saltiness, sourness and chile pepper heat. It is not reserved for cake, candy and cookies, but rather included at all levels of eating. A little palm sugar slips into curries, sauces and stews to balance the equation of flavors. Sweetness even stars in some dishes such as Mee Grop (page 147) and Son-in-Law Eggs (page 124). By Western standards, these dishes are savory main-course foods, but your palate will tell you that you are in Asia, where no clear line is drawn between savory and sweet.

Sweet dishes designed for eating apart from rice abound in Thai cuisine. They are enjoyed not as dessert following a main course, but as snacks to satisfy hunger or whims between meals, as food for children or as breakfast-time treats. These treats come under the general category of *kanome,* which can be translated as both "snack" and "sweet treat," although it also covers bread, certain kinds of noodles and other dishes made mostly from flour.

The majority of traditional Thai sweets involve coconut milk, palm sugar and an array of substantial ingredients, including tapioca pearls, sticky rice, squiggly little rice flour noodles, cooked mung beans or black beans, shreds of freshly grated coconut and gelatins made with the seaweed extract agar-agar. Both fruits and vegetables play a role in Thai sweets. Kabocha pumpkins are hollowed out and filled with custard for steaming, and taro root, potatoes, cassava, fresh ginger and several varieties of bananas are candied and preserved in sugar syrup in a process called *chu-am.* Dishes of sweetened coconut milk, chopped fruits, jellies, and ice in small bowls are typically served as an afternoon snack or in the night market, where you perch on a stool at the vendor's rickety table and enjoy a cool, sweet treat before strolling home. This dish acts as a refreshing dessert after nearly any Thai meal, particularly since sweet coconut milk can quell the fires of chile pepper heat.

While the traditional sweets of Thailand appear throughout the day as snacks rather than following a meal, Thais do love a simple dessert of the season's freshest, ripest fruits, carefully prepared and presented so that guests are relieved of the hassle of peeling it or dealing with seeds. I remember my first experience of this brilliant, healthful custom in the northernmost Thai town of Chiang Rai, where I joined a group of diners for a late lunch at a restaurant where we feasted away the heat of the day. As we lingered, enjoying the company and the lacy shade of a tamarind tree protecting our alfresco table, the dishes were cleared away and replaced with an enormous platter. It held juicy chunks of sweet watermelon and triangles of ripe, perfect pineapple of the short, squat variety that thrives in the north. This red-and-yellow mountain was showered with crushed ice to keep it cold while we enjoyed it in the withering heat. While I am a dedicated fan of Western desserts, I cannot imagine a better ending to that meal.

This chapter is an intriguing collection of sweets, some of them from the repertoire of traditional Thai *kanome* and some my Thai-inspired creations. Each and every one would work beautifully as a dessert course to your Thai or Western feast. Cool, Crisp Rubies in Coconut Milk and Maengluk Basil Seeds in Coconut Milk are two old-time Thai sweet things that I adore for a summertime breakfast, as well as for a snack or dessert. Coconut Ice Cream is spectacular, providing the owners of an ice cream maker with an unbelievably good, completely authentic Thai sweet treat in exchange for a very small amount of time and work.

Additional desserts are my East-West inventions. You will also find a lovely sorbet infused with the heavenly flavor of lemongrass and another with the delicate, delectable notes of galanga and wild lime leaves. These two Asian herb confections can also be made into granitas, which are a bit grainier than sorbets but every bit as good.

Winding up this sweet parade is a rice pudding made with coconut milk and toasted coconut that can be eaten hot or cold. To ease your thirst, I have included Thai Iced Coffee and Thai Iced Tea, with instructions on making them in a drip coffee maker or straining them more traditionally. Finally, for those of you with a lemongrass patch in a pot or yard, there is Fresh Lemongrass Lemonade.

Cool, Crisp Rubies in Coconut Milk

This beloved traditional sweet is called tuptim grop *and it has delighted Thais for centuries. Made from the most ordinary of Asian ingredients, its name embodies a double pun for both eye and ear.* Tuptim *can be translated both as "ruby" and as "pomegranate seed," and the dessert looks very much like the jewels or seeds, shimmering in a bowl of snowy, sweet coconut milk.*

SERVES 5

Tips

I use canned coconut milk in lieu of freshly made. For the traditional version, use fairly thick coconut cream from the first pressing (page 196), as this dish calls for that level of richness.

These "pomegranate seeds" are best made within a few hours of serving. They cling together into a gelatinous mass as time passes and as they chill. If you make them ahead, cover and chill for up to 2 days and then turn the cool red blob out onto a cutting board and gently separate it into individual "seeds" with your fingers.

	Red food coloring	
1	can (8 oz/250 g) whole water chestnuts, drained and cut into pea-size chunks	1
1 cup	tapioca flour (approx.) (see Tip, right)	250 mL
⅔ cup	water	150 mL
⅔ cup	granulated sugar	150 mL
1¼ cups	unsweetened coconut milk	300 mL
	Crushed ice	

1. Fill a medium bowl with water, add a few drops of red food coloring and stir well. Add water chestnuts and let stand until red color is absorbed fully, 15 to 20 minutes. Drain well.

2. Place tapioca flour in a medium bowl and add water chestnut pieces, a handful at a time, tossing gently with your fingers to coat evenly with flour. Scoop out with a slotted spoon, shake gently to remove any excess flour and set aside on a plate in a single layer.

3. Place a saucepan filled with water over medium heat and bring to a rolling boil. Add water chestnut pieces in handfuls, stirring well to discourage clumping. Boil until flour coating is clear and red, 3 to 4 minutes. Drain well. Add cool water to cover and let stand for 1 minute. Then drain well again. Set aside in a bowl.

Tip

Tapioca flour has the gelatinous property needed to give the water chestnut pieces a colorful and plump jellylike coating. Store extra tapioca flour in an airtight container, where it will keep indefinitely.

Variation

If you want to use fresh water chestnuts in this recipe, purchase 30 to 40 firm chestnuts. Using a very sharp knife, peel to remove the thick, tough brown exterior. Boil peeled chestnuts in water to cover, until tender enough to bite but still nicely crunchy and firm, about 30 minutes. Drain and immerse in cold water until cooled to room temperature, then use as directed.

4. In another saucepan over medium heat, combine water and sugar and bring to a rolling boil. Cook, stirring once, until sugar dissolves completely into a light syrup, about 3 minutes. Remove from heat and let cool.

5. To serve, divide "rubies" evenly among 5 small shallow serving bowls, preferably made of glass to show off the colors of the finished dish. Stir coconut milk well and divide among the bowls, putting about ¼ cup (60 mL) in each bowl. (The "rubies" should still be quite visible and appear to be floating in the coconut milk.) Add 3 tbsp (45 mL) of the syrup to each bowl and then sprinkle with a tbsp or two (15 to 30 mL) of crushed ice. Serve at once.

❀ Thai Tales

In Thailand, *tuptim grop* is purchased from a sweets vendor, either in individual serving bowls for eating at a market stall or in separate plastic bags for transporting home. Thais add crushed ice to each bowl at serving time, but if you prefer, simply chill the coconut milk and syrup well and serve it cold.

Maengluk Basil Seeds in Coconut Milk

Bai maengluk, *a member of the Thai basil trio, has a delicate lemony aroma and tang. The delicately sweet, translucent meat of young green coconuts is the classic companion to this dessert of swollen basil seeds in coconut cream. You can also use any other sweet, ripe fruit or a combination of several if young, green coconut is difficult to find. Once you have the seeds in hand, you are minutes away from a down-home Thai-Chinese treat beloved by children and grown-ups alike. This is best served within a few hours after chilling.*

SERVES 6

Tips

The tiny black *maengluk* seeds are sold in Asian markets year-round, often labeled "dried sweet basil" in English and "*hot e*" in Vietnamese.

Some fruits that would work well here are banana, cantaloupe, honeydew melon, mango, papaya or pineapple or whole strawberries, raspberries or blueberries.

To chill the sweet coconut milk quickly, nestle the bowl into a bigger bowl about three-fourths full of ice. Or try the traditional Thai method of chilling sweets: Add a handful of crushed ice to each bowl just before serving.

Variation

Use tiny tapioca pearls cooked until clear and tender if you cannot find maengluk seeds.

1 tbsp	*maengluk* basil seeds (see Tips, left)	15 mL
1½ cups	water	375 mL
½ cup	young coconut meat or 1 cup (250 mL) bite-size chunks sweet, ripe fruit (see Tips, left)	125 mL
1 cup	unsweetened coconut milk, stirred to combine well before measuring	250 mL
⅓ cup	palm sugar or brown sugar	75 mL

1. Place basil seeds in a medium bowl and add ¾ cup (175 mL) of the water. Let stand, stirring occasionally, until seeds absorb water and transform into about 1 cup (250 mL) tiny gray-blue "eggs" with a clear gelatin encasing each one. This should take about 15 minutes. Set aside along with prepared fruit.

2. In a medium bowl, combine coconut milk with remaining ¾ cup (175 mL) of water and stir well. Add sugar and mix well, stirring and mashing to dissolve sugar completely. (If some chunks refuse to dissolve, strain, place in a small saucepan with a little water, heat and stir just until dissolved. Then stir liquid into bowl of sweetened coconut milk.) Cover and place in refrigerator until well chilled, 1 to 2 hours.

3. To serve, set out small, individual bowls and pour about ⅓ cup (75 mL) of the chilled sweet coconut milk into each bowl. Place 2 tbsp (30 mL) or so of basil seeds in each bowl and then divide fruit among the bowls. Serve at once.

Sticky Rice with Mangos

This is heavenly. It is also simple to make once you are in possession of some sweet, ripe mangos, which are worth their weight in gold on a sweltering day in Thailand. During mango season, Thai people often skip supper and instead stroll to the night market to indulge in this local treat. Plan ahead, as the sticky rice needs 3 hours to soak and then an hour or so to cool to room temperature after steaming. Thais sometimes use black sticky rice, which actually has a gorgeous purple hue after cooking.

SERVES 6

Tips

You can keep the coconut rice for 6 to 8 hours at room temperature. Do not refrigerate, as it will harden.

For a traditional presentation, sprinkle each serving of sticky rice with toasted *tua tong* or "golden beans," which are the tiny, bright yellow oval centers that are at the heart of mung beans. They are widely available in Asian markets in small cellophane bags. To toast them, put a handful in a small skillet, place over medium heat and toast, shaking the pan often, until lightly browned, 5 to 10 minutes. Then divide them among the servings of rice.

Variation

If you do not have wonderful mangos handy to pair with the sticky rice, use summer's sweetest peaches, nectarines or plums, or a red, white and blue rainbow of strawberries, bananas and blueberries. Use about 1½ cups (375 mL) per person.

Sticky Rice with Coconut Sauce (page 138)

¾ cup	unsweetened coconut milk	175 mL
½ tsp	salt	2 mL
6	ripe, sweet mangos	6

1. Prepare sticky rice as directed and let cool to room temperature.

2. In a saucepan over medium heat, heat coconut milk gently until a gentle boil. Add salt, stir well and cook until coconut milk is fragrant and thickens slightly, about 3 minutes. Transfer to a small bowl and let cool.

3. Shortly before serving, peel and slice mangos, removing as much meat as you can in large, tender pieces. Avoid cutting very close to the seed, where the meat is quite fibrous. For each serving, arrange a fist-size serving of coconut rice on a dessert or salad plate along with several chunks of mango or other fruit. Spoon about 2 tbsp (30 mL) of the coconut milk over rice and serve at once.

Coconut Ice Cream

Here is the classic Thai ice cream that sweetens the hottest evening in Thailand's upcountry small towns. It could not be simpler and it could not be better. You can jazz it up with flavors and additions in the modern manner, but in my opinion it is perfect as is. Thais love it sprinkled with chopped peanuts and served in tiny bowls or in Thai Ice Cream Sandwiches (page 166).

**MAKES ABOUT
1 PINT**

SERVES 4

Tips

You can make the ice cream base in advance, cover, and chill for up to 1 day before you churn it into ice cream.

If the ice cream loses its pleasing texture and becomes grainy, break it into chunks and briefly process in a food processor fit with a metal blade to restore its creaminess.

◆ Ice cream maker

2	cans (each 14 oz/400 mL) unsweetened coconut milk (about 3½ cups/875 mL)	2
1 cup	granulated sugar	250 mL
½ tsp	salt	2 mL

1. In a heavy saucepan, combine coconut milk, sugar and salt. Place over medium-high heat and bring to a boil, stirring often to dissolve sugar and salt. Remove from heat and pour into a bowl.

2. Cover bowl and refrigerate until very cold, about 2 hours. Freeze in an ice cream maker according to the manufacturer's directions. Serve at once or transfer to an airtight container and freeze for up to 3 weeks.

Thai Coffee Ice Cream

I adore the flavor of Thai iced coffee, with its deep, dark coffee kick fortified with ground dried corn and sesame seeds that have been roasted to a robust turn. In the spring of 1989, I returned to Thailand to research my first cookbook, Real Thai. *My dear friend and fellow former Peace Corps volunteer Sandi Younkin joined me on this mission and together we survived the fierce heat of Thailand's April afternoons by collapsing into chairs in Chiang Mai's hyper-air-conditioned Black Mountain Cafe and swilling Thai iced coffee from enormous frosty mugs. Had they served this ice cream, we might be there still.*

MAKES ABOUT 1 PINT

SERVES 4

Tips

Allow plenty of time to prepare the ice cream, since it needs to be heated and then chilled until very cold so that it will freeze well. If possible, make the base a day in advance, as it keeps well and will then be ready when you are. It is also ideal to return the frozen ice cream to the freezer to "ripen" and set for an hour or two before you serve it. Leftover ice cream may freeze solid after a day or more in the freezer. In this case, cut it into large chunks and process in a food processor fitted with the metal blade until smooth.

To cool mixture quickly, nestle the bowl into a bigger bowl about three-fourths full of ice.

- ◆ Instant-read thermometer
- ◆ Ice cream maker

1½ cups	milk	375 mL
1½ cups	heavy or whipping (35%) cream	375 mL
¼ cup	Thai coffee powder (page 227)	60 mL
1 cup	granulated sugar, divided	250 mL
3	egg yolks	3

1. In a heavy saucepan over medium-high heat, combine milk and cream and bring to a boil. Quickly remove from heat and stir in powder. Let steep for 20 minutes.

2. Strain cream through a fine-mesh sieve into a bowl to remove coffee powder. Rinse out saucepan to remove any grounds, return strained coffee cream to pan and whisk in ½ cup (125 mL) of the sugar. Set aside.

3. Place egg yolks in a medium bowl and, using a whisk or an electric mixer at medium speed, whisk in remaining sugar, beating until mixture is smooth, lightened in color and as thick as softly whipped cream. Keep whisking egg-sugar mixture as you pour about one-third of the warm coffee cream into the bowl, to heat the egg-sugar mixture gently and combine everything well.

4. Return saucepan containing remaining coffee cream to the stove over medium heat. Using a wooden spoon, stir constantly as you pour egg-sugar mixture into warm coffee cream. Stir constantly in a figure 8 motion, cook coffee cream until thickened and coats back of a spoon, 2 to 3 minutes. The mixture should register 190°F (88°C) on the thermometer (do not allow it to come to a boil) (see Tips, left). Pour into a bowl and let cool to room temperature.

5. When ice cream base has cooled to room temperature, cover and chill for several hours until very cold. Then freeze in an ice cream maker according to manufacturer's directions.

Thai Ice Cream Sandwiches

This East-West snack exhibits Thai ingenuity in translating two Western imports, ice cream and sliced white bread, into a sweet and portable treat. Thailand's urban centers now have ice cream parlors with many flavors and a choice of plain or chocolate sprinkle cones, but in the countryside you may still find night markets where the flavor is coconut and your serving dish and spoon is washable rather than disposable. Use minuscule scoops of firm ice cream and soft white bread rather than the proverbial crusty peasant loaf for best results.

SERVES 4

Tip

Use any flavor ice cream you like. I am partial to coconut ice cream purely for sentimental reasons, and it is the traditional Thai choice in a land where dairy products are a recent addition to the market and remain relatively rare.

Vegan Variation

Vegans can use coconut milk–based ice creams or fruit-based sorbets for their sandwiches.

12	small scoops very firm ice cream, preferably Coconut Ice Cream (page 164) (approx.)	12
4	slices soft white bread	4
½	recipe Sticky Rice (page 137) (approx.), warm or at room temperature	½
2 cups	coarsely chopped salted, dry-roasted peanuts	500 mL

1. For each sandwich, scoop out 3 small, golf-size lumps of ice cream and line them up in the center of a slice of bread. Shape a handful of sticky rice into a plump, finger-length log and place it on the bread alongside the ice cream. Sprinkle with ½ cup (125 mL) of the peanuts, fold up into a rectangle and serve at once. Repeat with remaining ingredients to make 4 sandwiches.

❀ Thai Tales

As a greenhorn Peace Corps volunteer, I remember my surprise on being handed my first coconut ice cream sandwich, since it broke one of my Western culinary rules (bread equals savory; ice cream equals sweet). But as I devoured this revelation while meandering home through the steamy summer night, I decided many a culinary concept gains something in the translation.

Thai Tea Ice Cream

If you love Thai iced tea as I do, you will love this ice cream, too. Soft and creamy, it has the intriguing flavor of Thai black tea laced with cinnamon and vanilla, as well as the trademark pumpkin color Thai tea fans adore.

MAKES ABOUT 1 PINT

SERVES 4

- Instant-read thermometer
- Ice cream maker

1½ cups	milk	375 mL
1½ cups	heavy or whipping (35%) cream	375 mL
¼ cup	Thai tea (see page 227)	60 mL
1 cup	granulated sugar, divided	250 mL
3	egg yolks	3

1. In a heavy saucepan over medium-high heat, combine milk and cream and bring to a boil. Quickly remove from heat and stir in tea. Set aside and let steep for 20 minutes.

2. Strain cream through a sieve lined with a triple thickness of cheesecloth or a clean kitchen towel into a bowl. (Whatever you use will take on a terra-cotta hue.) Rinse out saucepan to remove any tea leaves. Return strained mixture to pan, whisk in ½ cup (125 mL) of the sugar and set aside.

3. Place egg yolks in a medium bowl and, using a whisk or an electric mixer at medium speed, whisk in remaining sugar, beating until mixture is smooth, lightened in color and as thick as softly whipped cream. Keep whisking egg-sugar mixture as you pour about one-third of warm tea cream into bowl, to heat egg-sugar mixture gently and combine everything well.

4. Return saucepan containing remaining tea cream to the stove over medium heat. Using a wooden spoon, stir constantly as you pour egg-sugar mixture into saucepan of warm tea cream. Stirring constantly in a figure 8 motion, cook tea cream until thickened and coats the back of a spoon, 3 to 4 minutes. The mixture should register 190°F (88°C) on thermometer (do not allow it to come to a boil). Pour into a bowl and let cool to room temperature. (To cool it quickly, nestle the bowl into a bigger bowl about three-fourths full of ice.)

5. When ice cream base has cooled to room temperature, cover and chill for several hours until very cold. Then freeze in an ice cream maker according to manufacturer's directions.

Lemongrass Ginger Sorbet

Track down fresh lemongrass and make this even if you never use lemongrass in soups and curry pastes. It is fabulous, taking the incomparable essence of lemongrass from the savory side to the sweet. You can make this tangy celebration of Southeast Asian herbs even if you do not have an ice cream maker. This sorbet needs only a food processor to transform it from syrup to icy perfection. Or you can make it into a wonderfully grainy confection called a granita (see Tips, below).

**MAKES ABOUT
1 PINT**

SERVES 4

Tips

If the sorbet has become too hard when you are ready to serve it, simply break it into big chunks and reprocess it in the food processor.

If you do not have a food processor, you can make a granita, which is a delicious icy version of ice cream made by a wonderfully low-tech, old-fashioned method. Pour the warm lemongrass-ginger base into a pie plate and place in the freezer until slushy but not frozen solid, about 30 minutes. Using a fork, reach into the freezer and quickly "rake" the granita to break it up and encourage it to form small ice crystals. Repeat this step every 30 minutes until the granita is uniformly frozen yet somewhat creamy, about 2 hours. Then freeze for at least 1 hour or overnight and serve ice cold.

◆ Food processor

4	stalks lemongrass	4
¼ cup	thin strips peeled fresh gingerroot (3-inch/7.5 cm chunk)	60 mL
1½ cups	water	375 mL
1 cup	granulated sugar	250 mL
1 cup	freshly squeezed lemon juice (about 5 lemons)	250 mL

1. Cut away and discard any tough root portions from lemongrass stalks, leaving a smooth, flat base just below the bulb. Trim away tops, including any dried brown leaf portions. (You should have handsome stalks about 6 inches/15 cm long, including the bulbous base.) Slice each stalk crosswise into thin rounds and place in a heavy saucepan along with ginger, water and sugar. Stir well and bring to a boil over medium heat. Adjust heat to maintain a gentle boil and cook, stirring occasionally, until sugar is dissolved, about 5 minutes. Remove from heat and let steep for 10 minutes. Strain through a fine-mesh sieve into a bowl. Stir in lemon juice.

2. Pour sorbet base into 2 ice cube trays and freeze until almost completely set but not rock hard, 2 to 4 hours. Remove from freezer and place in a food processor fitted with metal blade. Process until creamy and uniformly combined. Transfer to an airtight container and return to freezer to harden for at least 1 hour or overnight. Serve ice cold.

Wild Lime Leaf Sorbet

Wild lime leaves are a treasure of the Southeast Asian kitchen. These shiny, emerald-green ovals poke up from the branches of their thorny mother tree in chic pairs attached seamlessly end to end. Tear one and smell it to understand the pleasure Thai cooks take in having some on hand. Seldom eaten outright due to their toughness, they are tossed into soups, curries and stir-fries for the incomparable explosion of delicate citrusy aroma and flavor they impart to a dish.

**MAKES ABOUT
1 PINT**

SERVES 4

Tips

You can substitute 5 pieces dried galanga in place of the fresh galanga or ginger.

When I was a child, lime sherbet was my favorite ice cream and I still love its cool, green color, even though I now know the truth. Limes create lots of flavor but no color, so the folks at the ice cream factory used green food coloring to do the job. If you are nostalgic for that look, add 1 or 2 drops green food coloring to the sorbet base along with the lime juice.

Variation

If you do not have wild lime leaves, simply leave them out. If you omit the wild lime leaves and lemongrass, you will still have a lovely lime sorbet with fresh ginger. See Tips, page 168 on how to make a granita.

◆ Food processor

20	wild lime leaves	20
2	stalks lemongrass	2
1	piece fresh galanga, or ginger, about 3 inches (7.5 cm) long, thinly sliced (see Tips, left)	1
2 cups	water	500 mL
1 cup	granulated sugar	250 mL
½ cup	freshly squeezed lime juice	125 mL

1. Using kitchen scissors or a sharp knife, cut lime leaves crosswise into very thin strips. Cut away and discard any tough root portions from lemongrass stalks, leaving a smooth, flat base just below the bulb. Trim away tops, including any dried brown leaf portions. (You should have handsome stalks about 6 inches/15 cm) long, including the bulbous base.) Slice each stalk crosswise into thin rounds and place in a heavy saucepan along with lime leaves, galanga, water and sugar. Stir well and bring to a boil over medium heat. Adjust heat to maintain a gentle boil and cook, stirring occasionally, until sugar is dissolved, about 5 minutes. Remove from heat and let steep for 10 minutes. Strain through a fine-mesh sieve into a bowl. Stir in lime juice.

2. Pour sorbet base into 2 ice cube trays and freeze until almost completely set but not rock hard, 2 to 4 hours. Remove from freezer and place in a food processor fitted with metal blade. Process until creamy and uniformly combined. Transfer to an airtight container and return to freezer to harden for at least 1 hour or overnight. Serve ice cold.

Speedy Mango Sorbet

Frozen mangos are the secret of this quick treat, which is made in a food processor. You could also use frozen peaches or strawberries with great results, so check the freezer case at your supermarket to see what your options are.

MAKES ABOUT
1 PINT

SERVES 4

Variations

Speedy Peach or Strawberry Sorbet: If you use peaches and/ or strawberries you will need more sugar and lemon juice than mangos. Add 1 to 2 tbsp (15 to 30 mL) of each until you have a balance you like, up to a total of ½ cup (125 mL) sugar and 3 tbsp (45 mL) lemon juice.

◆ Food processor

1	bag (1 lb/500 g) frozen mangos	1
¼ cup	granulated sugar, or as needed	60 mL
1 tbsp	freshly squeezed lemon juice, or as needed	15 mL
1	can (12 oz/375 mL) lemon-lime soda	1

1. In food processor fitted with the metal blade, place still-frozen mango and process until finely chopped. If mango is very hard, let thaw slightly before processing, about 5 minutes.

2. Stop machine and add ¼ cup (60 mL) sugar and lemon juice. Process again and with machine running, add soda through the feed tube. Continue processing until creamy and well combined. Do not overprocess or sorbet will melt. Taste and adjust with lemon juice and sugar. Quickly transfer to an airtight container and freeze for 1 to 2 hours. If sorbet freezes longer, you may need to break it into chunks and process again until soft enough to eat.

Coconut Rice Pudding

Thais cook and eat rice in almost every form, but the traditional rice pudding I adore is a Western creation. Deliciously creamy and rich, my Thai-inspired version of this tempting comfort food classic has a tropical twist, with coconut milk in the custard and a confetti of toasted coconut on top. Almost any type of rice can be used, including sticky rice and jasmine rice. You can enjoy the pudding as is, serve it with chunks of fresh ripe pineapple or mango or pair it with Orange Salad in Ginger Syrup with Fresh Mint (page 66).

SERVES 6 TO 8

Tip

If you want to prepare the pudding in advance and serve it warm, reheat it gently in a warm oven or microwave.

Vegan Variation

Vegans can omit egg yolks and substitute soy milk for the dairy milk.

1 cup	long-grain sticky rice or jasmine rice	250 mL
3 cups	unsweetened coconut milk	750 mL
5 cups	milk	1.25 L
¾ cup	granulated sugar	175 mL
¾ tsp	salt	3 mL
2	egg yolks	2
1 tsp	vanilla extract	5 mL
1 cup	sweetened shredded dried coconut	250 mL
¼ cup	Toasted Coconut (page 199)	60 mL

1. In a large, heavy saucepan over medium-high heat, combine rice, coconut milk, milk, sugar and salt and stir well. Bring to a boil, stirring often and well. Reduce heat to medium, adjusting to maintain a gentle boil without burning and cook, stirring often, until rice is tender and pudding thickens, about 25 minutes.

2. Remove from heat. In a small bowl, combine egg yolks and vanilla and stir well. Slowly stir yolk mixture into pudding to combine well, then add coconut. Return pan to stove and cook over medium heat until pudding is smooth and well combined, 3 to 4 minutes.

3. Remove from heat and pour into a medium bowl, gratin dish or an oval baking pan. Sprinkle with Toasted Coconut. Serve warm or at room temperature or cover and chill until shortly before serving time and serve cold.

Thai Iced Coffee

Dark, rich and sweet, with an earthy note created by the addition of roasted corn and roasted sesame seeds to the coffee, Thai coffee powder is a Chinese legacy. Imported from China and packed in 1-lb (500 g) cellophane packages, it is widely available in Asian grocery stores. The label may read "Thai coffee powder" or "oliang," the latter a Chinese dialect name for the flavored coffee powder as well as the beverage when it is served cold and sweetened but without milk. The Thai version, with a luxurious crown of evaporated milk cascading into the dark iced brew, is extraordinary. The electric coffee maker does a great job on Thai iced coffee, so I have given you two methods.

SERVES 6 TO 8

Tips

Thais always serve this iced coffee very sweet, but you can adjust the amount of sugar to suit your taste.

Crushed ice is ideal for Thai iced coffee because it enhances the pleasing visual effect of a glass when the milk is added. Crushed ice captures the dollop of milk and holds most of it aloft as tendrils of it drift down into the dark coffee in mesmerizing swirls. Ice cubes do a good job, too.

Evaporated milk is the traditional choice, since fresh dairy products are a luxury in Thailand, but half-and-half also works well.

¼ cup	Thai coffee powder	60 mL
¾ cup	granulated sugar	175 mL
	Ice, preferably crushed	
1 to	evaporated milk or	250 to
1½ cups	half-and-half	375 mL

Electric Drip Coffee Maker Method

1. Place a paper filter in basket of an electric drip coffee maker. Add Thai coffee and fit basket into place on coffee maker. Fill coffee pot with water up to the 8-cup (2 L) mark and pour into coffee maker as directed. This will be about 6 cups (1.5 L) of water. Turn coffee maker on and let Thai coffee brew.

2. When brewing cycle is completed, add sugar to coffee and stir well to dissolve completely. Transfer to a serving pitcher and let cool to room temperature. Refrigerate until serving time or for up to 1 week.

3. To serve, fill tall glasses with ice, add coffee almost to the top of each glass and carefully float about ¼ cup (60 mL) evaporated milk on top of each glass. Serve at once.

Regular Method

1. In a medium saucepan over high heat, bring 4 cups (1 L) water to a rolling boil. Add coffee powder and stir gently to moisten the grounds fully. Reduce heat and simmer gently for 3 minutes. Remove from heat, add sugar and stir well to dissolve. Taste and add more sugar if needed. Let cool to room temperature.

2. Strain coffee through a coffee filter basket or a fine-mesh sieve into a pitcher and refrigerate until serving time or for up to 1 week.

3. To serve, fill tall glasses with ice, add coffee almost to the top of each glass and carefully float about ¼ cup (60 mL) evaporated milk on top. Serve at once.

Thai Iced Tea

There is nothing in the world quite like Thai iced tea. Thai tea is simply finely chopped black tea that is spiced with cinnamon, vanilla, star anise and a bit of food coloring to give it that trademark cinnamon-rose hue. While it is not to everyone's liking, I adore it and feel lucky that it is remarkably simple to make. While it is traditionally sweetened in advance with sugar and served with a dollop of evaporated milk, you can enjoy it hot or iced with honey and lemon. The electric coffee maker does a great job on Thai iced tea, so I have given you two methods for making it. See Tips (page 172) since it applies to tea as well.

SERVES 6 TO 8

Tip

The only challenge is securing the tea itself, which can be ordered by mail (see Resources, page 230) if you do not live near an Asian market. The powdery leaves keep for months so buy a good supply so that you can keep a pitcher of tea on hand in your refrigerator at all times.

½ cup	Thai tea (see Tip, left)	125 mL
¾ cup	granulated sugar	175 mL
	Ice, preferably crushed	
1½ cups	evaporated milk or half-and-half	375 mL

Electric Drip Coffee Maker Method

1. Place a paper filter in the basket of an electric drip coffee maker, add tea and fit basket into place on coffee maker. Fill coffee pot with water up to the 8-cup (2 L) mark and pour into coffee maker as directed. This will be about 6 cups (1.5 L) of water. Turn coffee maker on and let tea brew.

2. When brewing cycle is completed, add sugar to tea and stir well to dissolve completely. Transfer to a serving pitcher and let cool to room temperature. The tea will be a brilliant orange. Refrigerate until serving time or for up to 1 week.

3. To serve, fill tall glasses with ice, add tea almost to the top of each glass and carefully float about ¼ cup (60 mL) evaporated milk on top. Serve at once.

Regular Method

1. In a medium saucepan over high heat, bring 4 cups (1 L) water to a rolling boil. Add tea and stir gently to moisten leaves fully. Reduce heat and simmer gently for 1 minute. Remove from heat, add sugar and stir well to dissolve. Taste and add more sugar if needed. Let cool to room temperature. The tea will be a brilliant orange.

2. Strain tea through a coffee filter basket or a fine-mesh strainer into a pitcher and refrigerate until serving time or for up to 1 week.

3. To serve, fill tall glasses with ice, add tea almost to the top of each glass and carefully float about ¼ cup (60 mL) evaporated milk on top. Serve at once.

Maengluk Basil Seed Drink with Fresh Fruit and Honey

Cooling beverages similar to this one are popular throughout Southeast Asia, having spread from southern China down through Vietnam, Thailand and beyond. Soaking the maengluk *basil seeds creates an amazing transformation you must see to believe. Provide a spoon when you serve this in tall glasses. I like to pour it over ice cubes, but if you chill it well, you can serve it without them, which is the traditional way.*

SERVES 4 TO 6

Tip

You will find tiny black *maengluk* basil seeds sold in small cellophane bags at Asian markets, possibly labeled "sweet basil" or with the Vietnamese name, *hot e.*

3 cups	water	750 mL
3 tbsp	honey	45 mL
3 tbsp	palm sugar or brown sugar	45 mL
1 tbsp	*maengluk* basil seeds (see Tip, left)	15 mL
2 cups	ripe bananas, strawberries and pineapple, cut into chunks	500 mL
	Ice cubes	

1. In a saucepan over medium heat, combine water, honey and sugar, stirring well, until honey and sugar dissolve completely. Remove from heat and let cool to room temperature.

2. Stir in basil seeds. They will swell from tiny black sesame seed-like bits into countless little blue-gray balloons, with a gelatin-like coating enclosing each seed. Chill until very cold.

3. When you are ready to serve, fill 4 to 6 tall glasses halfway with ice cubes. Add a few chunks of banana, strawberries and pineapple to each glass. Fill to the top with sweet basil seed drink and serve at once with spoons.

✳ *Thai Tales*

In Thailand, *maengluk* basil leaves are tossed into soups and curries just before serving. The black seeds are purchased not only for planting in herb gardens, but also for their unique capacity to swell into gelatin-like pearls for serving in Thai soups and sweets. In addition to its pleasing, caviar-like texture, basil seeds have another strong appeal to Thai people. No scientific research studies have hit the journals, but Thai market ladies always assured me that eating soaked *maengluk* basil seeds causes one to *lote nahm nahk* or "release unwanted pounds."

Fresh Lemongrass Lemonade

I first enjoyed this pleasing Thai herbal version in the lovely northern city of Chiang Mai, seated on the patio of a restaurant called Takrai. Takrai means "lemongrass" in the central Thai dialect and the restaurant was graced with numerous large pots of its namesake herb, placed among the outdoor tables as a portable and accessible herb garden.

SERVES 4

Tip

Lemongrass is invariably sold with its willowy leaves trimmed away. If you can't find the long, slender leaves for this recipe, use about 2 cups (500 mL) finely chopped lemongrass stalks for a tasty version with a milder flavor and color.

♦ Blender

3¼ cups	cold water	800 mL
¼ cup	granulated sugar	60 mL
2 cups	coarsely chopped fresh lemongrass, preferably soft, grassy tops from 4 or 5 stalks (see Tip, left)	500 mL
	Ice cubes	

1. In a small, heavy saucepan over medium heat, combine ¼ cup (60 mL) of the water with sugar and bring to a gentle boil. Stir to dissolve sugar and remove from heat.

2. In a blender, combine remaining 3 cups (750 mL) water with chopped lemongrass leaves and add warm sugar syrup. Blend at high speed until water is intensely green and lemongrass leaves are reduced to a fine, aromatic mush, 1 to 2 minutes. Stop once or twice to scrape down sides and grind lemongrass evenly. Strain through a fine-mesh sieve into a pitcher, discarding the residue in the sieve.

3. Let cool and then chill for up to 1 day. To serve, fill tall glasses with ice cubes and fill with lemongrass drink. Serve at once.

Basic Recipes

Red Curry Paste 180

Green Curry Paste 182

Yellow Curry Paste 184

Mussamun Curry Paste 186

Quick-and-Simple Curry Paste 188

Everyday Vegetable Stock. 189

Asian Vegetable Stock 190

Tamarind Liquid 191

Mushroom Mince 192

Wheatballs 194

Fresh Coconuts for Coconut Milk
and Grated Coconut 196

Roasted Rice Powder 198

Toasted Coconut. 199

Pressed or Firm Tofu 200

Seasoned Tofu 201

Salty Eggs 202

Crispy Garlic in Oil 203

Roasted Chile Paste. 204

Sweet and Hot Garlic Sauce 206

Tangy Tamarind Sauce 207

Chile-Vinegar Sauce 208

Red Chile Purée 209

Sriracha Sauce 210

Roasted Tomato-Chile Sauce 211

Basic Recipes

IN THIS CHAPTER ARE RECIPES FOR PREPARATIONS YOU WILL NEED to cook the dishes in this book. Look here for instruction on making curry pastes and coconut milk from scratch, as well as for Roasted Rice Powder, Toasted Coconut and other ingredients called for throughout the book. You will also find a fantastic array of sauces, including Roasted Chile Paste, Tangy Tamarind Sauce and Sweet and Hot Garlic Sauce. In some cases you can purchase a shortcut, such as canned or frozen unsweetened coconut milk and chile garlic sauce. In other cases you will need to rely on these basic recipes or improvise a substitute on your own.

Vegetarian cooks have an extra incentive for taking the time to make their curry pastes from scratch, since shrimp paste, known in Thailand as *gapi,* is a basic ingredient in traditional Southeast Asian curry pastes and is included in almost all the commercial pastes imported from Thailand or made in the Thai manner. Homemade curry paste offers a great return on the time and energy you spend transforming my recipes into jars of flavor-filled curry paste standing by in your kitchen. You will need such uncommon ingredients as lemongrass, galanga, wild lime peel and cilantro roots, although you can make a good adapted version by substituting widely available items for these Asian treasures. You must chop it all and pound or grind it into a paste, which takes time and elbow grease, whether you use a blender, food processor or Thai-style mortar and pestle. Although most of the commercial curry pastes are of good quality, the fruit of your labors in grinding your own from scratch will be worlds better than anything you can buy.

Thai curry pastes call for lemongrass, galanga, wild lime peel and wild lime leaves, which have a sturdy, often fibrous texture that is difficult to chew. For this reason, Thai cooks add them to soups and stews in large pieces to infuse their flavor and aroma into the food. These pieces may be fished out or left in a dish, where they are clearly not to be eaten. Sometimes these herbs are minced or very thinly sliced before they are added to a dish. For curry paste, they are ground beyond recognition. A large food processor chops curry paste ingredients into bits that are small but still unpleasant to eat. If you prefer to use a large food processor, check the texture of the finished paste and if it is still too coarse, consider finishing off the batch of curry paste with a whirl in the blender. If you add water to help with grinding, your paste will be softer and moister and tend to separate a little as it stands. Give it a stir before you use it.

If you make your own curry pastes, you will benefit from the fact that they keep well in the refrigerator or freezer and have many uses beyond the basic Thai curry made with coconut milk. Consider making several pastes at once, since the basic ingredients are the same, with variations only in the type of chile and inclusion of certain spices. Even more important, take the authentic Thai step of recruiting help in the form of extra hands and good company to lighten the burden of cooking alone. In exchange for a portion of the curry paste or a curry feast, you will probably have a flock of volunteers.

Red Curry Paste

Red curry paste takes its name from the dried red chiles peppers that set it on fire. Thais use hot chiles known collectively as prik haeng, *which simply means "dried chiles." You can find dried red chiles in cellophane bags and sometimes loose in Asian markets. I often use the chiles sold in many supermarkets alongside ingredients for cooking Mexican food. Chiles de árbol or chiles japones will work nicely in this recipe. You can also experiment with a combination of large and small dried red chiles, keeping in mind that the smaller chiles are the hottest.*

MAKES ABOUT 1 CUP (250 ML)

Tip
For tips on making the paste, see chapter introduction (page 178).

♦ Mini food processor or mortar and pestle

20	dried red finger-length chiles such as *chiles de árbol* or *chiles japones*	20
1 tbsp	whole coriander seeds	15 mL
1 tsp	whole cumin seeds	5 mL
10	white or black peppercorns or 1 tsp (5 mL) freshly ground black pepper	10
3	stalks lemongrass	3
¼ cup	coarsely chopped fresh cilantro roots or leaves and stems	60 mL
¼ cup	coarsely chopped shallots	60 mL
2 tbsp	coarsely chopped garlic (8 to 12 cloves)	30 mL
1 tbsp	coarsely chopped peeled fresh galanga or fresh gingerroot	15 mL
1 tsp	finely minced fresh wild lime peel or domestic lime peel	5 mL
1 tsp	salt	5 mL

1. Stem chiles and shake out and discard most of the seeds. Break into large pieces. Place chiles in a small bowl, add warm water to cover and set aside to soften, about 20 minutes.

2. In a small dry skillet over medium heat, fry coriander seeds until darkened a shade or two, shaking pan or stirring often, 2 to 3 minutes. Tip out onto a saucer. Toast cumin seeds in same way, until darkened and fragrant, 1 to 2 minutes. Add to saucer along with peppercorns. In a mini processor or mortar and pestle, grind the three spices to a fine powder. Set aside.

Tip
You can substitute the same amount of ground spices, dry-frying the ground coriander and cumin together for a minute or two, stirring often to prevent burning and then combining with ground pepper.

3. For lemongrass, trim away and discard any root section below bulb base and cut away top portion, leaving a stalk about 6 inches (15 cm) long, including base. Remove any dried, wilted and yellowed leaves. Finely chop stalk.

4. Drain chiles. In a blender or mini food processor, combine chiles, lemongrass, ground toasted spices, cilantro, shallots, garlic, galanga, lime peel and salt and grind to a fairly smooth purée, stopping often to scrape down sides and adding a few tbsp (30 mL) of water as needed to move the blades. Transfer to a jar, seal airtight and store at room temperature for up to 1 day or refrigerate for up to 1 month.

Green Curry Paste

Green curry paste takes its name from the vibrant color of the fresh hot chile peppers from which it is made, rather than from the color of the finished paste and curry, which are an earthy brown with a greenish tinge. I like the idea of green curry actually being green, so I sometimes grind in ½ cup (125 mL) or so of fresh cilantro leaves or even Italian parsley, to give it a burst of emerald color. Thais make this with the petite, pointy chile peppers called prik kii-noo *or Thai bird's eye chiles. Available in Asian markets, they are among the world's hottest peppers. I like to use chopped fresh serranos or jalapeños, since they are easy to come by and plenty hot for a fiery curry paste.*

**MAKES ABOUT
1 CUP (250 ML)**

Tip
For tips on making the paste, see chapter introduction (page 178).

♦ Mini food processor or mortar and pestle

5	fresh green serrano chiles, 4 fresh green jalapeños or 10 fresh green Thai bird's eye chiles	5
1 tbsp	whole coriander seeds	15 mL
1 tsp	whole cumin seeds	5 mL
5	white or black peppercorns or ½ tsp (2 mL) freshly ground black pepper	5
3	stalks lemongrass	3
¼ cup	coarsely chopped fresh cilantro roots or leaves and stems	60 mL
¼ cup	coarsely chopped shallots	60 mL
2 tbsp	coarsely chopped garlic (8 to 12 cloves)	30 mL
1 tbsp	coarsely chopped peeled fresh galanga or gingerroot	15 mL
1 tsp	finely minced fresh wild lime peel or domestic lime peel	5 mL
1 tsp	salt	5 mL

1. Stem chiles, chop coarsely and set aside. In a small dry skillet over medium heat, fry coriander seeds until darkened a shade or two, shaking pan or stirring often, 2 to 3 minutes. Tip out onto a saucer. Toast cumin seeds in same way, until darkened and fragrant, 1 to 2 minutes. Add to saucer along with peppercorns. In a mini processor or mortar and pestle, grind the three spices to a fine powder. Set aside. To use ground spices, see Tip, right.

Tip
You can substitute the same amount of ground spices, dry-frying the ground coriander and cumin together for a minute or two, stirring often to prevent burning and then combining with ground pepper.

2. For lemongrass, trim away and discard any root section below bulb base and cut away top portion, leaving a stalk about 6 inches (15 cm) long, including base. Remove any dried, wilted and yellowed leaves. Finely chop stalk.

3. In a blender or mini food processor, combine lemongrass, chopped chiles, ground toasted spices, cilantro, shallots, galanga, lime peel and salt and grind to a fairly smooth purée, stopping often to scrape down sides and adding 2 tbsp (30 mL) of water as needed to move the blades. Transfer to a jar, seal airtight and store at room temperature for up to 1 day or refrigerate for up to 1 month.

Yellow Curry Paste

Yellow curry paste is red curry paste with a little less heat and the addition of pong kah-ree, *which is the standard curry powder we know in the West. It also includes extra turmeric, ginger's most colorful cousin and a regular component of curry powder. Like King Midas, turmeric turns everything it touches gold. Since gold is an auspicious color throughout Asia, turmeric is often used to transform plain food into an inviting dish with a handsome golden sheen.*

**MAKES ABOUT
1 CUP (250 ML)**

Tip

For tips on making the paste, see chapter introduction (page 178).

♦ Mini food processor or mortar and pestle

15	dried red finger-length chiles such as *chiles de árbol* or *chiles japones*	15
1 tbsp	whole coriander seeds	15 mL
1 tsp	whole cumin seeds	5 mL
10	white or black peppercorns or 1 tsp (5 mL) freshly ground black pepper	10
3	stalks lemongrass	3
¼ cup	coarsely chopped fresh cilantro roots or leaves and stems	60 mL
¼ cup	coarsely chopped shallots	60 mL
2 tbsp	coarsely chopped garlic (8 to 12 cloves)	30 mL
1 tbsp	coarsely chopped peeled fresh galanga or fresh gingerroot	15 mL
1 tsp	finely minced fresh wild lime peel or domestic lime peel	5 mL
1 tbsp	curry powder	15 mL
1 tsp	ground turmeric	5 mL
1 tsp	salt	5 mL

1. Stem chiles and shake out and discard most of the seeds. Break into large pieces. Place chiles in a small bowl, add warm water to cover and set aside to soften, about 20 minutes.

2. In a small dry skillet over medium heat, fry coriander seeds until darkened a shade or two, shaking pan or stirring often, 2 to 3 minutes. Tip out onto a saucer. Toast cumin seeds in same way, until darkened and fragrant, 1 to 2 minutes. Add to saucer along with peppercorns. In a mini processor or mortar and pestle, grind the three spices to a fine powder. Set aside. To use ground spices, see Tip, right.

3. For lemongrass, trim away and discard any root section below bulb base and cut away top portion, leaving a stalk about 6 inches (15 cm) long, including base. Remove any dried, wilted and yellowed leaves. Finely chop stalk.

4. Drain chiles. In a blender or mini food processor, combine chiles, lemongrass, ground toasted spices, cilantro, shallots, garlic, galanga, lime peel, curry powder, turmeric and salt and grind to a fairly smooth purée, stopping often to scrape down sides and adding 2 tbsp (30 mL) of water as needed to move the blades. Transfer to a jar, seal airtight and store at room temperature for up to 1 day or refrigerate for up to 1 month.

Mussamun Curry Paste

Mussamun *means "Muslim style," and this curry paste is used for making a popular curry that originated in the provinces of southern Thailand where many Thais follow the teachings of Islam. This classic variation on red curry paste includes heavenly spices such as cinnamon, cardamom, nutmeg and cloves. The finished curry is a luscious, spicy stew of coconut milk seasoned with this curry paste and studded with peanuts, cinnamon sticks and cardamom pods.*

MAKES ABOUT 1 CUP (250 ML)

Tip

For tips on making the paste, see chapter introduction (page 178).

* Mini food processor or mortar and pestle

15	dried red finger-length chiles such as *chiles de árbol* or *chiles japones*	15
1 tbsp	whole coriander seeds	15 mL
1 tsp	whole cumin seeds	5 mL
10	white or black peppercorns or 1 tsp (5 mL) freshly ground black pepper	10
3	stalks lemongrass	3
¼ cup	coarsely chopped fresh cilantro roots or leaves and stems	60 mL
¼ cup	coarsely chopped shallots	60 mL
2 tbsp	coarsely chopped garlic (8 to 12 cloves)	30 mL
1 tbsp	coarsely chopped peeled fresh galanga or fresh gingerroot	15 mL
1 tsp	finely minced fresh wild lime peel or domestic lime peel	5 mL
1 tsp	ground cinnamon	5 mL
1 tsp	ground cloves	5 mL
1 tsp	ground nutmeg	5 mL
1 tsp	ground cardamom	5 mL
1 tsp	salt	5 mL

1. Stem chiles and shake out and discard most of the seeds. Break into large pieces. Place chiles in a small bowl, add warm water to cover and set aside to soften, about 20 minutes.

Tip

You can substitute the same amount of ground spices, dry-frying the ground coriander and cumin together for a minute or two, stirring often to prevent burning and then combining with ground pepper.

2. In a small dry skillet over medium heat, fry coriander seeds until darkened a shade or two, shaking pan or stirring often, 2 to 3 minutes. Tip out onto a saucer. Toast cumin seeds in same way, until darkened and fragrant, 1 to 2 minutes. Add to saucer along with peppercorns. In a mini processor or mortar and pestle, grind the three spices to a fine powder. Set aside. To use ground spices, see Tip, left.

3. For lemongrass, trim away and discard any root section below bulb base and cut away top portion, leaving a stalk about 6 inches (15 cm) long, including base. Remove any dried, wilted and yellowed leaves. Finely chop stalk.

4. Drain chiles. In a blender or mini processor, combine chiles, lemongrass, ground toasted spices, cilantro, shallots, garlic, galanga, lime peel, cinnamon, cloves, nutmeg, cardamom and salt and grind to a fairly smooth purée, stopping often to scrape down sides and adding 2 tbsp (30 mL) of water as needed to move the blades. Transfer to a jar, seal airtight and store at room temperature for up to 1 day or refrigerate for up to 1 month.

Quick-and-Simple Curry Paste

Here is my stripped down version of Thai curry paste, using ingredients available in many supermarkets. Make it in a flash and then turn a few spoonfuls of your freshly made paste into tonight's pot of curry. This will work in any recipe calling for a Thai-style paste.

MAKES ABOUT 1 CUP (250 ML)

♦ Blender or mini food processor

5	fresh serrano chiles, 3 fresh green jalapeños or 7 long, slender dried red chiles	5
1 cup	coarsely chopped cilantro leaves and stems	250 mL
½ cup	chopped onion	125 mL
⅓ cup	coarsely chopped peeled fresh gingerroot	75 mL
¼ cup	chopped garlic (15 to 20 cloves)	60 mL
1 tbsp	grated lime zest	15 mL
1 tbsp	ground coriander	15 mL
1 tsp	ground cumin	5 mL
1 tsp	freshly ground black pepper	5 mL
1 tsp	salt	5 mL

1. Stem chiles and discard some of the seeds. Chop fresh chiles coarsely. Soak dried chiles in hot water to cover, about 10 minutes.

2. Drain dried chiles, if using. In a blender or mini processor, combine chiles, cilantro, onion, ginger, garlic, lime zest, coriander, cumin, black pepper and salt and grind to a fine, fairly smooth purée, stopping often to scrape down sides and adding a few tbsp (30 mL) of water as needed to move the blades. Transfer to a jar, seal airtight and keep in the refrigerator for up to 2 weeks.

Everyday Vegetable Stock

Make up a batch of this simple stock and keep it on hand for Thai soups or any recipe calling for vegetable stock. You can add other vegetables if you like. It is best to avoid sweet peppers, eggplant, celery leaves and the members of the cabbage family such as broccoli, cauliflower and kale, as these vegetables do not take well to long simmering. If you have freezer space, make a double batch so that you will have a half gallon or so on hand.

**MAKES ABOUT
5 CUPS (1.25 L)**

Tip

You can freeze this stock in airtight containers for 2 months. Freeze in 1- or 2-cup (250 or 500 mL) portions so that you can defrost only the amount you need for a given recipe. Freeze some in ice cube trays, too, and then transfer to a resealable bag. You will then have portions of 1 tbsp (15 mL) available as well.

4	large carrots (about 1 lb/500 g)	4
6	stalks celery without leaves	6
2	onions	2
1	bunch fresh parsley	1
1	head garlic	1
10 cups	water	2½ L
1 tbsp	soy sauce	15 mL
½ tsp	salt	2 mL

1. Coarsely chop carrots, celery, onions and parsley and combine in a large stockpot. Cut garlic head in half crosswise to expose cloves and add to stockpot along with water. Bring to a rolling boil over medium heat. Boil for about 5 minutes as you skim away and discard any scum that rises to the top. Reduce heat to maintain a gentle boil and simmer, uncovered, stirring occasionally, for 1½ hours.

2. Remove from heat and strain through a fine-mesh sieve into a clean container. Stir in soy sauce and salt. Let cool to room temperature, cover and refrigerate for up to 4 days.

Asian Vegetable Stock

Here is a vegetable stock fortified with the deep, earthy flavor of dried Chinese mushrooms and a pleasing jolt of fresh ginger. You can use it for Thai vegetarian dishes or for any other recipe calling for vegetable stock. Use other vegetables if you like, but avoid sweet peppers, eggplant, celery leaves and members of the cabbage family such as broccoli, cauliflower and kale, as these do not take well to long simmering.

MAKES 7 TO 8 CUPS (1.75 TO 2 L)

Tip

You can freeze this stock in airtight containers for 2 months. Freeze in 1- or 2-cup (250 or 500 mL) portions so that you can defrost only the amount you need for a given recipe. Freeze some in ice cube trays, too, and then transfer to a resealable bag. You will then have portions of 1 tbsp (15 mL) available as well.

4	large carrots (about 1 lb/500 g)	4
6	stalks celery without leaves	6
2	onions or 10 shallots	2
½	bunch fresh cilantro	½
1	bunch green onions	1
2	heads garlic	2
3	thumb-size hunks fresh gingerroot	3
5	dried shiitake mushrooms or Chinese mushrooms	5
10 cups	water	2½ L
1 tbsp	soy sauce	15 mL
1 tsp	salt	5 mL

1. Coarsely chop carrots, celery, onions, cilantro and green onions and combine in a large stockpot. Cut garlic heads in half crosswise to expose cloves and slice ginger crosswise into coins. Add to stockpot along with dried mushrooms and water. Bring to a rolling boil over medium heat. Boil for about 5 minutes as you skim away and discard any scum that rises to the top. Reduce heat to maintain a gentle boil and simmer, uncovered, stirring occasionally, for 1½ hours.

2. Remove from heat and strain through a fine-mesh sieve into a clean container. Stir in soy sauce and salt. Let cool to room temperature, cover and refrigerate for up to 4 days.

Tamarind Liquid

Thai cooks make frequent use of this liquid, pressed from the fruit of the tamarind tree. Its flavor is fabulous, sharp and fruity, sweet and smoky, like a marriage of raisins and limes. You can use fresh ripe tamarind pods if you find them in the market, but the mahogany-colored 1-lb (500 g) bricks of tamarind pulp, minimally processed to remove the tamarind's brittle peel and many of its seeds, work just as well and taste great with less mess. You handle both of them the same way.

MAKES ABOUT 1 CUP (250 ML)

½ cup	tamarind pulp	125 mL
1 cup	warm water	250 mL

1. Place sticky, gooey tamarind pulp in a small bowl and add warm water. Let stand, poking and mashing occasionally with your fingers or a spoon to break the sticky lump into pieces and help dissolve, 20 to 30 minutes.

2. Pour tamarind pulp and water through a fine-mesh sieve into another bowl. Use your fingers or back of a spoon to work tamarind pulp well, pressing softened pulp against sieve to extract as much thick brown liquid as you can. Scrape outside of sieve often to capture the thick purée that accumulates there. Discard pulp, fibers and seeds that have collected in sieve and thin tamarind liquid with water as needed until about consistency of pea soup or softly whipped cream.

3. Use as directed in recipes or seal airtight and refrigerate for up to 3 days. It sours and sharpens as it stands, so if it has stood for several days, taste and adjust flavor with some sugar.

Tips

If you want to use fresh tamarind rather than prepared tamarind pulp, be sure you have ripe, not young green tamarind. The latter is prized by Southeast Asians for its ferociously sour flavor; it is hard and smooth outside and a pale cream color with a greenish tinge inside. Fresh ripe tamarind looks tired, with its thin, brittle, cocoa-colored peel cracking and exposing its raisiny-brown flesh to the world.

There is no excellent substitute for tamarind, but you could get by using freshly squeezed lime juice, softened with a little and sugar, honey or molasses, to impart a sweet-sour flavor.

Several Thai companies now market a prepared tamarind liquid, which is more like a purée in texture and good enough to stand in for the freshly made tamarind liquid. Keep it airtight and refrigerated, just as you would your own batch, for several days.

❀ *Thai Tales*

Tamarind trees are large, graceful hardwoods that flourish throughout Thailand, but particularly in the northern and northeastern regions. Their trunks are cut crosswise into thick disks to provide the standard cutting board for traditional Thai kitchens. I remember bicycling to the market early in the morning, under a canopy of their generous branches. My neighbors' children often shouted greetings from on high, hidden from my view by the tamarind tree's lacy leaves and the profusion of J-shaped beanlike pods enclosing its tangy, sweet-sour fruit.

Mushroom Mince

You will find this delicious mixture used in recipes throughout this book whenever a rich, garlicky filling is needed. I based it on the classic French mushroom concoction called duxelles, *fortifying it with tofu and revving up the flavors with garlic, cilantro and Asian seasonings. It keeps well for 2 days in the refrigerator and freezes beautifully for up to 1 month. Double the recipe if you like and if you have any left over, enjoy it as you would Italian pesto.*

MAKES ABOUT 1 CUP (250 ML)

- ♦ Mini food processor

2 tbsp	coarsely chopped garlic (8 to 12 cloves)	30 mL
1 tbsp	coarsely chopped cilantro root or cilantro stems and leaves	15 mL
½ tsp	freshly ground black pepper	2 mL
8 oz	fresh button mushrooms, chopped	250 g
4 oz	firm tofu	125 g
3 tbsp	vegetable oil, divided	45 mL
2 tbsp	minced shallots	30 mL
1 tbsp	palm sugar or brown sugar	15 mL
1 tbsp	water	15 mL
2 tsp	regular soy sauce	10 mL
½ tsp	dark soy sauce	2 mL
½ tsp	salt	2 mL

1. In mini processor, combine garlic, cilantro and pepper and grind to a fairly smooth paste. Set aside. (Or combine garlic and cilantro in a Thai-style mortar along with ¼ tsp/1 mL whole peppercorns instead of ground pepper. Pound and grind to a fairly smooth paste.)

2. Chop mushrooms until reduced to a crumbly pile and set aside. Chop tofu into tiny cubes and set aside as well.

3. In a skillet over medium heat, warm 2 tbsp (30 mL) of the oil until a bit of mushroom added to pan sizzles at once, about 1 minute. Add garlic-cilantro paste and toss until fragrant and shiny, 2 to 3 minutes.

4. Add mushrooms and cook, tossing often, for 5 to 7 minutes. The mushrooms will soften, release their liquid and brown as they cook. When liquid has cooked away and mushrooms are shiny and tender, scrape to sides of pan and add remaining 1 tbsp (15 mL) of oil to the center. Add tofu and shallots and toss until thoroughly combined with mushrooms and heated through, about 1 minute. Add sugar, water, regular and dark soy sauces and salt and cook, tossing often, until mixture is moist, evenly colored and well combined, 2 to 3 minutes. Remove from heat, let cool to room temperature and refrigerate in a tightly covered container until needed.

Wheatballs

This recipe is my adaptation of Madhur Jaffrey's recipe for wheat gluten balls, which appears in her classic cookbook, Madhur Jaffrey's World-of-the-East Vegetarian Cooking. Wheatballs are terrific little fritters that seem born to enhance Thai stir-fries and curries. You can use almost any wheat flour, keeping in mind that the greater the gluten content, the easier your task of extracting the gluten and the more pleasing your results will be (see Tips, below). Plan ahead, as the dough needs to soak overnight before you squeeze out the starch and cook it up into balls.

MAKES ABOUT 48 WHEATBALLS

Tips

Gluten flour or bread flour is best for creating chewy-tender little pillows that take on curry flavors with delicious ease. Whole-wheat flour works well and browns beautifully, although like whole-wheat bread, its balls are sturdier and chewier than those made with high-gluten white flour. All-purpose flour is acceptable, but cake flour is too delicate for this task and flours made from anything other than wheat will not work at all.

You will need a gallon or so of clean water in which to rinse the dough, so consider pouring it off into a bucket and anointing your garden with this starchy white water while your gluten relaxes in the strainer.

- ◆ Baking sheet, lined with paper towels
- ◆ Asian-style wire strainer or 2 metal slotted spoons
- ◆ Candy/deep-fry thermometer

3 cups	flour (see Tips, left)	750 mL
1 tsp	salt	5 mL
1 cup	water	250 mL
	Vegetable oil for deep-frying	

1. In a large bowl, combine flour and salt and mix well. Pour water over flour and using your hands combine everything into a soft dough that pulls cleanly away from sides of bowl and is not sticky. Transfer to a lightly floured board and knead for about 10 minutes. Cover with a clean kitchen towel and let rest for about 1 hour.

2. Knead dough again for about 1 minute and then place in a small, deep bowl and add cold water to cover. Let stand 6 to 8 hours or for up to overnight.

3. Drain off water and place bowl in sink. Add enough fresh water to cover dough and work it as you would a sponge, squeezing and wringing it to extract starch and leave behind a rubbery, squishy, slippery, fibrous mass of gluten. Squeeze dough through 3 batches of water, which will turn milk white with the starch and then place ball of gluten in a strainer to rest and drain for about 10 minutes.

You can bake the wheatballs, rather than fry them. Arrange on a lightly greased baking sheet and bake at 375°F (190°C), turning once early on to discourage sticking and encourage browning, 15 to 20 minutes. Use and store as directed for fried wheatballs. I find them inferior to fried ones, however, because they puff less, brown unevenly and have a tough, hard texture.

Check the Asian market or Resources (page 230) for an array of wheat gluten products, from soft wheatballs packed in seasoned oil or broth, to mock duck and other imitation meat products molded into particular shapes and textures, to firm hunks of wheat gluten that you can cut into any shape you desire. You will also find wheat gluten in health food stores, often in the refrigerator case alongside tofu and tempeh.

4. Divide squishy dough into 1-inch (2.5 cm) lumps and set aside on a tray. Place prepared baking sheet near stove along with a long-handled Asian-style wire strainer or 2 metal slotted spoons. Fill a small bowl with water to keep your fingers moist while transferring sticky dough from tray to skillet.

5. Pour oil into a wok or large, deep skillet to a depth of 3 inches (7.5 cm). Place over medium heat until oil is hot but not smoking. The oil is ready when a bit of dough dropped into it sizzles at once. (The oil should register 325° to 350°F/160° to 180°C on the thermometer.) Moisten your fingers and then carefully add 5 to 7 balls to oil. Let cook, gently stirring to keep separate and to keep tiny waves of oil flowing over them, turning at least once to brown evenly, about 3 minutes. The balls will swell, blister, puff up and out and begin to darken. When ready, they will be appealingly asymmetrical fritters, crusty and golden brown. Scoop out these little clouds, hold briefly over oil to drain and then transfer to prepared baking sheet to drain and cool. Continue until all dough is cooked.

6. When balls are cool, use in recipes as directed or seal airtight and refrigerate for 3 days or freeze for about 1 month. Use frozen balls in recipes directly from the freezer; do not thaw first.

Fresh Coconuts for Coconut Milk and Grated Coconut

This is trouble, in terms of the physical effort you spend to open and grate the coconut and the mess it leaves in its wake. Most days I avail myself of the ease of unsweetened coconut milk in canned or frozen form. Both work well and save a tremendous amount of time and work; I would seldom enjoy coconut milk if I had to make it from scratch every time. But there is something that I love about fresh coconut and there are times when it seems like another job that gives back more than takes away. If you should be so inspired, see instructions below on how to handle a coconut. Select a dry, brown hairy coconut heavy with juice that sloshes when you shake the nut.

MAKES ABOUT 4 CUPS (1 L) GRATED COCONUT AND 4 CUPS (1 L) COCONUT MILK

Tip

When making coconut milk, I like to combine the grated coconut and the water in a blender and blend it for a minute or two before squeezing out the milk, for a somewhat richer yield.

◆ Large food processor

1	coconut	1

Cracking coconut

1. Place coconut on a baking sheet on a counter or a table and have a hammer handy. If possible, do this outside so that the inevitable mess of hairy fibers and bits of shell will be a gift to Mother Earth and not a clean up job for you. Examine coconut and note teardrop shape, with three eyes on the rounded bottom of the drop. Note also the faint ridges that run from between this trio of eyes all the way up the coconut, intersecting at the pointed tip. Picture the coconut as a hairy little globe, with a pointy north pole and a triple-eyed south pole and an equator encircling its fattest part.

2. Nestle coconut in your palm with pointed tip aiming away from you and the three eyes facing toward your tummy. Aim your hammer at the point on the coconut's equator closest to you and strike a mighty blow. Continue giving it whacks around the equator, striking on one of the three aforementioned ridge lines whenever possible, as these are weak points where cracking may occur first.

3. Listen for a change in the sounds your mighty blows create and you will know when you have struck home by a deep, ringing thud as the first crack opens. Keep striking until clear juice gushes out and coconut shell breaks open or can be separated into two or more pieces. Do not despair if you do not get results at once. It can take one or two blows or several trips around the nut, depending on the particular coconut and your aim and confidence. Practice helps, so do it

Tip

Most books instruct you to pierce the coconut, drain out its juice and then bake it in a hot oven for a while to crack its shell. The coconut-loving people of the world do not traditionally have ovens and they have cracked coconuts in a straightforward way for many generations. I not only prefer to omit the oven step for sentimental reasons, but I also find it extra trouble, because you must poke a hole, shake out the juice and then deal with a hot, hairy coconut, only to arrive at the very same step of having at it with a hammer to crack it open. The hot oven does get the crack started for you, however, if the prospect of striking mighty hammer blows to split open a hard, brown hairy globe is not something you want to do.

often if you want to become handy with this everyday Asian task. Thais discard the clear juice from inside the coconut, but I like to strain it well through a fine-mesh sieve or a coffee filter and use it in cooking sweets or add to juice drinks.

4. Once you have opened the coconut, use hammer to break into pieces smaller than palm of your hand. Using a blunt table knife, pry thick white meat away from the hard, dark brown hairy outer shell. Discard hard shells and retain chunks of white meat, which have a thin brown skin on the side that was attached to the shell. You can leave this on or peel off. Left on, it will give the coconut milk a pleasant cream color; peeling it will yield pure white milk. Thais peel it if they feel fancy and leave it if they do not, as taste is not affected either way. To peel it, you need either a special sturdy peeler made for this purpose and found in some Asian markets. Or you can use a paring knife or chef's knife, working carefully on the cutting board.

Grating coconut

1. Chop coconut meat into $\frac{1}{2}$-inch (1 cm) chunks. In a large food processor with metal blade, with machine running, drop coconut chunks through large feed tube onto blade, stopping to scrape down sides once or twice, until workbowl is full of soft, moist grated coconut. You should have about 4 cups (1 L) finely grated coconut.

2. You can also leave coconut meat in large pieces and grate by hand on a box grater, taking great care to avoid scraping your knuckles as each piece becomes small. Or leave coconut in two bowl-shaped halves and use a claw-bladed hand-held grater or stool-mounted coconut grater, both found in Asian markets, to scrape the white meat from the shell.

Making coconut milk

1. Place grated coconut in a bowl and add about 3 cups (750 mL) warm water. Squeeze with your hands to mix well and let stand for about 15 minutes. Then place a fine-mesh sieve over a bowl and pour coconut mixture through it. Squeeze grated coconut left behind in strainer well, to extract as much white coconut milk as you can. Use at once or cover and refrigerate for up to 2 days. You should have about 4 cups (1 L) unsweetened coconut milk.

Roasted Rice Powder

This crunchy, rustic condiment adds a toasty flavor and textural spark to Issahn-style dishes. In the Pahk Issahn region, located in Thailand's northeast, cooks roast a handful of raw sticky rice in a dry wok and then pound it to a sandy powder for the hearty, hot and spicy salads known as yum. *Long-grain sticky rice is the standard choice, but any raw white rice will work well. Since their flavor and aroma fade quickly once they are ground, I store the roasted grains whole and grind them as needed. If you like, however, you can grind it all and store the powder in an airtight container away from heat and light.*

**MAKES ABOUT
¼ CUP (60 ML)**

- Mortar and pestle or coffee or spice grinder

¼ cup	long-grain sticky rice or other white rice	60 mL

1. In a small dry skillet over high heat, fry rice grains until a wheaty golden brown, 3 to 5 minutes. Shake pan back and forth frequently to turn grains and color evenly. Remove from heat and set aside. When rice is cool, transfer to a jar, seal tightly and keep at room temperature until needed.

2. To use in recipes, transfer roasted grains to a heavy mortar and pound with a pestle to a fine, sandy powder. Or, using on-off pulses, grind in a coffee grinder or spice grinder, until rice powder is fairly smooth but still boasts something of a rough texture and an interesting degree of crunch.

Toasted Coconut

This condiment is used in traditional salads and snacks such as Delectable Lettuce Bites (page 28) and Kao Yum Rice Salad, Southern-Style (page 58). In these build-your-own savory dishes, toasted coconut gives a deep, sweet crunch to a rainbow of ingredients bound together with a sweet and tangy sauce.

MAKES 1 CUP (250 ML)

Tip

I like to use the easy-to-find sweetened, shredded coconut available in the baking section in supermarkets, since toasted coconut is used in dishes with a strong sweet note. You could also used the unsweetened grated or shredded coconut that is sold in health food stores or crack open and grate a coconut (page 196). Note that unsweetened coconut, freshly grated or not, will take a little longer to brown than the sweetened coconut, since the sugar caramelizes more quickly.

| 1 cup | sweetened shredded dried coconut (see Tip, left) | 250 mL |

1. Set a plate near the stove where the toasted coconut can cool. In a small dry skillet over medium heat, fry coconut until lightly browned and fragrant, 3 to 5 minutes. Toss often as it browns, to color evenly and discourage it from burning. When rich brown with white-to-brown specks remaining, transfer to plate and let cool to room temperature. Use as directed or seal in an airtight container and store at room temperature away from heat and light for up to 1 week.

Pressed or Firm Tofu

If you have exquisite, silken tofu on hand and need to transform it into something that is sturdy enough to stir-fry or boil without crumbling to mush, here is a simple, speedy technique. The resulting tofu will lose its straight, organized shape in the process, along with up to half its weight in water, so buy twice the amount of tofu you will need after it is pressed. You can use the pressed tofu in recipes calling for firm tofu, although it will be a good bit sturdier and flatter than the firm tofu available in grocery stores.

**MAKES
8 OZ (250 G)
PRESSED TOFU**

| 1 lb | soft tofu | 500 g |

1. Cut block of tofu in half both horizontally and vertically, so you have 4 smaller blocks. Cover a plate with a clean kitchen towel folded in half. Center a second kitchen towel, unfolded, on top of the first towel and arrange tofu blocks in center. Fold in towel to enclose tofu and then put a second plate of about the same size on top. Place a heavy weight on the plate, such as a teakettle filled with water or a few heavy cans. Place this makeshift press in a spot where it will remain balanced and steady. Let stand for a few minutes or an hour, depending on how sturdy and flat you want the tofu to be. The longer the time, the firmer and flatter the tofu.

2. When tofu is ready, remove weight and top plate. Unwrap the now-damp towel enclosing tofu (the towel will have absorbed the water given up by the soft tofu). Transfer pads of pressed tofu to a plate. Use at once or cover and refrigerate, either as is or immersed in water. Use within 2 days.

Seasoned Tofu

Many forms of tofu are widely available, from silken bricks floating in water to very firm soy sauce-seasoned blocks, fried tofu and dried tofu skin. You can find seasoned or firm baked tofu in most Asian markets; here is a way to make your own at home. The flavor is mild, but the mahogany color is an appealing change from the standard pale product and it can be used in lieu of firm tofu in any recipe.

MAKES ABOUT 2 CUPS (500 ML)

Tip

The dark soy sauce provides a depth of color more than flavor, so if you do not have it, you can still make seasoned tofu in a lighter shade of brown.

2 tbsp	Vegetable Stock (pages 189 and 190) or store-bought	30 mL
2 tsp	regular soy sauce	10 mL
1 tsp	dark soy sauce (see Tip, left)	5 mL
½ tsp	granulated sugar	2 mL
¼ tsp	salt	1 mL
8 oz	firm tofu, cut into ½-inch (1 cm) pieces (about 2 cups/500 mL)	250 g

1. In a medium skillet, combine vegetable stock, regular and dark soy sauces, sugar and salt and stir to mix well. Add tofu and place pan over medium heat and cook until tofu is evenly browned and heated through, 2 to 3 minutes.

2. Remove from heat and let cool to room temperature. Cover and refrigerate for up to 2 days. Use in recipes as you would plain tofu.

Salty Eggs

Thais employ this traditional Chinese method of preserving and flavoring duck and chicken eggs. While salty eggs are widely available in Asian markets, I provide this recipe for those who will need to make their own or will simply enjoy doing so. The eggs shine alongside a hot curry and a tangy dish of Pickled Cabbage (page 62) or pickled garlic.

MAKES 9 EGGS

Tips

If the eggs float to the top of the crock or jar, place a small, clean stone or other weight on top to hold the eggs down in the brine.

You can buy salted eggs in Asian markets. Often you will find them covered with a thick layer of charcoal ash, which is traditionally used to cushion them from one another once they are removed from their salt brine and packed for market in large crocks. Simply soak in cold water for 5 minutes and then rub each egg gently to remove the ash coating without breaking the egg. Cook the eggs as directed in the recipe.

You can also fry the eggs and eat them with Dao Jiow Lone Dipping Sauce with Vegetables (page 30).

4 cups	water	1 L
1 cup	salt	250 mL
9	duck or chicken eggs	9

1. In a medium saucepan over medium heat, combine water and salt, stirring well, and bring to a rolling boil. Boil brine, stirring often, for 1 minute. Remove from heat and let cool to room temperature.

2. Meanwhile, wash eggs gently in cool water and place in a pickling crock or a large jar with a tight-fitting lid. When salt brine has cooled, pour over eggs to immerse completely. Cover jar and set in a cool place for 1 month.

3. To cook eggs, remove number you want from brine and place in a small saucepan. Add water to cover and bring to a rolling boil over medium heat. Reduce heat to maintain a very gentle boil and cook for 9 minutes. Remove from heat, drain well, rinse in cool water and then let cool to room temperature. Peel and cut as desired to serve.

Crispy Garlic in Oil

Thais use a dollop of this simple condiment to light up a steaming bowl of rice noodles in broth. You can also try it in salad dressings and marinades for a pleasing garlic note. It will keep refrigerated in an airtight jar for 2 to 3 days. Be sure to refrigerate it as soon as it has cooled, as garlic in oil spoils quickly when left at room temperature. Or you can make a fresh batch while your soup simmers. Either way, your kitchen will glow with its garlicky aroma and your soups will be enhanced with its toasty perfume and tasty, rustic crunch.

**MAKES ABOUT
¼ CUP (60 ML)**

Tip

Avoid chopping the garlic to a fine mince for this recipe, as that would increase its tendency to burn. Double the recipe if you want a larger batch, but use a larger pan and expect a slight increase in cooking time. The line between heavenly toasting and bitter burning is easy to cross, so stay by the stove as the garlic cooks.

| ¼ cup | vegetable oil | 60 mL |
| 3 tbsp | coarsely chopped garlic | 45 mL |

1. Heat a small skillet briefly over low heat. Add oil and heat until a bit of garlic added to pan sizzles at once, 1 to 2 minutes. Add garlic and stir to separate any clumps. As garlic begins to turn golden and release its perfume, stir gently until half of garlic is a soft, wheaty color, 3 to 4 minutes. Remove from heat and let cool to room temperature.

2. Transfer garlic and fragrant oil to a glass jar with a tight-fitting lid and store in the refrigerator.

Roasted Chile Paste

Nahm prik pao *or "roasted chile paste," is a rustic, spectacularly tasty condiment made from easy-to-find ingredients. The trick to this simple recipe is to keep the herbs on the pleasing side of burnt, while allowing them to blossom into the robust, charred concoction beloved by Thais. Use the chile paste in Tome Yum Soup with Mushrooms and Tofu (page 72), Zucchini and Tofu in Roasted Chile Paste (page 119) and Crispy Rice Cakes (page 44).*

MAKES ABOUT 1¼ CUPS (300 ML)

Tip

This sauce has two incarnations, one as a pure chile shallot–garlic paste roasted in oil and the other as a rich, tangy chile-tamarind paste softened by palm sugar's voluptuous kiss. You can stop after frying the paste and have the former or complete the recipe and have the latter. Either will work in recipes in which *nahm prik pao* is used.

• Mini food processor or blender

½ cup	small dried red chiles such as *chiles de árbol* or *chiles japones* (about 32), stemmed, halved crosswise and loosely packed (see Tips, right)	125 mL
½ cup	unpeeled shallots, cut lengthwise into chunks	125 mL
¼ cup	unpeeled garlic cloves (8 to 10 large cloves)	60 mL
½ cup	vegetable oil, divided	125 mL
3 tbsp	palm sugar or brown sugar	45 mL
3 tbsp	Tamarind Liquid (page 191)	45 mL
1 tbsp	soy sauce	15 mL
1 tsp	salt	5 mL

1. In a wok or a small dry heavy skillet, fry chiles over medium-low heat, shaking pan and stirring frequently, until darkened, fragrant and brittle, 3 to 5 minutes. Remove from heat and transfer to a plate and let cool.

2. Increase heat to medium and dry-fry shallots and garlic, turning occasionally, until softened, wilted and blistered, about 8 minutes. Remove from heat and transfer to plate and let cool.

3. Stem chiles and shake out and discard most of seeds. Crumble chiles into small pieces. Trim shallots and garlic, discarding peel and root ends and chop coarsely. In a mini food processor or blender, combine chiles, shallots and garlic and pulse to a coarse paste, stopping to scrape down sides as needed. Add ¼ cup (60 mL) of the vegetable oil and grind to a fairly smooth paste. Transfer to a small bowl and set aside. You can also do this in a mortar and pestle.

Tips

You can purchase this condiment in Southeast Asian grocery stores, but check the ingredients list. In its traditional form, the seasonings added after frying include fish sauce and dried shrimp.

If you adore fiery food, add more chiles up to $\frac{1}{2}$ cup (125 mL). If you want to cut the heat, you can reduce the amount of chiles to about 2 tbsp (30 mL) coarsely chopped chiles. Handle chiles with care, avoiding touching your eyes and other tender areas for a few hours after handling them. When you are roasting chiles, the fragrant smoke from the pan may make you cough a little.

4. Pour remaining $\frac{1}{4}$ cup (60 mL) of oil into wok or skillet. Place over medium heat until a bit of paste added to pan sizzles at once, about 1 minute. Add ground chile paste and cook, stirring occasionally, until paste gradually darkens and releases a rich fragrance, about 5 minutes. Remove from heat and let cool to room temperature.

5. In a small bowl, combine sugar, tamarind, soy sauce and salt and stir well. Add mixture to cooled chile paste and stir to combine. The paste will be quite oily and must be well stirred before each use. Transfer to a jar, cap tightly and refrigerate for up to 1 month. Use at room temperature in recipes or as a condiment.

❀ Thai Tales

Traditionally this preparation is made by roasting the chiles, shallots and garlic in or over the feisty coals of charcoal stoves used in upcountry kitchens. If you have a lively bed of coals or a good grill, roast or grill the chiles, shallots and garlic to a handsome darkness, turning with tongs or chopsticks before they incinerate.

Sweet and Hot Garlic Sauce

Thais enjoy this simple, delectable sauce with foods that are deep-fried or grilled. Its hot, sharp flavor makes a piquant contrast to the rich crunch of spring rolls and the deep, earthy taste of onions, eggplant and sweet peppers hot off the grill. My friend Charlisa Cato makes this sauce in gallon-sized batches in her Arkansas kitchen so she can have it on hand for sharing with friends.

MAKES ABOUT ¾ CUP (175 ML)

Tips

This sauce keeps well, although it tends to thicken as it stands. Heat it briefly and gently before serving or add a little water if it is too thick.

Chile-garlic sauce is a rust-colored paste of dried red chiles studded with seeds and seasoned with garlic and vinegar. It is widely available in supermarkets and Asian grocery stores. It keeps indefinitely and makes a great addition to your hot-sauce shelf. If you like things hot, increase the amount of chile-garlic sauce used in this recipe. If you do not have chile-garlic sauce, make Red Chile Purée or simply add coarsely chopped dried red chiles or another hot sauce to taste.

1 cup	granulated sugar	250 mL
½ cup	water	125 mL
½ cup	distilled white vinegar	125 mL
2 tbsp	minced garlic	30 mL
1 tsp	salt	5 mL
1 tbsp	chile-garlic sauce or Red Chile Purée (page 209) (see Tips, left)	15 mL

1. In a medium saucepan, combine sugar, water, vinegar, garlic and salt. Bring to a boil over medium heat, stirring until sugar dissolves.

2. Reduce heat to medium-low and simmer until sauce is thickened and syrupy, 18 to 25 minutes. Remove from heat and stir in chile-garlic sauce. Let cool to room temperature. Transfer to a jar and seal airtight. Refrigerate until serving time, then heat gently until thinned to original consistency. Serve at room temperature. It will keep in the refrigerator for up to 3 weeks.

Tangy Tamarind Sauce

This sauce accentuates the natural dance of sweet and sour flavors in tamarind, the dark, rich fruit of the ubiquitous lacy-leafed tamarind trees that grace the kingdom's upcountry landscape. Use it with any deep-fried or grilled foods, against which its sharp, gingery notes make a perfect foil. Add more chile-garlic sauce if you want to fan the culinary flames.

MAKES ABOUT 1 CUP (250 ML)

Variation

You can substitute another hot sauce or hot pepper flakes for the chile-garlic sauce or Red Chile Purée.

♦ Mini food processor or blender

2 tbsp	coarsely chopped garlic (8 to 12 cloves)	30 mL
2 tbsp	coarsely chopped shallots	30 mL
1 tbsp	peeled and coarsely chopped fresh gingerroot	15 mL
1 cup	Tamarind Liquid (page 191)	250 mL
½ cup	palm sugar or brown sugar	125 mL
½ cup	Vegetable Stock (pages 189 and 190) or store-bought	125 mL
2 tbsp	freshly squeezed lime or lemon juice	30 mL
¼ tsp	chile-garlic sauce or Red Chile Purée (page 209) (see Tips, page 209)	1 mL
¼ tsp	salt	1 mL

1. In mini processor or blender, combine garlic, shallots and ginger and grind to a smooth paste, adding a little of the vegetable stock as needed to move the blades. In a small saucepan over medium heat, combine tamarind, sugar and vegetable stock and bring to a gentle boil, stirring often to dissolve sugar and combine well, about 1 minute. Add garlic mixture. Let sauce return to a boil and then cook, stirring often, for 2 minutes more.

2. Remove from heat and stir in lime juice, chile-garlic sauce and salt. Taste and adjust flavors to your liking with a little more lime juice, salt or hot sauce. Let cool to room temperature and serve. Or cover and refrigerate for up to 3 days.

Chile-Vinegar Sauce

Look for this tangy little explosion of flavor on the tables in Thai restaurants that take pride in their noodle dishes. With luck it will be in a little carousel of seasonings known as krueng broong, *which every Thai uses to tailor noodles to his or her taste. You will usually find crushed dried red chiles, white sugar and ground peanuts along with this sauce. Serve with rice and noodle dishes.*

**MAKES ABOUT
½ CUP (125 ML)**

Tip

For extra chile heat, finely chop the chiles and/or increase the amount you use.

½ cup	distilled white vinegar	125 mL
2 tbsp	Vegetable Stock (pages 189 and 190) or store-bought	30 mL
½ tsp	salt	2 mL
10	fresh green chiles such as serrano, jalapeño or Thai bird's eye chiles, thinly sliced crosswise	10

1. In a small bowl, combine vinegar, vegetable stock and salt and stir well to dissolve salt. Stir in chiles. Cover and store at room temperature for a day or so or in the refrigerator for 2 to 3 weeks. Pour into small bowls or tiny saucers to serve, so guests can spoon it on to taste.

Red Chile Purée

Here is a homemade version of chile-garlic sauce, the five-alarm condiment used to set noodles, sauces and other dishes on fire in Southeast Asian cuisine. You will often find it among the table condiments in Asian noodle cafés, along with chiles in white vinegar (page 208), ground dried red chiles, white sugar and ground peanuts. It is often available in supermarkets that boast a large Asian food section, but you can make your own in a flash. You can use it in marinades and dipping sauces or whenever you want some chile sizzle.

(page 208)

MAKES ABOUT ¼ CUP (60 ML)

Tips

Leaving in some seeds not only gives this volcanic condiment an appealing look and texture, but it also reminds you not to overgrind the sauce. When it is ready, you should still have some whole seeds visible, so grind in pulses and check often to avoid turning everything into a smooth red mush. What you want is textured red mush with a diminutive confetti of seeds.

A half portion of this recipe will produce enough to spike my Sweet and Hot Garlic Sauce (page 206) and you will have enough left over to fire up a few sandwiches or bowls of Asian noodle soup.

(page 206)

You can double or triple this recipe, but since it is so simple to make and a little goes a long way, I like to grind out a fresh batch as needed.

◆ Mini food processor or blender

20	dried red finger-length chiles such as *chiles de árbol* or *chiles japones*	20
2	large cloves garlic	2
1 tbsp	water	15 mL
2 tsp	distilled white vinegar	10 mL
½ tsp	salt	2 mL

1. Stem chiles and shake out and discard some of the seeds. Break in half and place in a small bowl. Add warm water to cover and let soften for 30 minutes.

2. Drain chiles. In a mini processor or blender, combine chiles, garlic, water, vinegar and salt and grind using on-off pulses and stopping to scrape down sides, until you have a bright red, nubby, coarse purée with some seeds still visible (see Tips, left). Transfer to a small bowl and add a little more water if needed to soften sauce, which should be a little thicker than applesauce. Cover or transfer to an airtight jar and refrigerate for up to 3 days.

Sriracha Sauce

This fire-engine red mild-to-incendiary hot chile sauce shows up alongside Thai omelets and other dishes. Unlike the popular chile purée with seeds, which goes by the same name, Thai Sriracha is smooth and liquid, pourable and delicate. I love both kinds, but the Thai sauce has my heart for its sweet notes and complexity, and because I fell in love with it soon after my arrival in Thailand.

MAKES ABOUT 2 CUPS (500 ML)			

◆ Food processor or blender

8 oz	fresh hot red chiles, such as red jalapeños, red serranos or red cayenne chile peppers	250 g
3 tbsp	coarsely chopped garlic	45 mL
½ cup	water	125 mL
¼ cup	distilled white vinegar	60 mL
1 tbsp	granulated sugar	15 mL
2 tsp	salt	10 mL

1. Stem and coarsely chop chiles and place in a large, heavy saucepan. Add garlic, water, vinegar, sugar and salt. Bring to a boil over medium-high heat, stirring often. Adjust heat to maintain a visible simmer and cook until chiles are softened and flavors have combined evenly, 20 minutes. Remove from heat and let cool to room temperature.

2. Transfer chile mixture to food processor or blender, in batches if necessary, and pulse to a fairly even coarse purée. Then process to a smooth purée, stopping often to scrape down the sides and grind everything evenly and well.

3. Scrape purée into a large wire mesh strainer placed over a medium bowl or large glass measuring cup. Press and scrape to gather the sauce and most of the pulp, leaving seeds and peel behind. Transfer to a glass jar, seal, and refrigerate for 2 days to allow flavors to develop. Serve as an accompaniment, condiment, or ingredient in sauces, marinades and dressings. Keep refrigerated for up to 3 weeks.

Roasted Tomato-Chile Sauce

Roasting shallots, garlic, tomatoes and chiles brings out a robust, intense flavor and fortifies them for this satisfying dipping sauce. This goes wonderfully with roasted vegetables such as butternut squash or sweet potatoes, or with crisp-fried tofu or a sticky rice–centered meal.

Tips

You could use whole dried red chile peppers, instead of fresh chiles, keeping in mind that they can burn very quickly and need careful attention and turning.

Thai cooks roast the tomatoes over glowing coals and tuck the unpeeled shallots and garlic right in among the coals to char. This version is how I make it on my home stove, for days when there are no coals to employ for this pleasing sauce.

◆ Roasting pan, lightly greased

	Vegetable oil	
6	large unpeeled shallots, cut in half lengthwise	6
8	large unpeeled garlic cloves, cut in half lengthwise	8
12	cherry tomatoes	12
6	fresh Thai bird's eye chiles or 1 fresh jalapeño	6
1 tbsp	palm sugar or brown sugar	15 mL
1 tsp	salt	5 mL
1 tbsp	freshly squeezed lime juice	15 mL

Oven Method

1. Heat a broiler until very hot. Place shallots and garlic, cut-side down, on roasting pan. Place tomatoes and chiles on pan and roast in preheated broiler, checking often and turning as needed, until softened and blackened but not burning. Remove vegetables when ready and keep turning and cooking remaining ones.

Stove-Top Method

1. Heat a large, heavy skillet over medium-high heat until very hot. Add enough oil to lightly coat skillet. Place shallots and garlic, cut-side down, in skillet. Add tomatoes and chiles and cook, turning as needed to cook on all sides, until softened and browned.

Both Methods

2. Set vegetables aside until cool enough to handle. Peel shallots and garlic, and stem chiles. Place shallots, garlic, tomatoes and chiles in bowl of a large mortar. Using a pestle, pound and grind together into a fairly smooth thick sauce, using a spoon to scrape and combine ingredients evenly and well. Or place in a blender or a mini food processor and pulse to combine into a pleasing, thick sauce.

3. Transfer to a bowl and stir in sugar, salt and lime juice. Taste and adjust seasonings. Transfer to a small bowl and serve at room temperature.

Suggested Menus

Here are ideas to get you started on putting Thai dishes together into menus you will enjoy. An asterisk (*) means the recipe is not included in this book. Vegan menus are noted with a (V).

Traditional Thai Feast (V)
Tome Yum Soup with Mushrooms and Tofu (page 72)
Panaeng Curry with Wheatballs and Wild Lime Leaves (page 98)
Pickled Cabbage (page 62)
Jasmine Rice (page 136)
A platter of sweet ripe fruit*

Northeastern Thai Barbecue (V)
Green Papaya Salad (page 54)
Mixed Grill (page 106)
Sticky Rice (page 137)
Roasted Eggplant Dip with Thai Flavors (page 35), served with vegetables
Fried Peanuts with Green Onions and Chiles (page 46)

Southern Thai Feast (V)
Mussamun Curry with Peanuts, Potatoes and Cardamom (page 96)
Brown Rice (page 140)
Kao Yum Rice Salad, Southern-Style (page 58)
Banana Splits*, made with Coconut Ice Cream (page 164) and sprinkled with Toasted Coconut (page 199)

Summertime Barbecue (V)
Satay Peanut Sauce with Grilled Vegetables, Fried Tofu and Toast (page 40)
Grilled Japanese Eggplant and Sweet Peppers*
Sweet-and-Sour Cucumber Salad (page 61)
Yellow Curry Fried Rice with Crispy Potatoes and Peas (page 142)
Wild Lime Leaf Sorbet (page 169)

One-Pot Party (V)
Kale Salad with Thai Flavors (page 64)
Tofu and Shiitakes Hidden in Curried Rice with Crispy Shallots (page 144)
Coconut Ice Cream (page 164) with Fresh Fruit*

Spicy Dining (V)
Butternut Squash in Fresh Green Curry (page 100)
Sticky Rice (page 137)
Pickled Cabbage (page 62)
Eggplant and Red Sweet Peppers in Roasted Chile Paste (page 118)
Firecracker Broccoli (page 123)
Coconut Ice Cream (page 164)

Cozy Winter Feast (V)
Burmese-Style Curry with Yams, Mushrooms and Ginger (page 97)
Garlicky Brussels Sprouts (page 114)
Jasmine Rice (page 136)
Coconut Rice Pudding (page 171)
Sweet and Spicy Nuts (page 47)

Too Hot to Cook (V)
Muslim-Style Salad with Peanut Dressing (page 56)
Sticky Rice (page 137) with Tangy Tamarind Sauce (page 207)
Orange Salad in Ginger Syrup with Mint (page 66)
Fresh Lemongrass Lemonade (page 175)

Do-Ahead Buffet (V)
Oyster Mushroom Salad with Chiles and
Lime (page 52)
Choo Chee New Potatoes with
Fresh Basil (page 99)
Everyday Fried Rice with Shiitakes
(page 139)
Thai Fruit Salad (page 65)
Lemongrass Ginger Sorbet (page 168)

Your Kids Will Love It
Crispy Spring Rolls with Sweet and Hot
Garlic Sauce (page 32)
Thai Omelet with Sriracha Sauce (page
129)
Coconut Rice with Cilantro and
Fresh Ginger (page 143)
Thai Ice Cream Sandwiches (page 165)

A Finger-Food Feast
Dao Jiow Lone Dipping Sauce
with Vegetables (page 30)
Roasted Eggplant Dip with Thai
Flavors (page 35), served on Crispy
Rice Cakes (page 44)
Pineapple Bites (page 20)
Garlicky Mushroom Turnovers
(page 23)
Crispy Spring Rolls with Sweet and Hot
Garlic Sauce (page 32)

Thai Dim Sum Party
Sweet Potato Shiao Mai (page 38)
Vegetable Curry Puffs (page 24)
Delectable Lettuce Bites (page 28)
Chewy "Pearl" Dumplings with
Mushroom Mince and
Crispy Garlic (page 26)
Curried Corncakes with Sweet and Hot
Garlic Sauce (page 22)

Sweet and Tangy Dinner (V)
Mee Grop (page 147)
Zucchini and Tofu in Roasted
Chile Paste (page 119)
Brown Rice (page 140)
Speedy Mango Sorbet (page 170)

Patio Supper
Shredded Bamboo Salad,
Issahn-Style (page 53)
Son-in-Law Eggs (page 124)
Thai Fruit Salad (page 65)
Pasta Salad*
Fresh Lemongrass Lemonade
(page 175)
Thai Coffee Ice Cream (page 165)

Vegan Delight (V)
Mung Bean Fritters (page 21) with
Tangy Tamarind Sauce (page 207)
Rice Noodles with Spinach in Shiitake
Mushroom Soup (page 80)
Speedy Mango Sorbet (page 170)

Speedy Stir-Fry Supper
Mushrooms and Tofu with
Fresh Mint (page 110)
Jasmine Rice (page 136)
Green Salad with Spicy Thai
Citrus Dressing (page 63)
Thai Iced Coffee (page 172)

Siam Sunday Brunch
Two-Potato Curry Potstickers (page 36)
with Sweet and Hot Garlic Sauce
(page 206)
Steamed Eggs with Cilantro and Crispy
Garlic (page 128)
Pineapple Fried Rice (page 141)
Thai Tea Ice Cream (page 167)
Cookies*

Sunday Night Supper (V)
Jasmine Rice Soup with Mushrooms,
Green Onions and Crispy Garlic
(page 82)
Green Papaya Salad (page 54)
Paht Thai (page 150)
Cool, Crisp Rubies in Coconut Milk
(page 160)

Glossary

Asian bean sauce/*dao jiow*

A pungent condiment made from salted, fermented soybeans. This astoundingly salty seasoning is an ancient Chinese recipe brought to Thailand with the original migration of people out of southern China nearly a thousand years ago. The English name on the label will in most cases read either "brown bean sauce" or "yellow bean sauce." If you buy a brand of Asian bean sauce imported from Thailand, it will probably be called "yellow bean sauce," not because of the color you see but because the Thai name for raw soybeans, which are yellowish, is *tua leuang* or "yellow bean." Thais use two types of Asian bean sauce. Most common is tall, long-necked bottles of a café au lait brown sauce, with whole dark beans in thick purée. The other is short, fat jars of whole pale yellow beans in a watery brine. Either will work fine in these recipes and the brown one is the most commonly available in upcountry Thai kitchens. I have used Asian bean sauce extensively in this book, as it works well in combination with salt and soy sauce as a vegetarian replacement for *nahm plah,* the fermented fish sauce that is ubiquitous in Thai cuisine.

Bamboo shoots/*naw mai*

Beloved in Asian cuisines for their crunchy texture and ability to absorb and deliver intense flavors from chile fire to herb-and-spice intensity, bamboo shoots appear in Thai soups, stir-fries, curries and salads. Some cooks buy or dig up fresh shoots and prepare them by parboiling, but mostly they are purchased from vendors who peel, trim and cook them to tenderness before sale. They vary in size and shape, with plump cones and slender rods the most common ones. In supermarkets, you'll find thinly sliced rectangles canned in water, while in Asian markets, you may find refrigerated tubs containing whole, chopped or shredded bamboo shoots, ivory to yellow in color. Rinse well and store in water in the refrigerator, changing water occasionally, for 3 to 5 days. Pickled and spicy-flavored bamboo shoots are enjoyed as a snack or condiment, while plain shoots work best in prepared dishes.

Banana leaf/*bai gluay; bai tong*

Thais use banana leaves to wrap food for steaming, roasting and boiling and as a beautiful tool for food presentation. *Bai gluay* means "banana leaf," but the same leaf is called *bai tong* or "leaf of gold," when used in cooking. Buy the leaves frozen in large packages at Asian markets and defrost at room temperature for about 30 minutes before using. The leaves are huge, so carefully unfold the amount you need, wipe clean with a wet cloth and cut to the size you like. Wrap extra leaves tightly and refreeze. Substitute fresh corn husks or dried corn husks from a Hispanic market, soaking the latter in cold water until pliable.

Basil/*bai horapah (Ocimum basilicum); bai graprao (Ocimum sanctum); bai maengluk (Ocimum canum)*

Thais use fresh basil extensively, along with cilantro and mint. Whole leaves are tossed into soups, curries and stir-fries, most often at the end of cooking time so the delicate burst of flavor and aroma shines through in the finished dish. Thais use particular types of basil in certain dishes, but you can substitute fresh Italian basil or sweet basil any time you do not have access to the ideal one, with good results. You can also use mint, since basils are members of the mint family. See *Graprao* basil, *Horapah* basil, *Maengluk* basil and Mint.

Bean curd/*dao hoo* See *Tofu*.

Bean sprout/*tua ngok*
Sprouted from mung beans, these are widely available in supermarkets in the West, but often neglected and allowed to wilt in the produce bin. Look for crisp, firm sprouts with little scent. If beautiful fresh ones aren't available, omit them.

Bean thread noodle/*woon sen*
Made from mung bean flour, these unusual noodles are also called glass noodles, silver noodles and cellophane noodles. Names abound, including the Chinese dialect word *saifun,* the Japanese *harusame* that means "spring rain" and the appetite-dulling English moniker "alimentary paste." These skeins of off-white dried noodle are usually wrapped up into small, oval bundles and enclosed in cellophane. They resemble fishing wire more than food and are about as tough until they are soaked in warm water for 15 to 20 minutes. Then they are limp and ready to be briefly stir-fried or dropped into soups just before serving. They cook quickly; as soon as they are translucent, they are done. They have no taste, but they have a lovely soft texture and absorb flavors well. When raw, bean thread noodles look a lot like thin rice noodles, so read the ingredients list on the packet; it should mention mung beans or even green beans, since the Thai name for mung bean is *tua kiow* or "green bean." You can substitute thin rice noodles, noting that they will need a little more cooking time and turn white rather than clear when cooked. Bean thread noodles are widely available in supermarkets, as well as in Asian markets and by mail.

Black sticky rice/*kao niow dahm*
See *Sticky rice*.

Brown bean sauce/*dao jiow*
See *Asian bean sauce*.

Cardamom/*luke gra-wahn*
A fragrant seedpod resembling in shape either a small plump garlic clove or a minuscule head of garlic. Thais use it whole in a few dishes of Indian origin, such as Mussamun Curry with Peanuts, Potatoes and Cardamom (page 96). In their natural state, cardamom pods are an ethereal shade of green, but you will also find white cardamom pods, which are green pods that have been bleached. Green are preferable, but either will work. Avoid black cardamom, which is a different spice, sold in large, dark, woody pods and used in Indian and South Asian cuisine.

Chee fah chile/*prik chee fah* (Capsicum annuum) See *Chiles*.

Chile-garlic sauce
An incendiary Vietnamese-style chile sauce made from fresh red chiles, vinegar, garlic and salt. It is a coarse, thick fire engine–red paste with visible seeds and pulp and is widely available in Asian markets. Look for small plastic jars with parrot-green lids; the sauce keeps well. Substitute a freshly made purée of hot red chiles, garlic and a little vinegar and salt (see Red Chile Purée, page 209) or use another chile sauce such as Sriracha Sauce (page 210) or Tabasco.

Chiles/*prik* (Capsicum sp.)
Thais adore hot chiles, both fresh and dried, whole and ground. Chiles contain oils that sting and burn, so cultivate the Thai cook's habit of not touching your eyes and other tender spots after handling them.

For fresh chiles, use the slender, tiny chiles called *prik kii noo* and *prik kii nok*

(*Capsicum frutescens*). They're often labeled "Thai chiles" or "bird's eye pepper" in Asian markets and are usually sold green, although they turn orange and red as they ripen. You can use other fresh chiles, such as serranos or jalapeños, in their place.

Also used frequently in Thai cooking are *chee fah chiles (Capsicum annuum),* which are long and slender like fingers and are usually a brilliant red. Although fiery, they are far milder than *kii noo chiles* and in most cases are sliced on the diagonal into ovals and added to Thai dishes as a garnish. For this reason, strips of red bell pepper make a good substitute, since *chee fah chiles* are difficult to find in the West.

Prik leuang (Capsicum annuum), which means "yellow chile," is a long, slender, mildly hot pepper that is extremely rare even in Thailand. It is used in *gaeng leuang,* a southern Thai curry, along with dried red chiles for heat and turmeric for yellow color. Substitute serrano chiles or omit altogether if you cannot find either in Asian markets.

Prik yuak (Capsicum annuum) is a mildly hot chile, pale green to pale yellow, 3 to 5 inches (7.5 to 12.5 cm) long, fat at the stem and tapering to a point. It is also called *prik noom* and is used in the northern Thai chile dipping sauce called *nahm prik noom.* It is difficult to locate in Asian markets in the West, but is often found in well-stocked supermarkets under the name banana pepper or Hungarian wax pepper.

For *prik haeng* or dried red chiles, use any dried red chiles imported from Thailand and sold in plastic bags or any other dried red chile you like as long as it is hot. For coarsely ground dried red chile or hot pepper flakes, buy it already ground, with seeds and pieces of red pepper still visible or grind your own. Dried chiles keep for months but not forever, so check carefully now and then to see if you need a new batch.

Chinese broccoli/*pahk ka-nah* (*Brassica sp.*)

A leafy, dark green vegetable of the cabbage family, known in Thai as *pahk ka-nah.* It resembles broccoli, though its stems are more tender and slender and it has large leaves and tiny flowers. When flowering it has beautiful tiny white blossoms, which are also edible. Dim sum parlors serve it blanched and seasoned with oyster sauce. Thais use it extensively for stir-frying and for combining with noodles. Substitute collard greens, Swiss chard, cabbage, Chinese mustard greens or any leafy Asian green or use spinach leaves, adding them toward the end of cooking since they're much more tender.

Chinese mustard green/*pahk kwahng-toong* (*Brassica sp.*)

A leafy, dark green vegetable of the cabbage family. It often has beautiful tiny yellow flowers, which are also edible. Like Chinese broccoli or *pahk ka-nah,* it has sturdy broccoli-like stalks and large, delicious leaves.

Cilantro/*pahk chee* (*Coriandrum sativum*)

Also called coriander and Chinese parsley, a beautiful, soft, leafy herb adored by Thais and used extensively to add its distinctive flavor to dishes and as a garnish. It's often available in supermarkets, as well as in Asian and Hispanic markets.

Cooks in many countries use cilantro leaves, but only Thai and Lao cooks appreciate the unusually fragrant and flavorful roots as a component of seasoning pastes. Increasingly, produce vendors are becoming aware of the benefits of leaving the roots intact, since the herb stays fresh much longer when the roots have not been removed.

If you can't find cilantro with roots attached, substitute chopped stems with some leaves.

Cloud ears/*heht hoo noo*
A thin, black mushroom with no flavor but a pleasing crunch and appearance. Thais use them in a few dishes of Chinese origin. The Thai name means "mouse ear mushroom," since that's what they look like when fresh or softened. Other common names are *mo-er* mushrooms, tree ears, wood ears and black fungus. They're seldom available fresh here, but dried ones work fine. They must be softened for about 30 minutes in warm water to cover and trimmed of their hard little navels, the spot at which they were attached to the tree or log on which they grew.

Coconut/*maprao*
Thais use coconuts extensively in cooking, particularly for sweets and to make coconut milk and coconut cream for curries and soups. See page 196 for instructions on opening coconuts and extracting and grinding their meat.

Coconut candy/*nahm tahn maprao*
See Palm sugar.

Coconut cream and coconut milk/ *nahm ga-ti*
Thais grate the sturdy, white flesh of hairy brown coconuts, soak it in water and then squeeze it through a fine-mesh sieve to make coconut cream and coconut milk. Cream is *hua ga-ti* or "the head," and milk is *hahng ga-ti* or "the tail." Unsweetened canned or frozen coconut milk is a good substitute for freshly made. It is such a rich essence that it would more properly be labeled "coconut cream." Throughout this book, I call for this rich coconut milk straight from the can or from the freezer, simply thawed. When it needs diluting, I have included stock or water

as needed among the recipe ingredients. If you encounter Southeast Asian recipes calling for coconut cream and coconut milk, use this formula. For coconut cream, stir the contents of a can well and use it undiluted. For coconut milk, stir the contents of a can of coconut milk well, dilute it by half, adding an equal amount of water to the coconut cream and then measure out the amount of coconut milk you need. "First pressing" refers to coconut cream and "second pressing" refers to coconut milk. In all its forms, unsweetened coconut milk is as perishable as the dairy products it resembles, so keep it chilled and use within 1 or 2 days. See page 196 for more on coconuts.

Coconut sugar/*nahm than maprao*
See Palm sugar.

Coriander seed/*luke pahk chee*
The whole seeds of cilantro, also known as coriander and Chinese parsley. Thais toast them in a dry skillet to bring out the flavor and then grind them for use in curry pastes and herb pastes.

Cucumber/*taeng kwah*
Use small pickling cucumbers or large hothouse or Japanese cucumbers if you can. Or use the huge, waxy torpedoes from the grocery store, but peel them well and also scrape out the seeds, as they tend to be large, tough and bitter.

Cumin seed/*meht yee-rah*
Used extensively in Thai cooking, usually dry-fried to bring out the flavor and then ground for use in fragrant herb pastes and curry pastes.

Curry paste/*krueng gaeng*
An intensely flavored paste of herbs and spices used to flavor curries, soups and other dishes. See Basic Recipes (pages 180 to 188) for how to make your own or purchase prepared curry pastes in Asian

markets. Homemade curry pastes take time and effort to prepare, but they taste wonderful and keep well. Store-bought curry pastes are a good alternative and they enable cooks to make tasty curries fast. In my kitchen I greatly enjoy using both.

The most common curry pastes are red, made from dried red chiles and known both as *krueng gaeng peht,* the latter word meaning "fiery hot," and as *krueng gaeng daeng,* the latter word meaning "red"; green, made from fresh green chiles and called *gaeng kiow wahn,* which means literally "green and sweet"; *krueng gaeng kah-ree,* a red curry paste enhanced with Indian spices and turmeric for golden color; and *krueng gaeng mussamun,* a rich, mildly hot red curry paste flavored with cinnamon, cloves and other spices. Curry pastes come in cans, plastic tubs and small and large plastic packets.

Dao jiow *See Asian bean sauce.*

Dark soy sauce/*si-yu dahm*
Available in bottles in Asian markets, dark soy sauce is valued mostly for the rich, deep color it lends to food and not for its flavor, which is mild.

Dark sweet soy sauce/*si-yu wahn*
Available in bottles in Thai and Southeast Asian markets, this is a combination of dark soy and molasses and is the secret of the delicious rice noodle dish Rice Noodles with Eggs, Broccoli and Dark Sweet Soy Sauce (page 152). If unavailable, substitute two parts dark soy sauce and one part molasses. You could use sorghum, pure cane syrup, honey or maple syrup.

Dried Chinese mushroom/
heht hohm *See Dried shiitake mushroom.*

Dried red chiles/*prik haeng*
See Chiles.

Dried shiitake mushrooms/
heht hohm
The Thai name means "fragrant mushroom," and shiitake are used along with other varieties of dried Chinese mushrooms in Chinese-Thai cooking. Soak in warm water for about 30 minutes, remove and discard the stem or use it in stock and then cook the softened caps whole or sliced, in soups, stir-fries and stews. The soaking liquid can be strained and used to flavor soups and sauces. You will find acceptable ones in small packages in supermarkets. If you use them often, buy a supply at an Asian market, where you will find excellent buys on a variety of top-quality mushrooms. They keep indefinitely, sealed airtight, at room temperature and away from light. Expect them to be costly, as they are a specialty ingredient within Asian cuisine.

Five spice powder/*pong pah-lo*
Thais enjoy this Chinese import, a ground mixture of cinnamon, cloves, fennel, Szechuan peppercorns and star anise, which imparts a deep, sweet and spicy aroma and flavor to the popular Chinese-style stews known in Thai as *pah-lo* dishes. Try *kai pah-lo,* Five-Spice Hard-Boiled Eggs in Sweet Soy Stew (page 126). See Star anise for further information.

Freshly ground black pepper/
prik thai pohn
Freshly ground white or black pepper has so much more flavor and aroma than pre-ground that I hope you'll buy yourself a good pepper mill. Many Thai cooks use pre-ground pepper, however, except in curry pastes, where there are other spices to grind as well. I specify black or white pepper in some recipes, but either will work fine.

Galanga/*kah (Alpinia galanga siamensis)*

This first cousin of ginger has a wonderful sharp, lemony taste and a similar hotness. Its Vietnamese name is *rieng* and it is also known as galanga, Java root, Siamese ginger, *laos, lengukual, languas* and galingae. Galanga is pale and creamy, much lighter than ginger and encircled with thin, dark rings. It's never eaten straight, but rather used in large, thin pieces to flavor soups, stews and curries or chopped fine to be pounded up in curry pastes and herb pastes. Frozen or dried galanga pieces make a reasonable alternative if you can't find fresh. You could also substitute fresh ginger, which has a different flavor from its cousin but makes a delicious, herbaceous alternative. Ground dried galanga powder has no taste and no scent, so leave it on the grocer's shelf.

Garlic/*gratiem (Allium sativum)*

Every recipe I was given in Thailand seemed to begin with *Hohm, gratiem . . .* ("Shallots, garlic . . .") and it is assumed a good cook knows how much to use and how to cut it up. I had to watch and write it down, so check the recipes for the details. Be sure to look for fresh, shiny heads of garlic that feel heavy in your hand and don't have soft or dusty, moldy cloves. To me there's no substitute for fresh garlic, crushed, peeled and chopped as I need it. I buy a dozen heads at a time when I find good ones and keep it handy in a big basket with shallots, plum tomatoes, an onion, a hunk of ginger and some chiles.

Garlic, pickled/*gratiem dong*

See *Pickled garlic.*

Garlic chives/*tone gooey chai*

These flat green chives have a strong smell and taste. Traditionally they're used in Thailand's two noodle classics, Paht Thai (page 150) and Mee Grop (page 147), but green onions make an excellent substitute.

Ginger/*king (Zingiber officinale)*

A delicious fresh seasoning with an extraordinary flavor—hot and spicy and yet cooling as well. Happily it's now widely available in the West in well-stocked supermarkets as well as Asian markets. Look for shiny, fat lobes that aren't shriveled or wrinkled. Thais don't use ginger as much as they do its cousins, galanga and turmeric, but they like it and it makes a good alternative if the others are hard to come by.

Glutinous rice/*kao niow*

See *Sticky rice.*

Grachai/*grachai (Kaempferia pandurata; Boesenbergia pandurata)*

This ginger cousin is also called *zerumbet, zeodary,* rhizome, camphor root, *kentjur* or *kencur* and lesser galanga. It has a thin, medium brown skin over a creamy interior and is shaped like a bunch of long, tapered fingers. Like all members of the ginger family, it's widely used in traditional Asian medicine as well as in food. It's sometimes available frozen, which makes an acceptable substitute, as does fresh ginger. Ground dried *grachai,* sometimes labeled "rhizome," is tasteless and scentless, so pass it by.

Graprao basil/*bai graprao (Ocimum sanctum)*

This is often called holy basil and it's my favorite member of the herb family to which all mints and basils belong. Although it's not easy to find outside Thailand, Asian markets in the West are gradually beginning to carry it. You're most likely to find *graprao* basil in Asian markets that cater to a Lao, Cambodian and Thai clientele and often only during the spring, summer and early fall months. The leaves of *graprao* basil are not shiny like most basils, nor are they textured like mint. They have a smooth, matte finish and a serrated edge and the color varies from pure green to a green-red-purple mixture, with or without flowers, all depending on the particular variety and the time of year. It's more fragile than other mints and basils, so when you find it, use it fast and use a lot of it. Any variety of fresh basil or mint makes a good substitute; unfortunately, dried mint and basil just don't work—no scent, no flavor.

Green onion/*tohn hohm* (*Allium fistulosom*)
Also called scallions, these are used extensively for flavor and garnish.

Holy basil/*bai graprao (Ocimum sanctum)* See Graprao basil.

Horapah basil/*bai horapah (Ocimum basilicum)*
The most widely available Asian basil, it's used extensively in Vietnamese cuisine, as well as in the cooking of Cambodia and Laos. Sometime called Thai or Vietnamese basil, it looks and tastes like a basil, with its shiny, pointy leaves and anise flavor. It usually has purple stems, sometimes tipped with lovely purple flowers; the latter are a nice addition to any recipe that calls for the leaves. Thais use *horapah* basil more than the other types of basil, tossing a handful onto curries, soups and stir-fries just before serving so that its delicate perfume and flavor are released but not extinguished. *Rau hung* is its Vietnamese name.

Hot pepper flakes/*prik pong*
These coarsely ground dried red chiles are widely used in Thai cooking for a fiery blast, particularly in sauces and dips. Look for small flakes of red pepper punctuated with a small proportion of whole seeds. Look for them in cellophane bags in Asian markets, in jars in supermarkets or grind up your own in a Thai mortar or in a mini food processor or a blender.

Hungarian wax pepper/*prik yuak; prik noom (Capsicum annuum)*
See Chiles, Banana pepper.

Jasmine rice/*kao hohm mali*
A naturally aromatic, long-grain white rice widely available in Asian markets in the West. Its scent is subtle, somewhere between toasty and nutty and it's wonderful for general cooking as well as for Thai food. It's sometimes called Thai basmati rice, since basmati is another exotic aromatic, long-grain white rice, albeit a bit different in texture, aroma and taste. I buy jasmine rice in 25-lb (11 kg) sacks because it keeps well and I use it often; many Asian grocers break it down into smaller lots. The large sacks will usually have been marked "jasmine rice, imported from Thailand" in English, somewhere beneath the brand name and various inscriptions in Vietnamese, Khmer, Chinese, Lao and Thai. See page 136 for instructions on cooking jasmine rice.

Kabocha pumpkin/*fahk tong (Cucurbita moschata)*
Beloved by Thais for use in curries and sweets, these chubby, dark green pumpkins are widely available in supermarkets and Asian markets. Any winter squash will make a fine substitute, although I think kabocha has an especially sweet, pleasing taste. Sweet potatoes work, too, but need shorter cooking time.

Kaffir lime leaves/*bai makrut*
See Wild lime leaves.
The word "kaffir" is a racial slur, and as awareness of this fact grows, its use is declining quickly. The word can

mean wild, as in not domesticated or cultivated, and in this context it was used to identify this particular fruit, distinguishing it for cooks from the more commonly available varieties of lime. You will encounter it in older reference sources. Names in use today include wild lime, clear and expressing the non-pejorative meaning; makrut lime or magrood lime, using the Thai language name for the tree and its leaves and fruit; or simply, lime leaves, as there is no tradition of using any other sort of lime leaves in Asian cooking, since they lack the transcendent aroma and flavor of wild lime leaves.

Kii noo chile/prik kii noo (Capsicum frutescens) See Chiles.

Lemongrass/takrai (Cymbopogon citratus)
Lemongrass grows in long, pale green stalks with a woody texture and a lovely lemony scent. It is shaped like a green onion but is stiff and quite fibrous. Its Vietnamese name is *xah* (pronounced *zah*) and it is also called *serai, sereh, zabalin,* citronella and fever grass. Thais use only the bulbous base, trimmed of roots and any dry outer leaves. If your lemongrass is fresh, you'll see lovely purple concentric rings inside when you cut it crosswise. Like galanga, lemongrass is seldom eaten because it has such a coarse, fibrous texture and delicate flavor and scent. Instead it is used like bay leaves in Western cooking, to infuse a sauce, a soup or a curry with its delicate flavor and scent. It is sliced very thin and then finely chopped before being pounded with other ingredients in curry pastes. Try to do any cutting and pounding of lemongrass at the very last minute, as its perfume and flavor quickly fade away. You'll find dried lemongrass, chopped and in powder form, in Asian markets and I strongly suggest you leave it there; it has no taste

and no scent. Soaking it won't help, since there's nothing left once it's dried.

Lemongrass freezes fairly well, so when you find fresh stalks, buy an extra dozen or so, trim away the tops and wrap tightly before freezing. Don't defrost it; use it straight from the freezer, just about doubling the amount you would use if it were fresh. If you can't find lemongrass, substitute some juice and zest of lime or lemon.

If your lemongrass is tired, brown and pliable rather than fresh, green-tinged and stiff, use a few more stalks to intensify its flavor. I like to split open the lemongrass to expose its fragrant core and then remove it after it has infused the soup with its flavor and perfume. This creates lots of tiny fibrous pieces that need to be strained out. Asian cooks usually smash the lemongrass with a cleaver, leaving it in large chunks and then let it remain in the soup, since this saves a step and everyone knows not to try and eat it.

Leuang chile/prik leuang (Capsicum annuum) See Chiles.

Lime/manao
Fresh lime juice is a basic ingredient in Thai cooking, but fresh lemon juice is a good substitute.

Lime leaf/bai makrut
See Wild lime leaf.

Maengluk basil/bai maengluk (Ocimum canum)
This basil has a heavenly lemon scent and flavor and it's used in soups, tossed into the classic *gaeng liang* just before serving. It is also used in some curries and noodle dishes, including the northeastern version of the steamed curried custard called *haw moke.* It's difficult to find in the West and it fades quickly, so if you come across some at a market, enjoy it right away. Substitute

another fresh basil or mint if you like or any lemony herb such as lemon balm.

Maengluk basil seed/ meht maengluck (Ocimum canum)

These tiny black seeds resemble sesame seeds in size and shape and are sold in markets catering to Thai, Lao, Cambodian and Vietnamese cooks. Not only can you plant them to raise a crop of lemony *maengluk* basil, you can use them Asian style in sweets. Soak them in water for about 5 minutes and watch each seed enclose itself within a bubble of bluish-gray jelly. In this swollen form, *maengluk* basil seeds are used in sweet puddings and cool fruity drinks. The word in the Thai marketplace is that eating basil seeds causes one to *"lote nahm nahk,"* which means "to release unwanted pounds." I cannot vouch for this but I do love the peculiar pillowed crunch these seeds provide in sweets and drinks. Look for small cellophane packets of seeds, which may be labeled "sweet basil" or with the Vietnamese words *"hot e."*

Mint/bai saranae (Mentha arvensis)

Thais adore fresh mint, especially in their hot and spicy salads called *yums.* Any type of mint will do nicely in Thai recipes or you could substitute any form of basil as a second choice.

Mung bean centers/tua tong

See *Yellow mung bean centers.*

Noom chile/prik noom (Capsicum annuum) See Chiles.

Oyster mushroom/heht nahng lome

Beautiful clusters of dove-gray mushrooms that resemble oysters in both color and shape. They are increasingly available in Asian markets and some supermarkets here. Substitute any fresh mushroom.

Palm sugar/nahm tahn beep, nahm tahn maprao

An absolutely delicious, robust sugar made from the fruit of the palmyra palm tree called *toen pahm* or from the coconut palm, *toen maprao. Beep* refers to the tall tin can in which palm sugar is sold in Thailand, so the package doesn't always specify which type of sugar is inside. Whether it is labeled palm sugar, coconut sugar or coconut candy, it's a wonderful addition to sauces, curries and sweets. You can substitute brown sugar or white sugar or jaggery from India.

Peanut/tua lisong

Used more in the south than in other regions. Peanuts are called groundnuts in some Asian cookbooks. Use roasted peanuts, either salted or unsalted and then salt the dish you're making to taste. Buy small jars and keep them in the freezer, as they quickly go stale.

Pepper/prik thai See Freshly ground black pepper.

Peppercorn/luke prik Thai (Piper nigrum)

The original Thai hot seasoning. Thais use both white and black whole peppercorns, particularly in curry pastes and herb pastes, and ground pepper to season stir-fries, sauces and soups.

Pickled garlic/gratiem dong

Thais pickle diminutive heads of garlic in a simple white vinegar, salt and sugar brine and use slices or whole cloves as a flavorful foil for salty dishes like *kai kem* or Salty Eggs (page 202). Pickled garlic is sold in jars in many Asian markets. For a classic Mee Grop (page 147) garnish, slice heads crosswise into 1/4-inch (0.5 cm) thick rounds and drape over the mound of noodles.

Pomelo/soem-oh

A delicious cousin of grapefruit, it has sturdier, drier flesh and much thicker skin. Unlike grapefruit, it has a round shape that is a trifle irregular, distended at the stem end and its ripe meat is much sweeter. Peel off the skin, separate the sections, gently cut them open to extract the glistening juicy flesh and enjoy it in chunks out of hand. For a palace-style presentation to a very important guest, a Thai chef might separate the peeled sections of pomelo into individual teardrops of fruit. Look for pomelos in Asian markets, especially around Chinese New Year in January and February. You can substitute a combination of peeled sections of grapefruit and orange.

Pressed tofu/dao hoo keng

Firm bean curd can be pressed under a heavy weight to extract a portion of its water content. This makes it sturdy enough to hold its shape, for use in recipes where it is vigorously tossed, stirred or stewed. You will find it shrink-wrapped in the refrigerator case in Asian markets and health food stores, either plain or seasoned with soy sauce and sometimes shredded into long thin strands. You can make it easily at home (page 200).

Rice/kao See Jasmine rice.

Rice crusts

If you find yourself with a layer of rice stuck but not burned onto the bottom of your cooking pot, scrape out all the soft rice to leave a shell of browned, hardened rice in the pot. Place the pot over low heat so that the crust can dry out and shrink a little, which helps it separate from the cooking pot, then carefully remove the shell and set it aside at room temperature for a day or two, until it is brittle and completely dry. Break it into pieces of 3 to 4 inches (7.5 to 10 cm) each and fry them as directed in the recipe. You can also collect these natural rice crusts over time, combine them in a resealable bag and store in the freezer for a month or so before frying them.

Rice flour/baeng kao jow

Ground from long-grain white rice and available in Asian markets, this soft, chalk-white powder is made into the tender white rice noodles used in Asian cuisines. It is also widely used in various sweets and savory snacks and can be substituted for sticky rice flour in a pinch.

Rice noodles/kwaytiow

Wonderful white noodles, sold fresh in large, soft sheets folded into packets or dried, cut into various widths from angel-hair size *(sen mee)* used for Mee Grop (page 147), to linguine size *(sen lek)* used for Paht Thai (page 150), to 1-inch (2.5 cm) wide size, my personal favorite, which one Thai restaurant menu translated perfectly as "big fat noodle" *(sen yai)*. To prepare dried rice noodles for stir-frying, soak them in warm water to cover until they are limp, pliable and stark white, 15 to 20 minutes. Drain and proceed according to recipe.

While I've specified particular noodle widths for particular recipes, you needn't be bound by that in your kitchen. Use what you can find and what you like. All dried rice noodles are softened in the same way and cook in a similar amount of time. You can use dried rice noodles of any size, from wire-thin vermicelli to medium linguine-like threads to wide, flat fettuccine-like ribbons in any recipe in this book, just as you could interchange pasta shapes and sizes at home. You can also use fresh soft rice noodles if you live in a community large enough to support an Asian shop that carries the delicate product.

Fresh rice noodle sheets are highly perishable and in Asia they are sold and used on the same day. Here you may find them refrigerated or even frozen. If you find a fresh source, buy either precut noodles, which are in wide ribbons or a flat rectangular packet, which is a gigantic noodle sheet folded into a 1-lb (500 g) pad the size of a book. Cut the noodle pad lengthwise into strips about 1 inch (2.5 cm) wide and then gently separate the strips into noodles. Some will break apart and this is fine, but strive to keep the noodles intact as long as possible. Taste one and if it is pleasingly tender, use the noodles as they are, adding them to the serving bowls to be bathed in hot soup. If they are a little dry, stiff or firm, they are old enough to have needed refrigeration, so refresh them with a quick dip in boiling water before serving them. You can also use dried rice flakes, which are found with other dried noodles in Asian markets and look like white but translucent tortilla chips. Add them to boiling water, stir well and watch them turn white and curl into little scrolls.

Roasted chile paste/*nahm prik pao*

A fiercely delicious amalgam of dried roasted chiles, garlic and shallots, seasoned with tamarind and palm sugar. This condiment is used in the wildly popular Thai soup, *tome yum* (see page 72 for my version, Tome Yum Soup with Mushrooms and Tofu). *Nahm prik pao* is available in small jars in many supermarkets, and in large jars or big flat packets in Asian markets, where its English-language name will likely be "Chile Paste in Soybean Oil," rather than "roasted chile paste." You can make your own (page 204), with delicious results, and I urge you to do so. This condiment has many uses in your kitchen, from *tome yum* soup and stir-fries to marinades and oven-roasted tofu or winter squash. Once you have it handy and enjoy its pleasures, you may want to keep a batch on hand always.

Note that commercial *nahm prik pao* usually includes ground dried shrimp and fish sauce, so making your own may be a necessity rather than an option.

Roasted rice powder/*kao kua pone*

Raw grains of sticky rice are dry-fried until wheaty brown and then ground to a fragrant powder with a pleasing crunch and toasty flavor. A traditional ingredient in *yum,* the hearty salads of the northeastern region. Either make your own (page 198) or omit.

Salty egg/*kai kem*

Sometimes labeled "salted eggs," this is a traditional way of preserving duck eggs. Buy in Asian markets and hard cook just before using or preserve your own (page 202). Salty eggs are often sold coated with a cushioning ¼-inch (0.5 cm) thick layer of gray ash. Soak these in cold water for about 5 minutes and then gently rub off the ash with your fingers under running water.

Sataw bean/*look sataw (Parkia sp.)*

These unique fat beans look a lot like peeled, shelled lima beans or fava beans, but they have a peculiar taste and aroma. Sataw beans are immensely popular in southern Thailand, where they grow on trees in huge, ladder-like pods. Often available frozen in Asian markets and of surprisingly good quality. Or substitute fresh young fava beans, shelled and peeled; fresh lima beans, shelled and peeled or frozen lima beans, thawed and peeled; fresh sugar snap peas; or fresh snow peas. Nothing tastes quite like sataw beans, though.

Seitan

This traditional Asian form of wheat gluten or wheat protein is widely available in health food stores, sold like tofu in the refrigerator case, sealed in small tubs basted by a spiced soy broth rather than water. Like other types of wheat gluten, it is made from a simple wheat flour dough that is kneaded well and then rinsed to remove the starch and the bran. Sometimes called "wheat meat," the variously shaped hunks of firm, chewy seitan can be cut to your liking into strips or bite-size pieces and used as a protein source instead of tofu or other forms of wheat gluten in many Asian-style recipes. See also Wheat gluten.

Shallot/*hohm daeng* or *hohm lek* (*Allium ascalonicum*)
The first Thai name means "red onion," because the tiny shallots of Thailand have a gorgeous pinkish purple color. Thais also call them *hohm lek* or "tiny onion," and they use them extensively, usually along with garlic. Look for small, hard, shiny shallots without green shoots. Unfortunately, often the only kind you'll find here are huge, wrinkly shallots with green shoots. But they'll do.

Soy sauce/*saus si-yu*
Thais use soy sauce as a background seasoning in many dishes, often for color as well as taste. See also Dark soy sauce and Dark sweet soy sauce.

Spring roll wrappers/*paen boh biah*
Square, ivory-colored sheets sold at Asian markets in 1-lb (500 g) packets of about 30 or so 8-inch (20 cm) square sheets. They are usually sold frozen. They are made of flour and water and usually do not contain egg. They can dry out quickly, so keep them frozen until shortly before you plan to fill and wrap them. The wrapper package needs about 30 minutes to thaw and it is best to keep unused raw wrappers covered with a damp kitchen towel or plastic wrap while you work. Rewrap leftover wrappers airtight and freeze. Since quality can vary and the wrappers keep well and use little freezer space, I buy several packages of different brands

rather than the one package I need. Then if I encounter the occasional dried out, useless batch, I can go to the freezer rather than back to the Asian market. The doughy refrigerated kind widely available in supermarkets will do, too. Note that these usually contain egg and have a heavier, oilier texture when cooked.

Sriracha sauce
A terrific five-alarm chile sauce made in the seaside town of Sriracha. Thais love it as an accompaniment to egg dishes and seafood. Disregard designations on the slender bottles that say "mild" and "hot"—they are all very, very hot. To make your own see page 210.

Star anise/*poy kaek bua* (*Illicium verum*)
Used in Thai cooking mostly in dishes of clear Chinese origin, such as Five-Spice Hard-Boiled Eggs in Sweet Soy Stew (page 126), known in Thai as *kai pah-lo*. This gorgeous spice is a reddish brown star with eight pointy pods, each housing a shiny, pungent seed. Botanically it belongs to the magnolia family. Though unrelated to anise, the two spices share a similar licorice flavor and aroma. Thais commonly make use of it in five-spice powder, but whole star anise is often tossed into *pah-lo* dishes along with cinnamon sticks for an extra spice spark.

Sticky rice/*kao niow*
In its long-grain form, this opaque, bright-white strain of rice is the daily bread of northeastern and northern Thailand and of Laos. Soaked for 3 hours and then steamed until tender, long-grain sticky rice plumps up and easily clings into bite-size lumps, which Laotians and many Thais eat out of hand along with curries, soups, stir-fries and salads. In English, sticky rice is also called glutinous rice and

sweet rice. Gluten, the protein in wheat that gives bread its appealing chewy quality, is not present in this rice, but since sticky rice has a unique chewiness, the name has stuck. Though this rice has no sweet taste, short-grain sticky rice is widely used in sweet snacks and desserts throughout Asia, sometimes ground into flour and sometimes in its whole-grain form. Its importance as an ingredient in sweet treats is probably the source of the term, "sweet rice." See page 137 for instructions on cooking long-grain sticky rice the Thai way. Some Asian markets and health food stores also carry black sticky rice, which is a handsome medium-grain rice that is black, brown and white in a calico pattern. Less sticky than its white cousin, it can be soaked and steamed or cooked as you would cook regular rice. However you cook it, you will enjoy seeing its earthy color transformed into a stunning deep-purple hue. Thais often toss cooked black sticky rice with coconut milk and sugar and serve it with ripe mangos or custard as a sweet course (page 163).

Sticky rice flour/*baeng kao niow*
Ground from sticky rice, this velvety white powder is widely used in sweets. Its natural stickiness in whole-grain form translates to a thick, chewy texture that is treasured in a rainbow of Asian treats, savory as well as sweet. Available in boxes and cellophane bags in Asian markets. Plain rice flour is an adequate substitute. See also Sticky rice.

Straw mushroom/*heht fahng*
Available fresh in Thailand. Buy whole, peeled canned ones or substitute any fresh mushroom.

Sweet potato/*mun*
You can use any kind of sweet potato or yam when cooking the curries and dumplings in this book. You could also substitute potatoes, kabocha pumpkin or any peeled variety of winter squash.

Sweet rice/*kao niow* See Sticky rice.

Sweet soy sauce/*si-yu wahn*
See Dark sweet soy sauce.

Tamarind/*makahm*
The ripe fruit of the tamarind tree, it has a complex, fruity sour taste that recalls a smoky combination of raisins and limes. Buy small blocks of tamarind pulp *(makahm biak)* in Asian markets, soak the pulp in warm water, mash to a thick soft paste, strain and use the liquid. See page 191 for specific directions for extracting the liquid. Thai cooks sometimes use freshly squeezed lime juice or distilled white vinegar as a substitute; although the flavor is not as wonderful, it will do.

Tapioca flour/*baeng mun*
Made from the dried tubers of the cassava plant, tapioca flour is found in Asian markets and health food stores. Valued for its power to thicken sauces in a clear, silken way, it is also used in combination with other flours to lend crispness to batters for deep-fried snacks. If it is unavailable, use an equal amount of rice flour, cornstarch or wheat flour.

Taro/*peuak (Colocasia antiquorum)*
A chubby tuber with fuzzy brown skin that is something like a potato in appearance and taste. There are many types, ranging in size from as small as a walnut to as large as a coconut. The flesh is ivory to gray and often spiked with purple. In Hawaii, taro is used for making *poi* and in Thailand it is used mostly in sweets such as *kanome maw gaeng,* the classic custard that is the signature sweet of the coastal town of Hua Hin. Since it is peeled and cut into 2-inch (5 cm) chunks before cooking, any variety and size will do for Thai recipes.

Tempeh

These nubby, rectangular patties are a traditional vegetarian protein source that originated in Indonesia. They are made from soybeans that are partly cooked, infused with a starter and then fermented until they are extremely rich in protein and easy to digest. Made from soybeans only or soybeans mixed with grains and seasonings, tempeh is widely available in health food stores, vacuum-packed and stored in the refrigerator case or the freezer. Its thick chewy texture takes well to frying and simmering in curries and its yeasty, earthy, mushroom-like flavor works well in Asian-style cooking.

Thai bird's eye chiles/*prik kii-noo; prik kii-nok (Capsicum annum)*
See Chiles.

Thai coffee/o-liang powder

Roasted sesame seed and corn kernels give this coffee a wonderful burnt flavor. Thais like their coffee ice cold and sweet with evaporated milk or hot with sweetened condensed milk.

Thai tea/*cha Thai*

Cinnamon, vanilla, star anise and a little food coloring give this finely chopped black tea its pleasing, unusual flavor and terra-cotta color. Brewed strong and served only cold and very sweet, topped off with evaporated milk

Tofu/*dao hoo*

In Thai cooking, fresh tofu, also called bean curd, is used especially in soups and Chinese dishes. Usually sold in large square or rectangular cakes packed in water and sealed in 1-lb (500 g) tubs. Purchase the firm type for use in recipes in this book. Store leftover tofu in water to cover in the refrigerator. Change the water every few days and use it as soon as possible.

Turmeric/*kamin (Curcuma longa; Curcuma domestica)*

A member of the ginger family, turmeric is an underground stem or rhizome. It grows in clusters of small, stubby fingers, with a dull, brown skin hiding its gorgeous fluorescent-orange meat. It has a faint, earthy taste, but the color is the point here and it's used in many dishes for that reason, particularly in southern Thailand. Today turmeric gives ballpark mustard and curry powder their characteristic yellow color and it is found with the ground spices on well-stocked supermarket shelves. It has been used extensively in Asian medicines since ancient times and is the natural dye traditionally used to color the robes of Theravada Buddhist monks. Since color is what matters in cooking with this herb, ground dried turmeric works fine.

Vegetarian "oyster" sauce/*saus nahmahn hoy jay*

This newcomer to the prepared Asian condiment market is a version of Chinese-style oyster sauce, with a rich essence of dried shiitake mushrooms used in place of oyster extract, along with soy sauce, sugar, salt and thickeners. Lee Kum Kee distributes its version to supermarkets, labeled "vegetarian stir-fry sauce," and Asian markets carry other brands labeled "vegetarian oyster sauce." This thick, silky and salty sauce pairs beautifully with stir-fried greens, mushrooms, bean sprouts and noodles.

Vegetarian stir-fry sauce/*saus nahmahn hoy jay* See Vegetarian "oyster" sauce.

Vinegar/*nahm som*

Thais use plain white vinegar, like the distilled white vinegar widely available in grocery stores. Japanese rice vinegar or white wine vinegar will work, although they are both more strongly flavored.

Water chestnuts/*haew* (*Elocharis dulcis*)

Fresh water chestnuts resemble giant, rustic Hershey kisses, walnut-size with rounded bottoms and a brittle yet pliable skin. Check Asian markets for firm, plump water chestnuts that are heavy for their size, and keep them loosely wrapped and chilled for about one week. Peeling away the brown outer covering is *lambahk,* a nifty Thai word meaning a bothersome task, but the result is a sweet crunchy nugget that outshines the canned ones. Slice off the tip and the rounded base and then peel the barrel-like sides with a paring knife. The crunchy white heart is somewhat like jicama in texture, though drier and denser. Peeled whole water chestnuts are widely available in cans and make a very good substitute for fresh. Rinse and drain well before using them and store any leftovers in water in the refrigerator for a week or so, changing the water every few days.

Water spinach/*pahk boong* (*Ipomoea aquatica*)

Also called swamp cabbage, water convolvulus, long green and morning glory, its Cantonese name is *ong choy,* its Vietnamese name is *rau muong* and its Malay name is *kang kong.* It has distinctive hollow stems with widely spaced, arrowhead-shaped leaves. It resembles watercress in color and spacing of the leaves, although water spinach is much larger. It comes in huge sheaves; don't worry, however, as it cooks down considerably. Substitute spinach, watercress or Chinese broccoli, adjusting cooking time according to the vegetable you use.

Wheatballs/*look baeng sah-lee*

See Wheat gluten and recipe (page 194).

Wheat gluten/*look baeng sah-lee*

This traditional Asian vegetarian protein source is a bland, chewy dumpling made by separating the gluten or protein from the starch and bran in wheat flour and cooking this elastic dough into sturdy little protein-packed lumps. Fried brown and crisp, boiled, simmered or baked, it is used in traditional Chinese vegetarian cooking in many dishes as a substitute for meat. Also known as wheat protein, wheat meat, wheatballs and seitan, you can buy it canned and sometimes fresh in Asian markets, usually marinating in a seasoned liquid, or you can make your own at home (page 194).

Wheat protein/*look baeng sah-lee*

See Wheat gluten.

Wild lime leaf/*bai makrut* (*Citrus hystrix*)

Gorgeous emerald leaves of the wild lime tree, used in soups and curries for their unique, citrusy flavor, exquisite aroma and beauty. Wild lime leaves are also called *djeroek poeroet, limau purut* and kaffir (or keffir) lime leaves. They grow attached to each other in pairs, end to end. Look for wild lime leaves in small plastic bags in Asian markets, usually in the refrigerator case. They are difficult to find, but the pleasure of their culinary presence makes it well worth the extra effort to track them down. Sealed airtight and chilled, they will keep four or five days. When the recipe calls for slicing them crosswise into thin threads, try to remove the sturdy vein that runs lengthwise through each wild lime leaf. Start at the pointed end rather than the thick stem end and use a paring knife to lift up the vein. Use fresh ones or omit them, as dried ones have only a faint memory of their former greatness. They freeze fairly well, so buy a lot and keep them frozen, using twice the amount called for, straight from the freezer. If you cannot find wild lime leaves, or if your supply has run out and you are ready to cook without a trip to the store, know that you can simply omit them from every recipe in this book where I have called for them except for Wild Lime Leaf Sorbet (page 169) where the lime leaf is integral to the recipe. They are a lovely note, but they are a crowning glory and not an essential ingredient. There is no substitute, but omitting them will not sink your curry or ruin your soup.

Wild lime peel/*piew makrut* (*Citrus hystrix*)

This extremely fragrant, flavorful peel of the wild lime is an important ingredient in curry pastes. Wild limes, which have a distinctive, knobby texture, are also referred to as kaffir (or keffir) limes. Inside there is only a little rather bitter juice, which has traditionally been used in shampoos and soaps rather than in the kitchen. Substitute domestic lime peel or use dried wild lime peel, sold in Asian markets in cellophane packets; soften it in a little warm water until pliable or break it into bits and grind to a powder.

Winged bean/*tua poo*

A pale green legume with four sharp-edged fins running lengthwise. The fins seem softly serrated along their edges, as if they have been gathered by a seamstress with a green thumb. According to Elizabeth Schneider, in her excellent reference book *Uncommon Fruits and Vegetables,* this delicate tropical vegetable is very nutritious and high in protein, but its fragility in the face of cool temperatures makes it difficult to cultivate outside Southeast Asia and the Pacific Islands. The flavor of the beans is quite mild, but southern Thais adore their raw, starchy or *faht-faht,* taste. It is difficult to find them in the West and they wilt quickly, so keep them wrapped and chilled and use as soon as possible. Green beans look

mighty plain by comparison, but they make an excellent substitute.

Yam/*mun*

You can use any variety of yam for the recipes in this book. Or substitute any kind of sweet potato, potato, kabocha pumpkin or any kind of winter squash.

Yellow bean sauce/*dao jiow kao*

See Asian bean sauce.

Yellow mung bean centers/*tua tong*

Known in Thai as "golden beans," these flat oval yellow pellets resemble petite, sturdy rolled oats. They are the split hearts of dried green mung beans, which are in turn the source of the big white bean sprouts that are ubiquitous in Asian cooking. Southeast Asian cooks are partial to these pretty little beans, using them whole in sweet coconut puddings and iced beverages and steamed and ground to fortify the batter for savory Indian-style fritters (page 21) and the crispy Vietnamese-style filled pancakes known in Thai as *kanome bueang*. Look for them in Asian markets in cellophane packets that may bear the Vietnamese name *dau xanh ca.*

Yuak chile/*prik yuak* (*Capsicum annuum*) *See Chiles.*

Resources

Here is information to put you in touch with vendors who carry everything you need to cook Thai food at home including resources for seeds and plants.

Evergreen Seeds
P.O. Box 17538
Anaheim, CA 92817
USA
(714) 637-5769
www.evergreenseeds.com
(Ships worldwide)

Superb source of seeds for Asian herbs and vegetables. You'll find holy basil and other Asian basil types, edamame beans, long beans, winged beans, Thai and other eggplant varieties, bok choy and other cabbage varieties, garlic chives, cilantro and many types of chile peppers.

Golda's Kitchen
2885 Argentia Road, Unit 6
Mississauga, ON L5N 8G6
Canada
(866) 465-3299 or (905) 816-9995
www.goldaskitchen.com
(Ships worldwide)

Thai granite mortar and pestle and woks.

Gold Mine Natural Food Company
13200 Danielson Street, Suite A-1
Poway, CA 92064
USA
(800) 475-3663 (U.S. only) or
(858) 537-9830
shop.goldminenaturalfoods.com
(Ships worldwide)

A good source for rice, noodles and soy sauce.

ImportFood.com
P.O. Box 2054
Issaquah, WA 98027
USA
(888) 618-8424 (U.S. only) or
(425) 687-1708
www.importfood.com
(Ships worldwide)

One of my favorite sources for all things Thai. Import Food stocks fresh herbs, as well as dried ones, curry pastes and sauces, and traditional equipment from granite mortars and pestles to Issahn-style sticky rice baskets. Video series features Thai street vendors making traditional dishes.

Penzeys Spices
12001 West Capital Drive
Wauwatosa, WI 53222
USA
(800) 741-7787 or (414) 760-7337
www.penzeys.com
(Ships to U.S. and Canada)

Penzeys offers a superb selection of whole spices and ground spices, particularly useful for making curry pastes such as mussamun curry paste at home.

Qualifirst Foods Ltd.
4-40 Ronson Drive
Toronto, ON M9W 1B3
Canada
(800) 206-1177
www.qualifirst.com
(Ships to U.S. and Canada)

Extensive selection of whole and
ground spices and spice mixtures,
Thai curry pastes and aromatic rice.

Richters Herbs
357 Highway 47
Goodwood, ON L0C 1A0
Canada
(905) 640-6677
www.richters.com
(Ships worldwide)

Excellent selection of both seeds and
plants for your home garden. Asian
treasures include lemongrass, garlic
chives, Thai basil, holy basil, cilantro,
various types of mint and an array of
chile peppers.

Temple of Thai
(877) 811-8773
www.templeofthai.com
(Ships worldwide)

Extensive selection of Thai curry
pastes, seasonings, sauces, rice
noodles and fresh herbs, along
with cooking equipment including
mortars and pestles and sticky
rice steaming sets. Features Thai
cookbooks in English and an archive
of traditional recipes.

Thai Kitchen
P.O. Box 13242
Berkeley, CA 94712-4242
USA
(800) 967-8424
www.thaikitchen.com
(Ships to U.S. only)

Thai curry pastes, coconut milk,
rice noodles, seasoning pastes
and sauces.

The Spice House
1941 Central Street
Evanston, IL 60201
USA
847-328-3711
www.thespicehouse.com
(Ships to U.S., Canada and Mexico.
Canadian orders please email
spices@thespicehouse.com)

Wide selection of whole and ground
spices for curry pastes, as well as
chile peppers.

The Spice Trader
877 Queen Street West
Toronto, ON M6J 1G3
Canada
(647) 430-7085
www.thespicetrader.ca
(Ships throughout Canada)

Fine quality whole and ground spices,
and a selection of salts.

Index

(v) = variation

A

Appetizers and snacks,
about, 18
Chewy "Pearl" Dumplings
with Mushroom Mince
and Crispy Garlic, 26, 213
Crispy Rice Cakes, 44, 213
Crispy Spring Rolls
with Sweet and Hot
Garlic Sauce, 32, 213
Curried Corncakes
with Sweet and Hot
Garlic Sauce, 22, 213
Dao Jiow Lone
Dipping Sauce with
Vegetables, 30, 213
Delectable Lettuce
Bites, 28, 213
Fried Peanuts with Green
Onions and Chiles, 46, 212
Garlicky Mushroom
Turnovers, 23, 213
Mung Bean Fritters, 21, 213
Pineapple Bites, 20, 213
Roasted Eggplant Dip with
Thai Flavors, 35, 212, 213
Satay Peanut Sauce with
Grilled Vegetables, Fried
Tofu and Toast, 40, 212
Spicy Cashews with Chiles,
Cilantro and Lime, 43
Sweet and Spicy Nuts, 47,
212
Sweet Potato Shiao
Mai, 38, 213
Two-Potato Curry Pot
Stickers, 36, 213
Vegetable Curry Puffs, 24, 213
Asian Vegetable Stock, 190

B

Baby Corn and Tofu
with Cashews, 109

Bamboo shoots, about, 214
Green Curry with Zucchini
and Bamboo Shoots, 94
Shredded Bamboo Salad,
Issahn-Style, 53, 213
Bamboo skewers, 40, 41
Beans
Bean Sprout Toss-Up,
113
Dao Jiow Lone
Dipping Sauce with
Vegetables, 30, 213
Kao Yum Rice Salad,
Southern-Style, 58, 212
Mung Bean Fritters, 21,
213
mung beans, 24
Red Hot Vegetable
Stir-Fry, 120
Bean sprouts, about, 215
Bean Sprout Toss-Up, 113
Kao Yum Rice Salad,
Southern-Style, 58, 212
Mee Ga-ti Rice Noodles with
Coconut-Bean Sauce, 154
Mee Grop, 147, 213
Muslim-Style Salad with
Peanut Dressing, 56, 212
Paht Thai, 150, 213
Beverages. See Drinks
Broccoli
Firecracker Broccoli, 123,
212
Garlicky Cabbage or
Broccoli (v), 114
Rice Noodles with Eggs,
Broccoli and Dark
Sweet Soy Sauce, 152
Brown Rice, 140, 212,
213
Brussels Sprouts,
Garlicky, 114, 212
Burmese-Style Curry
with Yams, Mushrooms
and Ginger, 97, 212

Butternut squash
Butternut Squash and
Spinach in Roasted
Chile Paste, 117
Butternut Squash in Fresh
Green Curry, 100, 212
Coconut Soup with Galanga
and Butternut Squash, 74
peeling, 100

C

Cabbage
Chinese Cabbage with Black
Pepper and Garlic, 116
Dao Jiow Lone
Dipping Sauce with
Vegetables, 30, 213
Garlicky Cabbage or
Broccoli (v), 114
Golden Cabbage with
Mushrooms and Peas, 121
Green and Purple
Cabbage Salad (v), 55
Pickled Cabbage, 62, 212
Shredded Bamboo Salad,
Issahn-Style, 53, 213
Carrots
Asian Vegetable Stock, 190
Crispy Spring Rolls
with Sweet and Hot
Garlic Sauce, 32, 213
Dao Jiow Lone
Dipping Sauce with
Vegetables, 30, 213
Everyday Vegetable Stock, 189
Pineapple Fried Rice, 141, 213
Vegetable Curry Puffs, 24, 213
Cashews
Baby Corn and Tofu
with Cashews, 109
Spicy Cashews with Chiles,
Cilantro and Lime, 43
Winter Vegetables Infused
with Coconut Milk
and Cashews, 91

Cauliflower, Sweet-and-Sour Tempeh with Cucumber and, 111
Celery
  Asian Vegetable Stock, 190
  Everyday Vegetable Stock, 189
Chewy "Pearl" Dumplings with Mushroom Mince and Crispy Garlic, 26, 213
Chiles
  Baby Corn and Tofu with Cashews, 109
  Chile-Vinegar Sauce, 208
  Fried Peanuts with Green Onions and Chiles, 46, 212
  Green Curry Paste, 182
  Minced Mushrooms and Tofu with Chiles and Holy Basil, 130
  Mussamun Curry Paste, 186
  Quick-and-Simple Curry Paste, 188
  Red Chile Purée, 209
  Red Curry Paste, 180
  Roasted Chile Paste, 204
  Roasted Tomato-Chile Sauce, 211
  Sriracha Sauce, 210
  Yellow Curry Paste, 184
Chinese Cabbage with Black Pepper and Garlic, 116
Choo Chee New Potatoes with Fresh Basil, 99, 213
Clear Soup with Roasted Portobello Mushrooms and Bean Thread Noodles, 78
Clear Soup with Spinach and Tofu, 76
Coconut
  Coconut Rice Pudding, 171, 212
  cracking, 196
  Delectable Lettuce Bites, 28, 213
  grating, 197
  Maengluk Basil Seeds in Coconut Milk, 162
  Pink Grapefruit Salad with Toasted Coconut, Fresh Mint and Lime, 67
  Toasted Coconut, 199, 212
Coconut milk
  Butternut Squash in Fresh Green Curry, 100, 212
  Choo Chee New Potatoes with Fresh Basil, 99, 213
  Coconut Ice Cream, 164, 212
  Coconut Rice Pudding, 171, 212
  Coconut Rice with Cilantro and Fresh Ginger, 143, 213
  Coconut Soup with Galanga and Butternut Squash, 74
  Cool, Crisp Rubies in Coconut Milk, 160, 213
  in curries, 89
  Eggplant and Sweet Pepper–Studded Red Curry, 92
  Green Curry with Zucchini and Bamboo Shoots, 94
  Hard-Boiled Eggs and Peas in Green Curry, 93
  homemade, 197
  Maengluk Basil Seeds in Coconut Milk, 162
  Mee Ga-ti Rice Noodles with Coconut-Bean Sauce, 154
  Muslim-Style Salad with Peanut Dressing, 56, 212
  Mussamun Curry with Peanuts, Potatoes and Cardamom, 96, 212
  Panaeng Curry with Wheatballs and Wild Lime Leaves, 98, 212
  Red Curry with Red Sweet Peppers, Snow Peas and Tofu, 90
  Satay Peanut Sauce with Grilled Vegetables, Fried Tofu and Toast, 40, 212
  Sticky Rice with Coconut Sauce, 138
  Sticky Rice with Mangos, 163
  Winter Vegetables Infused with Coconut Milk and Cashews, 91
  Yellow Curry with Pineapple and Peas, 95
Coffee
  Thai Coffee Ice Cream, 165, 213
  Thai Iced Coffee, 172, 213
Condiments. See also Sauces
  Crispy Garlic in Oil, 203
  Roasted Chile Paste, 204
  Roasted Rice Powder, 198
  Toasted Coconut, 199, 212
Cool, Crisp Rubies in Coconut Milk, 160, 213
Corn
  Baby Corn and Tofu with Cashews, 109
  Curried Corncakes with Sweet and Hot Garlic Sauce, 22, 212
Crispy Garlic in Oil, 203
Crispy Rice Cakes, 44, 213
Crispy Shallots, 144
Crispy Spring Rolls with Sweet and Hot Garlic Sauce, 32, 213
Cucumbers
  Dao Jiow Lone Dipping Sauce with Vegetables, 30, 213
  Everyday Fried Rice with Shiitakes, 139, 213
  Green Salad with Spicy Citrus Dressing, 63, 213
  Kao Yum Rice Salad, Southern-Style, 58, 212
  Muslim-Style Salad with Peanut Dressing, 56, 212
  Sweet-and-Sour Cucumber Salad, 61, 212
  Sweet-and-Sour Tempeh with Cucumber and Cauliflower, 111
Curried Corncakes with Sweet and Hot Garlic Sauce, 22, 213
Curries, about, 88
  Burmese-Style Curry with Yams, Mushrooms and Ginger, 97, 212
  Butternut Squash in Fresh Green Curry, 100, 212

Curries (continued)
Choo Chee New Potatoes
with Fresh Basil, 99, 213
Eggplant and Sweet Pepper–
Studded Red Curry, 92
Green Curry with Zucchini
and Bamboo Shoots, 94
Hard-Boiled Eggs and
Peas in Green Curry, 93
Mussamun Curry with
Peanuts, Potatoes and
Cardamom, 96, 212
Panaeng Curry with
Wheatballs and Wild
Lime Leaves, 98, 212
Red Curry with Red
Sweet Peppers, Snow
Peas and Tofu, 90
Winter Vegetables Infused
with Coconut Milk
and Cashews, 91
Yellow Curry with
Pineapple and Peas, 95
Curry pastes
Green Curry Paste, 182
Mussamun Curry Paste, 186
preparing, 178
Quick-and-Simple
Curry Paste, 188
Red Curry Paste, 180
Yellow Curry Paste, 184

D

Dao Jiow Lone Dipping Sauce
with Vegetables, 30, 213
Desserts. *See* Sweets
Dips
Dao Jiow Lone
Dipping Sauce with
Vegetables, 30, 213
Roasted Eggplant Dip with
Thai Flavors, 35, 212, 213
Drinks
Fresh Lemongrass
Lemonade, 175, 212
Maengluk Basil Seed
Drink with Fresh Fruit
and Honey, 174
Thai Iced Coffee, 172, 213
Thai Iced Tea, 173

Dumplings
Chewy "Pearl" Dumplings
with Mushroom Mince
and Crispy Garlic, 26, 213
Sweet Potato Shiao
Mai, 38, 213

E

Edamame beans,
Tofu and Shiitakes Hidden
in Curried Rice with
Crispy Shallots, 144, 212
Eggplant
Eggplant and Red Sweet
Peppers in Roasted
Chile Paste, 118, 212
Eggplant and Sweet Pepper–
Studded Red Curry, 92
Eggplant Paht Peht, 122
Red Hot Vegetable
Stir-Fry, 120
Roasted Eggplant Dip with
Thai Flavors, 35, 212, 213
Satay Peanut Sauce with
Grilled Vegetables, Fried
Tofu and Toast, 40, 212
Eggs
Five-Spice Hard-Boiled Eggs
in Sweet Soy Stew, 136
Hard-Boiled Eggs and
Peas in Green Curry, 93
Salty Eggs, 202
Son-in-Law Eggs, 124, 213
Steamed Eggs with Cilantro
and Crispy Garlic, 128, 213
in sweets, 158
Thai Omelet with Sriracha
Sauce, 129, 213
Everyday Fried Rice with
Shiitakes, 139, 213
Everyday Vegetable Stock, 189

F

Firecracker Broccoli, 123, 212
Five-Spice Hard-Boiled Eggs
in Sweet Soy Stew, 136
Fresh Lemongrass
Lemonade, 175, 212
Fried Peanuts with Green
Onions and Chiles, 46, 212

Fritters, Mung Bean, 21, 213
Fruit. *See also individual fruits*
for dessert, 158
Kao Yum Rice Salad,
Southern-Style, 58, 212
Maengluk Basil Seed
Drink with Fresh Fruit
and Honey, 174
Maengluk Basil Seeds in
Coconut Milk, 162
Pink Grapefruit Salad with
Toasted Coconut, Fresh
Mint and Lime, 67
Speedy Mango
Sorbet, 170, 213
Speedy Peach or Strawberry
Sorbet (v), 170
Thai Fruit Salad, 65, 213

G

Gaeng hahng ley, 97
Gaeng jeute, 71, 76
Galanga
Coconut Soup with Galanga
and Butternut Squash, 74
dried, 74
Kao Yum Rice Salad,
Southern-Style, 58, 212
Wild Lime Leaf
Sorbet, 169, 212
Garlic
Chewy "Pearl" Dumplings
with Mushroom Mince and
Crispy Garlic, 26,
213
Chinese Cabbage with Black
Pepper and Garlic, 116
Crispy Garlic in Oil, 203
Crispy Spring Rolls
with Sweet and Hot
Garlic Sauce, 32, 213
Curried Corncakes
with Sweet and Hot
Garlic Sauce, 22, 213
Garlicky Brussels
Sprouts, 114, 212
Garlicky Cabbage or
Broccoli (v), 114
Garlicky Mushroom
Turnovers, 23, 213

Jasmine Rice Soup with
Mushrooms, Green Onions
and Crispy Garlic, 82, 213
Kale with Black Pepper
and Garlic (v), 116
Mee Grop, 147, 213
Mushroom Mince, 192
Quick-and-Simple
Curry Paste, 188
Roasted Chile Paste, 204
Roasted Tomato-
Chile Sauce, 211
Son in Law Eggs, 124, 213
Sweet and Hot Garlic
Sauce, 206
Sweet Potato Wonton
Soup with Cilantro and
Crispy Garlic, 84
Thai pickled, 148
Ginger
Lemongrass Ginger
Sorbet, 168, 213
Orange Salad in Ginger
Syrup with Fresh
Mint, 66, 212
Oyster Mushrooms with
Red Sweet Peppers
and Ginger, 108
preparing, 108
Tofu and Shiitakes Hidden
in Curried Rice with
Crispy Shallots, 144, 212
Golden Cabbage with
Mushrooms and Peas, 121
Granitas, 168
Grapefruit
Pink Grapefruit Salad with
Toasted Coconut, Fresh
Mint and Lime, 67
Green and Purple Cabbage
Salad (v), 55
Green beans
Bean Sprout Toss-up,
113
Dao Jiow Lone
Dipping Sauce with
Vegetables, 30, 212
Red Hot Vegetable
Stir-Fry, 120
Green Curry Paste, 182

Green Curry with Zucchini
and Bamboo Shoots, 94
Green Papaya Salad,
54, 212, 213
Green Salad with Spicy
Citrus Dressing, 63, 213
gyoza wrappers, 37

H
Hard-Boiled Eggs and Peas
in Green Curry, 93

I
Ice cream
Coconut Ice Cream, 164, 212
Thai Coffee Ice
Cream, 165, 213
Thai Ice Cream
Sandwiches, 166, 213
Thai Tea Ice Cream, 167, 213

J
Jasmine Rice, 136, 212, 213
Jasmine Rice Soup with
Mushrooms, Green Onions
and Crispy Garlic, 82, 213

K
Kai pa-loh, 126
Kai toon, 128
Kale
Kale Salad with Thai
Flavors, 64, 212
Kale with Black Pepper
and Garlic (v), 116
Kanome jeep, 38
Kao taen, 44
Kao Yum Rice Salad,
Southern-Style, 58,
212

L
Lemongrass
Coconut Soup with Galanga
and Butternut Squash, 74
Fresh Lemongrass
Lemonade, 175, 212
Green Curry Paste, 182
Lemongrass Ginger
Sorbet, 168, 213

Lemongrass Soup with Rice
and Basil Chez Sovan, 77
Mussamun Curry Paste, 186
Red Curry Paste, 180
Tome Yum Soup with
Mushrooms and
Tofu, 72, 212
Wild Lime Leaf
Sorbet, 169, 212
Yellow Curry Paste, 184
Lettuce
Delectable Lettuce
Bites, 28, 213
Green Salad with Spicy
Citrus Dressing, 63, 213
Muslim-Style Salad with
Peanut Dressing, 56, 212
Lime leaves, wild, 228
Coconut Soup with Galanga
and Butternut Squash, 74
Eggplant and Sweet Pepper–
Studded Red Curry, 92
Eggplant Paht Peht, 122
Kao Yum Rice Salad,
Southern-Style, 58, 212
Panaeng Curry with
Wheatballs and Wild
Lime Leaves, 98
slicing, 98
Tome Yum Soup with
Mushrooms and Tofu, 72
Wild Lime Leaf
Sorbet, 169, 212

M
Maengluk Basil Seed
Drink with Fresh Fruit
and Honey, 174
Maengluk Basil Seeds in
Coconut Milk, 162
Mah haw, 20
Main dishes. *See also* Curries;
Noodles; Rice; about,
104
Baby Corn and Tofu
with Cashews, 109
Bean Sprout Toss-Up, 113
Butternut Squash and
Spinach in Roasted
Chile Paste, 117

Main dishes (continued)
  Chinese Cabbage with Black
    Pepper and Garlic, 116
  Eggplant and Red Sweet
    Peppers in Roasted
    Chile Paste, 118, 212
  Eggplant Paht Peht, 122
  Firecracker Broccoli, 123, 212
  Five-Spice Hard-Boiled Eggs
    in Sweet Soy Stew, 136
  Garlicky Brussels
    Sprouts, 114, 212
  Golden Cabbage with
    Mushrooms and Peas, 121
  Minced Mushrooms
    and Tofu with Chiles
    and Holy Basil, 130
  Mixed Grill, 106, 212
  Mushrooms and Tofu with
    Fresh Mint, 110, 213
  Oyster Mushrooms with
    Red Sweet Peppers
    and Ginger, 108
  Red Hot Vegetable
    Stir-Fry, 120
  Son-in-Law Eggs, 124, 213
  Spinach in Sweet-Sour
    Tamarind Sauce, 115
  Steamed Eggs with Cilantro
    and Crispy Garlic, 128, 213
  Stir-Fried Spinach with
    Garlic and Pepper, 131
  Sweet-and-Sour Tempeh
    with Cucumber and
    Cauliflower, 111
  Thai Omelet with Sriracha
    Sauce, 129, 213
  Triple Mushroom Feast, 112
  Zucchini and Tofu in Roasted
    Chile Paste, 119, 213
Mangos
  Speedy Mango Sorbet, 170
  Sticky Rice with Mangos, 163
Masalas, 89
Mee Ga-ti Rice Noodles with
  Coconut-Bean Sauce, 154
Mee Grop, 147, 213
Menus, suggested, 212
Miang kum, 28
Mixed Grill, 106, 212

Mung Bean Fritters, 21, 213
Mushrooms
  Asian Vegetable Stock, 190
  Burmese-Style Curry
    with Yams, Mushrooms
    and Ginger, 97, 212
  Chewy "Pearl" Dumplings
    with Mushroom Mince
    and Crispy Garlic, 26, 213
  Clear Soup with Roasted
    Portobello Mushrooms and
    Bean Thread Noodles, 78
  Coconut Soup with Galanga
    and Butternut Squash, 74
  Crispy Spring Rolls
    with Sweet and Hot
    Garlic Sauce, 32, 213
  Everyday Fried Rice with
    Shiitakes, 139, 213
  Garlicky Mushroom
    Turnovers, 23, 213
  Golden Cabbage with
    Mushrooms and Peas, 121
  Jasmine Rice Soup with
    Mushrooms, Green Onions
    and Crispy Garlic, 82, 213
  Lemongrass Soup with Rice
    and Basil Chez Sovan, 77
  Mee Grop, 147, 213
  Minced Mushrooms
    and Tofu with Chiles
    and Holy Basil, 130
  Mushroom Mince, 192
  Mushrooms and Tofu with
    Fresh Mint, 110, 213
  Oyster Mushroom Salad with
    Chiles and Lime, 52, 213
  Oyster Mushrooms with
    Red Sweet Peppers
    and Ginger, 108
  Pineapple Bites, 20, 213
  Rice Noodles with Eggs,
    Broccoli and Dark
    Sweet Soy Sauce, 152
  Rice Noodles with Spinach
    in Shiitake Mushroom
    Soup, 80, 213
  Rice Soup with Mushrooms
    and Fresh Herbs (v),
    77

Satay Peanut Sauce with
  Grilled Vegetables, Fried
  Tofu and Toast, 40, 212
Sweet Potato Shiao
  Mai, 38, 213
Sweet Potato Wonton
  Soup with Cilantro and
  Crispy Garlic, 84
Tofu and Shiitakes Hidden
  in Curried Rice with
  Crispy Shallots, 144, 212
Tome Yum Soup with
  Mushrooms and
  Tofu, 72, 212
Triple Mushroom Feast,
  112
Two-Potato Curry Pot
  Stickers, 36, 213
Muslim-Style Salad with
  Peanut Dressing, 56, 212
Mussamun Curry Paste, 186
Mussamun Curry with
  Peanuts, Potatoes and
  Cardamom, 96, 212

N
Nahm prik pao, 204, 224
Nahng leht, 44
Noodles
  Clear Soup with Roasted
    Portobello Mushrooms and
    Bean Thread Noodles, 78
  Crispy Spring Rolls
    with Sweet and Hot
    Garlic Sauce, 32, 213
  Mee Ga-ti Rice Noodles with
    Coconut-Bean Sauce, 154
  Mee Grop, 147, 213
  Paht Thai, 150, 213
  Rice Noodles with Eggs,
    Broccoli and Dark
    Sweet Soy Sauce, 152
  Rice Noodles with Spinach
    in Shiitake Mushroom
    Soup, 80, 213
Nuts
  Baby Corn and Tofu
    with Cashews, 109
  Sweet and Spicy Nuts, 47,
    212

Winter Vegetables Infused with Coconut Milk and Cashews, 91

O

Orange Salad in Ginger Syrup with Fresh Mint, 66, 212
Oyster Mushroom Salad with Chiles and Lime, 52, 213
Oyster Mushrooms with Red Sweet Peppers and Ginger, 108

P

Pahk boong fai daeng, 116
Paht Peht, Eggplant, 122
Paht Thai, 150, 213
Panaeng Curry with Wheatballs and Wild Lime Leaves, 98, 212
Papaya Salad, Green, 54, 212, 213
Peach,
    Speedy Sorbet (v), 170
Peanuts
    Delectable Lettuce Bites, 28, 213
    Fried Peanuts with Green Onions and Chiles, 46, 212
    Muslim-Style Salad with Peanut Dressing, 56, 212
    Mussamun Curry with Peanuts, Potatoes and Cardamom, 96, 212
    Pink Grapefruit Salad with Toasted Coconut, Fresh Mint and Lime, 67
    Satay Peanut Sauce with Grilled Vegetables, Fried Tofu and Toast, 40, 212
    Thai Ice Cream Sandwiches, 166, 213
Peas. *See also* Snow peas
    Golden Cabbage with Mushrooms and Peas, 121
    Hard-Boiled Eggs and Peas in Green Curry, 93
    Yellow Curry Fried Rice with Crispy Potatoes and Peas, 142, 212

Yellow Curry with Pineapple and Peas, 95
Peppers. *See also* Chiles
    Eggplant and Red Sweet Peppers in Roasted Chile Paste, 118, 212
    Eggplant and Sweet Pepper–Studded Red Curry, 92
    Oyster Mushrooms with Red Sweet Peppers and Ginger, 108
    Red Curry with Red Sweet Peppers, Snow Peas and Tofu, 90
Pickled Cabbage, 62, 212
Pineapple
    Pineapple Bites, 20, 213
    Pineapple Fried Rice, 141, 213
    Yellow Curry with Pineapple and Peas, 95
Pink Grapefruit Salad with Toasted Coconut, Fresh Mint and Lime, 67
Potatoes. *See also* Sweet potatoes
    Choo Chee New Potatoes with Fresh Basil, 99, 213
    Mussamun Curry with Peanuts, Potatoes and Cardamom, 96, 212
    Two-Potato Curry Pot Stickers, 36, 213
    Vegetable Curry Puffs, 24, 213
    Yellow Curry Fried Rice with Crispy Potatoes and Peas, 142, 212
    Yellow Curry with Pineapple and Peas, 95
Pot Stickers, Two-Potato Curry, 36, 213
Pressed or Firm Tofu, 200

Q

Quick-and-Simple Curry Paste, 188

R

Red Chile Purée, 209
Red Curry Paste, 180

Red Curry with Red Sweet Peppers, Snow Peas and Tofu, 90
Red Hot Vegetable Stir-Fry, 120
Rice, about, 134
    Brown Rice, 140, 212, 213
    Coconut Rice Pudding, 171, 212
    Coconut Rice with Cilantro and Fresh Ginger, 143, 213
    Crispy Rice Cakes, 44, 213
    crusts, 223
    Everyday Fried Rice with Shiitakes, 139, 213
    Jasmine Rice, 136, 212, 213
    Jasmine Rice Soup with Mushrooms, Green Onions and Crispy Garlic, 82, 213
    Kao Yum Rice Salad, Southern-Style, 58, 212
    Lemongrass Soup with Rice and Basil Chez Sovan, 77
    "new crop," 136
    Pineapple Fried Rice, 141, 213
    Rice Soup with Mushrooms and Fresh Herbs (v), 77
    Roasted Rice Powder, 198
    Sticky Rice, 137, 212
    Sticky Rice with Coconut Sauce, 138
    Sticky Rice with Mangos, 163
    Tofu and Shiitakes Hidden in Curried Rice with Crispy Shallots, 144, 212
    Yellow Curry Fried Rice with Crispy Potatoes and Peas, 142, 212
Rice Noodles with Eggs, Broccoli and Dark Sweet Soy Sauce, 152
Rice Noodles with Spinach in Shiitake Mushroom Soup, 80, 213
Roasted Chile Paste, 204
Roasted Eggplant Dip with Thai Flavors, 35, 212, 213
Roasted Rice Powder, 198
Roasted Tomato-Chile Sauce, 211

S

Salad dressings
  Peanut Dressing, 56
  Spicy Citrus Dressing, 63
Salads, about, 50
  Green and Purple
    Cabbage Salad (v), 55
  Green Papaya Salad,
    54, 212, 213
  Green Salad with Spicy
    Citrus Dressing, 63, 213
  Kale Salad with Thai
    Flavors, 64, 212
  Kao Yum Rice Salad,
    Southern-Style, 58, 212
  Muslim-Style Salad with
    Peanut Dressing, 56, 212
  Orange Salad in Ginger
    Syrup with Fresh
    Mint, 66, 212
  Oyster Mushroom Salad
    with Chiles and
    Lime, 52, 213
  Pickled Cabbage, 62, 212
  Pink Grapefruit Salad with
    Toasted Coconut, Fresh
    Mint and Lime, 67
  Shredded Bamboo Salad,
    Issahn-Style, 53, 213
  Sweet-and-Sour Cucumber
    Salad, 61, 212
  Thai Fruit Salad, 65, 213
Salaht kaek, 56
Salty Eggs, 202
Satay Peanut Sauce with
    Grilled Vegetables, Fried
    Tofu and Toast, 40, 212
Sauces
  Chile-Vinegar Sauce, 208
  Dao Jiow Lone
    Dipping Sauce with
    Vegetables, 30, 213
  Red Chile Purée, 209
  Roasted Tomato-
    Chile Sauce, 211
  Satay Peanut Sauce, 40
  Sriracha Sauce, 210
  Sweet and Hot Garlic
    Sauce, 206

Tangy Tamarind
    Sauce, 207, 213
Seasoned Tofu, 201
Sgnor chhrok moin, 77
Shallots, Crispy, 144
Shiao Mai, Sweet
    Potato, 38, 213
Shredded Bamboo Salad,
    Issahn-Style, 53, 213
Snacks. See Appetizers
    and snacks
Snow peas
  Red Curry with Red
    Sweet Peppers, Snow
    Peas and Tofu, 90
  Yellow Curry with
    Pineapple and Peas, 95
Som loy gaew, 66
Som tum, 54
Son-in-Law Eggs, 124, 213
Soop naw mai, 53
Sorbets
  Lemongrass Ginger
    Sorbet, 168, 213
  Speedy Mango
    Sorbet, 170, 213
  Speedy Peach or Strawberry
    Sorbet (v), 170
  Wild Lime Leaf
    Sorbet, 169, 212
Soups, about, 70
  Clear Soup with Roasted
    Portobello Mushrooms and
    Bean Thread Noodles,
    78
  Clear Soup with Spinach
    and Tofu, 76
  Coconut Soup with Galanga
    and Butternut Squash, 74
  Jasmine Rice Soup with
    Mushrooms, Green Onions
    and Crispy Garlic, 82,
    213
  Lemongrass Soup with Rice
    and Basil Chez Sovan, 77
  Rice Noodles with Spinach
    in Shiitake Mushroom
    Soup, 80, 213
  Rice Soup with Mushrooms
    and Fresh Herbs (v), 77

Sweet Potato Wonton
    Soup with Cilantro and
    Crispy Garlic, 84
  Tome Yum Soup with
    Mushrooms and
    Tofu, 72, 212
Speedy Mango Sorbet, 170, 213
Speedy Peach or Strawberry
    Sorbet (v), 170
Spicy Cashews with Chiles,
    Cilantro and Lime, 43
Spinach
  Butternut Squash and
    Spinach in Roasted
    Chile Paste, 117
  Clear Soup with Spinach
    and Tofu, 76
  Rice Noodles with Spinach
    in Shiitake Mushroom
    Soup, 80, 213
  Spinach in Sweet-Sour
    Tamarind Sauce, 115
  Spring Rolls, Crispy,
    with Sweet and Hot
    Garlic Sauce, 32, 213
  Stir-Fried Spinach with
    Garlic and Pepper, 131
Squash. See Butternut
    squash; Zucchini
Sriracha Sauce, 210
Steamed Eggs with Cilantro
    and Crispy Garlic, 128, 213
Sticky Rice, 137, 212
Sticky Rice with Coconut
    Sauce, 138
Sticky Rice with Mangos, 163
Stir-Fries. See Mains
Stocks
  Asian Vegetable Stock, 190
  Everyday Vegetable Stock, 189
  freezing, 189
Strawberry, Speedy
    Sorbet (v), 170
Sweet and Hot Garlic
    Sauce, 206
Sweet-and-Sour Cucumber
    Salad, 61, 212
Sweet-and-Sour Tempeh
    with Cucumber and
    Cauliflower, 111

Sweet and Spicy Nuts, 47, 212

Sweet potatoes. *See also* Yams
Mussamun Curry with Peanuts, Potatoes and Cardamom, 96, 212
Sweet Potato Shiao Mai, 38, 213
Sweet Potato Wonton Soup with Cilantro and Crispy Garlic, 84
Two-Potato Curry Pot Stickers, 36, 213

Sweets, about, 158
Coconut Ice Cream, 164, 212
Coconut Rice Pudding, 171, 212
Cool, Crisp Rubies in Coconut Milk, 160, 213
granitas, 168
Lemongrass Ginger Sorbet, 168, 213
Maengluk Basil Seeds in Coconut Milk, 162
Speedy Mango Sorbet, 170, 213
Sticky Rice with Mangos, 163
Thai Coffee Ice Cream, 165, 213
Thai Ice Cream Sandwiches, 166, 213
Thai Tea Ice Cream, 167, 213
Wild Lime Leaf Sorbet, 169, 212

T

Tamarind
fresh, 191
Son-in-Law Eggs, 124, 213
Spinach in Sweet-Sour Tamarind Sauce, 113
substitutes for, 191
Tamarind Liquid, 191
Tangy Tamarind Sauce, 207, 212, 213
Tangy Chile Sauce, 145
Tea
Thai Iced Tea, 173
Thai Tea Ice Cream, 167, 213

Tempeh, Sweet-and-Sour, with Cucumber and Cauliflower, 111
Thai Coffee Ice Cream, 165, 213
Thai Fruit Salad, 65, 213
Thai Ice Cream Sandwiches, 166, 213
Thai Iced Coffee, 172, 213
Thai Iced Tea, 173
Thai Omelet with Sriracha Sauce, 129, 213
Thai Tea Ice Cream, 167, 213
Toasted Coconut, 199, 212
Tod mun kao pode, 22
Tofu
Baby Corn and Tofu with Cashews, 109
Bean Sprout Toss-Up, 113
Clear Soup with Spinach and Tofu, 76
Coconut Soup with Galanga and Butternut Squash, 74
Dao Jiow Lone Dipping Sauce with Vegetables, 30, 213
Five-Spice Hard-Boiled Eggs in Sweet Soy Stew, 136
Lemongrass Soup with Rice and Basil Chez Sovan, 77
Mee Ga-ti Rice Noodles with Coconut-Bean Sauce, 154
Mee Grop, 147, 213
Minced Mushrooms and Tofu with Chiles and Holy Basil, 130
Mushroom Mince, 192
Mushrooms and Tofu with Fresh Mint, 110, 213
Oyster Mushrooms with Red Sweet Peppers and Ginger, 108
Paht Thai, 150, 213
Pressed or Firm Tofu, 200
Red Curry with Red Sweet Peppers, Snow Peas and Tofu, 90
Red Hot Vegetable Stir-Fry, 120

Rice Noodles with Eggs, Broccoli and Dark Sweet Soy Sauce, 152
Satay Peanut Sauce with Grilled Vegetables, Fried Tofu and Toast, 40, 212
Seasoned Tofu, 201
Tofu and Shiitakes Hidden in Curried Rice with Crispy Shallots, 144, 212
Tome Yum Soup with Mushrooms and Tofu, 72, 212
Zucchini and Tofu in Roasted Chile Paste, 119, 213

Tomatoes
Bean Sprout Toss-Up, 113
Everyday Fried Rice with Shiitakes, 139, 213
Green Papaya Salad, 54
Lemongrass Soup with Rice and Basil Chez Sovan, 77
Muslim-Style Salad with Peanut Dressing, 56
Roasted Tomato-Chile Sauce, 211
Sweet-and-Sour Tempeh with Cucumber and Cauliflower, 111
Triple Mushroom Feast, 112
Two-Potato Curry Pot Stickers, 36, 213

V

Vegetable Curry Puffs, 24, 213
Vegetables, mixed. *See also individual vegetables*
Asian Vegetable Stock, 190
Dao Jiow Lone Dipping Sauce with Vegetables, 30, 213
Everyday Vegetable Stock, 189
Mixed Grill, 106, 212
Satay Peanut Sauce with Grilled Vegetables, Fried Tofu and Toast, 40, 212
Winter Vegetables Infused with Coconut Milk and Cashews, 91

W

Water chestnuts
  Cool, Crisp Rubies in
    Coconut Milk, 160, 213
  preparing fresh, 161
Wheatballs, 194
  Jasmine Rice Soup with
    Mushrooms, Green Onions
    and Crispy Garlic, 82, 213
  Mussamun Curry with
    Peanuts, Potatoes and
    Cardamom, 96, 212
  Panaeng Curry with
    Wheatballs and Wild
    Lime Leaves, 98, 212
  Winter Vegetables Infused
    with Coconut Milk
    and Cashews, 91

Wheat gluten, 194.
  See also Wheatballs
Wild Lime Leaf
  Sorbet, 169, 212
Wonton Soup, Sweet
  Potato, with Cilantro
  and Crispy Garlic, 84

Y

Yams. *See also* Sweet potatoes
  Burmese-Style Curry
    with Yams, Mushrooms
    and Ginger, 97, 212
  Golden Cabbage with
    Mushrooms and Peas, 121
Yellow Curry Fried Rice
  with Crispy Potatoes
  and Peas, 142, 212

Yellow Curry Paste, 184
Yellow Curry with
  Pineapple and Peas, 95
Yums. See Salads

Z

Zucchini
  Green Curry with Zucchini
    and Bamboo Shoots, 94
  Mee Ga-ti Rice Noodles with
    Coconut-Bean Sauce, 154
  Satay Peanut Sauce with
    Grilled Vegetables, Fried
    Tofu and Toast, 40, 212
  Zucchini and Tofu in Roasted
    Chile Paste, 119, 213

Library and Archives Canada Cataloguing in Publication

McDermott, Nancie
[Real vegetarian Thai]
    Simply vegetarian Thai cooking : 125 real Thai recipes / Nancie McDermott.

Includes index.
Revised and expanded edition of: Real vegetarian Thai. San Francisco : Chronicle Books, 1997.
ISBN 978-0-7788-0505-2 (pbk.)

    1. Cooking, Thai. 2. Vegetarian cooking. 3. Cookbooks. I. Title.

TX724.5.T5M33 2015   641.59593   C2014-907263-5